THE BOOK OF
ROWING

THE BOOK OF
ROWING

D. C. CHURBUCK

THE OVERLOOK PRESS

The photographs appearing on the following pages are courtesy of:

page 14: The Bettmann Archive.
page 17: The Bettmann Archive.
page 20: The Bettmann Archive.
page 31: Author photo.
page 32: Harvard University Department of Sports Information.
page 38: Harvard University Department of Sports Information.
page 40: Harvard University Department of Sports Information.
page 41: Harvard University Department of Sports Information.
page 45: Dick Raphael, Harvard University Department of Sports Information.
page 51: The University of Washington.
page 61: The University of Washington.
pages 82-85: Peter Smith.
page 88: Peter Smith.
page 91: Peter Smith.
page 95: The Bettmann Archive.
page 96: Harvard University Department of Sports Information.
page 98: The University of Washington.
page 99: The University of Washington.
page 101: The Bettmann Archive.
page 104: Harvard University Department of Sports Information.
page 109: The Bettmann Archive.
page 110: The Bettmann Archive.
page 113: The Bettmann Archive.
page 114: The University of Washington.
page 115: The University of Washington.
page 117: Harvard University Department of Sports Information.
page 124: Scott Adams
page 129: Robert Stewart.
page 136: The Bettmann Archive.
page 139: The University of Washington.
page 140: Tim Morse, Harvard University Department of Sports Information.
page 142: Brian Hill.
page 149: Brian Hill.
page 151: The Bettmann Archive.
page 154: The University of Washington.
page 159: Robert Stewart.
page 161: Robert Stewart
page 166: Robert Stewart
page 173: The Bettmann Archive.
page 178: The University of Washington.
page 187: Harvard University Department of Sports Information.
page 188: Harvard University Department of Sports Information.
page 192: Harvard University Department of Sports Information.
page 193: Harvard University Department of Sports Information.
page 196: University of Washington.
page 199: Dick Moore, Harvard Department of Sports Information
page 200: Brian Hill.
page 201: Brian Hill.
page 202: Brian Hill.
page 205: Brian Hill.
page 211: Lowell Dory Shop.
page 214: Martin Marine.
page 224: Cliff Hurtz.

Pen and ink line drawing on page 37 © 1988 by Jaye Zimet.
All other line drawings © 1988 by Daphne Fullerton.

First published in the United States in 1999 by
The Overlook Press, Peter Mayer Publishers, Inc.
One Overlook Drive
Woodstock, New York 12498

Library of Congress Cataloging-in-Publication Data

Churbuck, D. C. (David C.)
The book of rowing / D.C. Churbuck, — Updated ed.
p.   cm.
Includes bibliographical references (p.) and index.
1. Rowing. I. Title
GV791.C55   1999   797.1′23—dc21   99-11455

Printed in Hong Kong
9 8 7 6 5 4 3 2
ISBN 1-58567-380-3

BOOK DESIGN BY JAY ZIMET

For teaching me how: to William W. Dunnell

ACKNOWLEGDGEMENTS

My deepest thanks to: My wife, Daphne Fullerton Churbuck, who drew the pen-and-ink illustrations; Charles Clapp III, who posed for many photographs and served as this book's technical adviser; my editors at the Overlook Press: Deborah Baker, Susan Bernard and Peter Holm; Maria "Fritz" Beshar for planting the seed that grew this book; my agent, Muriel Nellis; and in no significant order: Arthur Martin, Benjamin Riggs, Bill Ferguson, Burgess Smith, Christopher "Tiff" Wood, Christopher Blackwell, Cliff Hurtz, David Pew, David Swift, David Thorndike, Dick Dreissigacker, Dick Erickson, Dick Viall, Edward Hand, Eric Baade, Eric West, Fritz Hagerman, Grahame King, Hart Perry, Henry Riggs, Herb Bethony, J. Fletcher Chace, James Wyer, Jerry Dearborn, Jim Dreher, John Smith, Joseph Dearborn, Joseph Nickerson, Laurence Morgan, Malcolm Ripley, Mark D'Annolfo, Martha Bragdon, Maura Casey, Peggy O'Neal, Peter Smith, Peter Van Dusen, Richard Lovering, Robert Sturgis, Russell Bingham, Samuel Parkman, Scott Adams, Seth Bauer, Stuart Fullerton, Susan Carlson, Ted Towl, The Boston Public Library, The Brook School rowing alumni, The Cotuit Memorial Library, The Harvard University Department of Sports Information, The Philadelphia Maritime Museum, The Riverside Boat Club, The Union Boat Club, The United States Rowing Association, The University of Washington Department of Sports Information, Thomas Mendenhall III, Tony Johnson, Walter Demers, Warren Kraft, William Eggleston, William Smith, radio station WMVY.

CONTENTS

Pull, pull, my fine hearts-alive; pull, my children; pull, my little ones. Why don't you break your back-bones, my boys? What is it you stare at? Those chaps in yonder boat? Tut? They are only five more hands come to help us—never mind from where—the more the merrier. Pull, then, do pull; never mind the brimstone—devils are good fellows enough. So, so; there you are now; that's the stroke for a thousand pounds; that's the oil, my heroes! Three cheers, men—all hearts alive!

Moby Dick
by
Herman Melville

THE BOOK OF
ROWING

CHAPTER 1

THE START

There is an element of deception about rowing that makes it almost an invisible pastime. Like a person pedaling a bicycle, a person rowing a boat does little to catch the eye of a casual spectator. There is no flash to the act of pulling an oar, no fancy moves, no visible complication that helps it stand out from any other activity.

The deception lies in the act. Nearly everyone is familiar with the thrill of pedaling a bicycle hard and fast down a steep hill, the wind rushing by, the landscape blurring into a stream of color and noise. Yet how often does a person standing on a sidewalk see bicyclists enjoying the sensations of pushing themselves quickly along with their legs and feet? Cyclists are on the streets nearly everyday, each one getting some pleasure out of pedaling himself or herself along—yet the rest of the world, standing on the sidewalk, sitting in their cars, gazing out their windows, only sees a bicycle and its rider.

Put that same watcher on the same bicycle and the fun and flow of pedaling is theirs.

So it goes with rowing, only less often, as a rower is a rarer sight than a cyclist. Many cities founded near water—and most were—afford the facilities for rowing. On the coast, in the harbors, bays and coves, yachts owners and their guests and people on their way to commercial fishing boats still row small dinghys and skiffs to get to and from their larger craft, as well as to explore constricted waters too narrow or shallow for their larger craft to negotiate safely.

This book has one mission and that is to explain the appeal behind one of the oldest known forms of aquatic transportation and organized sport in the world. It cannot recreate the graceful sensation of rowing in a well-designed boat; but it will try, through photograph, drawing, and prose, to impart a sense of the romance and dedication that rowing brings to its participants.

Once the most popular sport in the world—a fact that will be borne out in a later chapter—rowing slipped into the obscurity of a sport accessible only to the rich, privileged, or very dedicated. Two world wars, the growth of spectator sports, and the organization of professional athletics all contributed to hide rowing behind the ivy covered walls of academia. Today, the sport is re-emerging.

Once the province of only young, wealthy men, rowing is now popular with women, youngsters, adults, the elderly, and the handicapped, it is a sport for everyman and everywoman. (At the outset, let me attempt to meet head on the criticisms of those who will object to the use of what might be deemed sexist language. For pure convenience and no other, I have tended to use the masculine pronoun when describing rowers, to refer to coaches as 'he', and to make use of such time-honored terms as 'oarsman' and 'freshmen'. I beseech oarswomen, female coaches, and freshwomen to accept the author's good faith.)

Rowing can be kind to the body. There are no jarring jolts or impacts, no danger at all save drowning. Like walking, rowing can be done at a lazy pace, slow enough to let the scenery sink in, easy enough so a person at the oars can keep up a conversation with a fellow rower or passenger. It can also be one of the most competitive endurance sports of all. It can extract a toll unlike that of any other sport, wracking a body with pains and exhaustion.

This sport of contrasts is a sport that more and more are coming to know and enjoy. All one needs is the desire to learn and a nearby body of water.

I came to the sport by default—even after proclaiming it would be the last sport in the world I would try—when I was fourteen years old and new to a small boys' school in New England. Because of its size the school could only support three spring sports: baseball, tennis, and crew. There was a rule that every student had to play one of those sports or be put to work with the grounds crew. I had learned to tend a lacrosse goal in junior high school, but I had never been much of a tennis or baseball player.

With the support of the school's handful of frustrated lacrosse players, I set about organizing a drive to establish lacrosse as the fourth spring sport. I researched the cost of equipping and transporting a full team through a season—I even contacted athletic directors at other schools to see if they would include a new team on their schedules. A petition was signed and presented to the authorities. A full report was prepared and submitted.

One afternoon in February, near the end of the winter sports season, I was invited to sit down with three members of the faculty: the coaches of the crew. Now I was very tall for my age and in fairly good condition from playing soccer and hockey. The entire school was aware of my determination to establish lacrosse as a sport that season. Yet the three coaches, seated across from me in the faculty lounge, had the audacity to inquire whether or not I would be interested in trying out for a seat in one of the five four-man shells.

I informed them that I hoped to be standing in the crease of a lacrosse goal within thirty days, defending the school's honor from its rivals' best bounce shots and one-on-one attacks.

Patiently, they explained that there would be no lacrosse team. They complimented me for my diligence but shook their heads. The reasons were obvious, they said. The school had an enrollment of only

250 boys and of those, the thirty strongest were needed for the crew. They went on to say that in the early days of the school's history, every boy was required to try out for the football team in the fall and the crew in the spring. Those selected by the coaches stayed; those rejected went off to staff the other sports. So important was rowing, they explained, that they could never allow lacrosse to be added to the spring schedule and in this they had the support of fifty years' worth of alumni and tradition behind them.

I felt betrayed, enraged, but wise enough to realize that I was battling a far greater force than I (or even the entire student body) could hope to overthrow.

I told the three coaches I would rather rake leaves with the grounds crew than admit defeat and take part in what appeared to be the most ridiculous sport in the world. Why, you faced backward to go forward! The crew practiced early in the morning, even in the dark, by flashlights and with icicles hanging off the oars. Crew members missed breakfast and were late to class.

The coaches didn't press me to reconsider. They were serene in the knowledge that the school's pool of potential rowers would be preserved from the lure of lacrosse. As for me...their smiles seemed to indicate their assurance that come March I would be standing on the docks, shivering in wet sweatpants along with the rest of the neophyte rowers.

My mind was changed late in February, as I walked from the locker room to dinner and passed a door opening into the basement of the school auditorium, a former barn. From it came the sound of rushing water and the measured beat of some device rushing back and forth. Outside, a group of upperclassmen were stretching out their muscles and joking. Catching sight of me, one of them called out and asked me if I would be playing tennis or baseball when spring vacation ended. I shrugged, not having made up my mind yet and still holding out hope that someone would miraculously announce that lacrosse practice would commence immediately.

The seniors asked me if I would at least think about rowing—give it a try—even take a few seconds to come inside and try the tank, a homemade swimming pool filled with very dirty water and fitted with two oars and sets of rolling seats mounted on the side. The two oars were modified with open blades so they would move through the stationary water without too much resistance, simulating on a prep school budget the sensation of rowing.

I watched for a few minutes, keeping myself in the shadows lest one of the two coaches notice me and force one of the oars into my hands. The motions of the two rowers seemed very simple, almost soothing. I have to admit that it was not long before I was completely bored with the spectacle of rowing. Why the school held such a monotonous sport in such high esteem was beyond me. The two rowers were apparently the best in the school; one was the captain of the team and the other had rowed on the first, or varsity, boat since he was a freshman. Yet they were doing nothing extraordinary; in fact, I thought, I probably knew how to row as well if not better because of my years of experience rowing to the sailboat my father kept moored off the beach on Cape Cod.

Finally, when the heat and the stench of the once-stagnant, but now roiled water was turning my stomach, I agreed to give it a try. I stepped out of the dark recesses of the basement and avoided meeting the gaze of the two coaches. I thought I detected a faint smile pass over the lips of the head coach as I pulled off my sweater and climbed onto the seat. But he was all business when I looked up for some help in lacing my feet into the leather foot straps.

The first question was have you ever done this before.

Sure, I said, thinking of the family skiff and its two short oars.

Well then let's see what you've got.

A crowd had formed around the tank. The sixteen rowers—the first four boats—had stopped stretching and exercising on the mats to stand and watch.

Today, nearly fifteen years later to the day, I can remember that first stroke. The seat, which rolled down steel tracks, shot forward, forcing my knees to jackknife upward in front of the oar handle. My hands hit the oar and the oar hit the dirty water, raising a splash that rose and hit the nearest onlookers. With a red face, I tried to pretend the mistake had been planned, like a few practice swings with a golf club, and got set to really show off my rowing skill.

The next stroke was a little better. At least I got the oar in and out of the water without dropping it or skinning my knees. I concentrated on the handle,

keeping an eye on the blade. Within a few strokes I was doing well enough to start putting some *oomph* behind it.

You've got the blade turned around backward and you are feathering upside down, the coach said, too busy to interject any laughs into his critique. I looked out at the blade and saw only a tulip-shaped piece of wood dipping in and out of the water.

Okay, try it again another time, the coach said after ten more strokes. I didn't want to get off. I still didn't understand what it was that I was doing "backwards," and I wanted the coach to tell me exactly what constituted a backward stroke. Didn't he know that I had been rowing since I could swim? What a joke! I climbed off the seat and even though dinner had started, I decided to hang around a while to see what made for a backward or a frontward stroke.

Every oarsman that afternoon was criticized by the coaches. Nitpickers, I thought. Perfectionists who couldn't leave well enough alone. Why, when two rowers were on the oars in tandem there wasn't any discernible difference between the two. They looked like images of each other, shadows that did the same thing, at the same speed, with the same expressions and the same muscles at the same time. But the coaches found something wrong in the way they held their heads, the speed they rolled the seats, the spacing of their fingers and the angle of their knees. I left, angry that I had somehow committed a "backward" stroke, determined that given the chance, in a real boat on real water against any of the so-called experts on the team, that I would come out the easy winner.

Two weeks later and I was in a real boat, or shell as the coach insisted on calling it, sitting with three other novices in the middle of a cold, cold lake. The coach sat in an aluminum launch, a big megaphone in one hand, a thermos of coffee in the other. He was explaining to us how to turn an oar with our hands so it would enter and exit the water quickly and efficiently. I couldn't figure it out, so he repeated himself, over and over, as I turned my wrists back and forth, back and forth—once more wondering why I was subjecting myself to such a mindless exercise.

We hadn't really rowed yet. I don't think any of us wanted to. For starters, the boat was so incredibly unstable that we moved around like four children sent out on skates for the first time. Everytime one of us moved his oar, the entire shell reacted in the most violent fashion, threatening to throw all of us over the side, where we would most surely drown as our feet were tied into the so-called stretchers.

The coach was a taciturn type (I would later learn that this was a prerequisite to successful crew coaching just as volatile mania was the watchword with college football coaches); he smoked a pipe and a pair of binoculars and two watches hung around his neck. He seemed to like playing mental games with us, harping on the most minute flaws until we were ready to unlace our feet, dive over the

side, and strike out for the shore in exasperation.

The practices began to blur and become indistinguishable. I would be yelled at for my hands, another in the boat would be harped on for looking at the scenery, another would get it for dipping one shoulder at a specific place in the stroke. We all loathed practice. Hated having to run the mile every day from the locker room to the boathouse. Hated putting on the same wet clothes every day only to spend three hours sitting in an impossibly fragile boat doing inane drills. But I kept going back, feeling trapped by the knowledge that the other three beginners would be back, just as trapped by me.

We had far to go, and our first race was only a month away. We knew the stakes were high: we had to buy our own racing shirts at ten dollars each, and if we lost, our shirts had to be forfeited to the winners. On the other hand, winning meant being able to parade around campus wearing the losers' shirts as a badge of victory. If we had a really good season, we could begin to accumulate a big collection of shirts—perhaps even enough to make a bedspread, like the one the captain of the team had on his bed.

I lost my first race, and in reflection I think I finished even throughout my entire rowing career. Of course one remembers the victories better than the losses, but more than the wins and the shirts kept me coming back to rowing. Perhaps it was the sensation of rowing under a bright blue sky, the riverbanks and lakesides tinged with a classic light that seemed best appreciated from a craft as fine and efficient as a shell. Perhaps it was the camaraderie of rowing with friends and teammates, or even the sheer solitude of sculling alone in the morning, tendrils of mist rising off of the water toward the pink dawn sky.

There was one thing—the one thing that every rower will say he or she enjoyed the most about rowing—that kept me coming back: to call on Duke Ellington, rowing don't mean a thing if it ain't got that swing. Swing is the payoff in rowing. It is the epiphany of the sport, a transcendental moment of bliss. The boat seems to accelerate on its own, balanced on a razor's edge, leaving friction and exhaustion behind in its wake.

I rowed for six years in prep school and college, rowing every season of the year on oceans, lakes, rivers, channels, sloughs, bays, coves, and sounds in everything from fiber glass ocean shells to the finest European built racing eights constructed from the latest in synthetic fibers and adhesives. I rowed on some great boats, I rowed on some pretty bad ones. I've been shot at with a BB gun, laughed at, cheered, and photographed while sitting in a shell. I've done some of my best thinking behind an oar and met some of my best friends there.

One summer I was wasting time on Cape Cod, sailing and making some spending money at various jobs like house painting, counter work at a fast food franchise, and giving private sailing lessons to vacationing businessmen. Although I was only sixteen, the summer seemed like the sixteen summers before

it, with no new friends or events to keep me excited. While sitting on a friend's porch for the umpteenth time, it occurred to me that in two months' time I would be back at school, depressed that nothing of note had happened to distinguish the summer.

I recalled a flier that had been posted in the school boathouse the spring before. It was an invitation to coaches to recommend their best rowers for a summer camp that would train junior rowers for the national trials and potentially the world championships in Montreal. Remembering that invitation, and feeling soft after three months of hard training, I resolved to call my coach the following morning and ask him if it was too late to try out for a seat in one of the camp's boats.

The next day I called and he promised to look into the situation. An hour later he called back and told me to get in touch with the head of the camp, who at the time was organizing a crew at the Kent School on the Housatonic River in northwest Connecticut, only miles from the New York state border.

As luck had it there was one spot left, and it was for a starboard stroke in the pair-with-coxswain. The eight and four had been picked, the first round of cuts had been made, and my spot was open only because another rower had quit unexpectedly. They wanted me there immediately, and that afternoon I was packed and on my way, driving across Connecticut in an old jeep that was permanently stuck in four-wheel-drive.

When I arrived in the early evening, the crews were practicing on the river. I launched a single and set out down the river, looking over my shoulder with every other stroke because of the failing light and the strange waters.

In the distance, down river near the next bend, came the faint sound of shouting—two coxswains urging their crews on in a race for the docks. I stopped and turned the scull back up stream, sidling over to the bank to wait for the boats to pass. At a slow paddle, with my oars and the frogs the only sounds, I slid quietly back toward the bridge where the boathouse was.

The shouts grew louder as the light dimmed over the high ridge to the west of the river. The buzzing noise of the coach launch jarred the dusk, still beaten in volume by the coxswains. I stopped, the handles of the oars crossed in my lap, and peered into the half-light over the needle stern of the varnished scull. Suddenly, I saw the flash of oar blades, wet and gleaming as they dipped and feathered into and out of the water.

An eight-oared shell, seventy-two feet of Spanish cedar and spruce, was pulling abreast of a four-man shell, three quarters its size and about as fast. The coach had given the four a head start, and now, with about a mile to go before the boathouse, the eight was making a move to pull ahead and leave the four behind.

As the light was all but gone, all I could see was the white of a few of the rowers' shirts and caps and the white chevron painted over the blue oar blades. The sound was stirring; a subdued roar of twelve wheeled seats rolling down their tracks and back,

the clack of the oars as they snapped in the oarlocks.

I suddenly felt guilty at watching and hearing such power from the shadows of the riverbank. But the coach, standing tall in the bow of the launch, noticed me, and hailed me through his megaphone.

A senior at Harvard, the coach had taken on the task of putting together three boats from the best rowers New England's prep schools had to offer. His reward, if the crews were successful, would be the experience and reputation as a good coach—the only goal of many serious rowers. He told me to wait a few minutes, that the person I would row the pair with was behind in another single.

There was no hello. No question of who I was. Simply a quick order to start rowing and start rowing hard.

Four weeks later and I was in the best shape I had ever been in my life. Our pair with cox, considered by most rowers to be the hardest and slowest class of shell to row, was moving well, although the coach would only tell us we had a long way to go before we could be considered fast. As there was no other pair to gauge our speed against, we had nothing to judge our progress on other than our individual times over a 2,000-meter course. We were improving. Each one of us was responsible for one side of the boat. Each held one oar, and at first our mismatched size, style, and strength caused the boat to veer in one direction or another. But a month later we were rowing in perfect concert, swinging together at least once each practice for at least thirty strokes, the first time I had ever been able to count on that phenomenon becoming a common and expected event. We felt ready, a month of three practices a day in the oppressive heat and humidity of the Housatonic Valley had transformed us from lackadaisical teenagers to determined young men.

We were to have only one race and that was the trial that would select the pair-with-cox to represent the United States in the world championships in late August. It was held in Camden, New Jersey, on a manmade course not far from Philadelphia.

That race was the most important athletic event of my life. Ten pairs-with-coxswain were backed into the starting blocks at one end of the long course. Each lane was marked by a row of buoys spaced fifty feet apart, and we had drawn the first lane, the one closest to the edge of the course. My heart was jumping in my throat with anticipation. All my legs and arms wanted to do was drive the tension out of my body and through the oar. For five minutes, the starters positioned all ten boats directly down the course, before giving the international starting command, "Etre vous prêt? Partez!"

We left the starting blocks at a cadence of 40 strokes per minute, far too high as we were rushing the oars into the water and neglecting the business of applying our strength to the drive. As stroke, the pacesetter of the shell, it was my responsiblity to drop the stroke count, so I did, down four to thirty-six beats per minute, settling the boat and myself into a pattern of long, even, fluid strokes that milked every pound of potential pressure from the drive. I fixed my eyes on a spot above the horizon, letting my peripheral vision tell me that we had, in fewer than ten strokes, left the rest of the competition two boat lengths behind.

Never had I rowed so well. Never had any boat I sat in moved ahead so fast and decisively. I took note of all these surprises but kept driving down, almost with anger at the month of hard training, angry that so much preparation and cautious coaching was resulting in such an easy victory against the so-called best rowers the rest of the country had to offer.

At the 1500 meter mark, with 500 meters to go, I brought the stroke back up to a fast forty strokes per minute, sprinting the last two minutes into the finish. The boat was perfectly set, or balanced. We were pulling evenly and far behind us, a good six to eight boat lengths back, was the rest of the fleet.

Or so I thought. Again, we were rowing in the first lane, stuck all the way over to one side of the course, with nine lanes and nine boats on our starboard side and nothing but the bank to port. Looking out of the boat is prohibited in rowing, especially if there is a coxswain aboard to look around and keep the shell on course. Our coxswain was a ten-year-old boy, the son of the Kent School headmaster, selected because of his familiarity with the sport and his light weight. He lay on his back in a well in the bow of the boat, rather than sitting in the stern facing the stroke as coxswains usually do in eights, fours, and some pairs.

His task was to keep the boat steered down the center of the course. He was not expected to talk to

Sculling along the Charles River, Boston.

us, to tell us to try harder, or to point out flaws in our style. His job was to steer, nothing more.

As we entered the sprint, my teammate and I began to talk. Talking, like looking around, is also prohibited during a race, but we were winning and so we began to congratulate ourselves, looking forward to receiving our official American team uniforms and sweats.

As we talked, still sprinting along at a high cadence, I started to look around, determined to let the moment sink into my memory forever. As I looked hard to my left, what I saw will never leave my memory. Dead even with us, in the tenth lane against the far bank, was the entry from the Detroit Boat Club. The race was far from won. Instead it was nearly lost, for the finish line was about fifteen strokes away, and we were rowing easily along.

I shouted to my bowman and we set back to the hard determined pace that had put the rest of the fleet far behind us at the start. We both swore and shouted at each other and especially at the coxswain for not telling us what was happening in the far lane. It was bitter, bitter to know that had we not assumed victory and kept rowing as hard as a month of hard training had prepared us to do, we might have been even farther ahead, and in a much better position to win.

The race was coming down to which boat would have its oars in the water at the precise instant when our bows crossed the line. There was no time to look around, no time to look back over at the far lane. There were only the shouts of the spectators, our teammates, our coaches, parents, and friends to let us know that the race was impossibly close and that the winner would be decided in a fraction of a second.

We flashed past the docks where we had launched our shell a half hour before. It was almost submerged with the weight of dozens of rowers and spectators caught up in such a close, important contest.

The faces of those we knew told us all we needed to know.

We rowed through the finish and collapsed across the oars, breathing as hard as we could to try to fill our lungs with more oxygen than they could hold. I was sick over the side, my stomach cramped after eight minutes of folding back and forth with every stroke.

The tone of the cheers told us we had lost. Lost by less than a second. Second to Detroit by four feet, a finish so close that there was argument among the watchers as to who had won.

But it wasn't us. We recovered and paddled across the course to congratulate Detroit. As we rowed we were silent, stricken with the horror of having lost to our assumptions.

There were many more races in my rowing career. I watched some that were as close, but nowhere nearly so exciting nor important. For that small race, one of a dozen that July day more than ten years ago, was an event that hammered home for me the importance of rowing, an importance that at times was a devotion and at others a hatred.

This book is about that sport.

THE HISTORY
OF ROWING

There is a scene in *Ben Hur* most rowers nervously laugh about. It isn't a scene recommended for viewing by a group of naive freshmen eager to sign up for crew. Charlton Heston, in the role of a Roman centurion converted to Christianity, has been pressed into service as galley slave on a Roman bireme. Chained to the thwarts, crude oars in their hands, Heston and the rest of the galley slaves pull mightily to the beat of an enormous drum while overseers roam among them cracking whips. Faster and faster the crew of slaves row, some bleeding from cracked hands, others expiring with foaming lips, only to be tossed to the sharks.

It is a scene that has replayed many a time in an oarsman's mind as his coxswain screams for more power and the coach announces another hour at full speed during an early morning practice. It is also a scene that has played through the minds of many a spectator.

For a sport that demands such a high degree of devotion, and one that imparts such a fine sense of accomplishment, rowers by and large profess little knowledge of the history of rowing. Mention such races as Doggett's Coat and Badge, or the Summer Bumps, and most American rowers will shrug. Ask them who Michael Davis, George Faulkner, or George Pocock were and the most likely response will be a blank look.

Most ancient civilizations depended on natural, and in a few rare instances manmade, waterways for commerce and transportation. Mayans, Babylonians, Phoenicians, Sumerians, Greeks, Malays, and Polynesians all developed their own unique system of shipbuilding and navigation, often drawing from adjacent cultures and eras for ideas and development to incorporate into their own indigenous designs.

If the history of sport were to be traced to its beginnings, the fundamental truth is that the origin of competition lies in the marketplace and in war.

Horses were prized not for the ability to win a race and wager for their owners, but for their ability to arrive at a destination before any other, delivering their passenger or cargo before any other. So too was the case with boats, whether sail or oar. Competitive and bellicose behavior demands speed first, and only later was the sport conceived.

Archaeologists have unearthed and raised from the deeps countless artifacts that depict ancient marine activity. Full Viking longboats, preserved by the peat in which they were buried, give maritime historians invaluable data on the details of ancient naval architecture and building techniques.

The Egyptian civilization, founded on the banks of the Nile, both worshipped the river and depended on it for survival and cultural coherence. As royal dynasties thrived, barges were constructed to carry nobility from palace to palace along the watery highway. As far as can be determined from surviving records, oars were used to power the barges, with poles used in shallow waters and in marshland.

Rowing thrived for centuries as the most common form of power for river, lake, and coastal trips. It was only when the Phoenicians expanded the scope of their coastal trading that sail took over much of the burden from men. Those early oarsmen lived a hard existence compounded by superstition, cruel conditions, and uncharted waters. Sails were a relief, but it wasn't for many centuries that oars were removed altogether. Small boats (those used by fishermen and lighters in a port) carried oars for maneuverability; larger ships, (those used for cargo and coastal trips) also depended on oars to augment the sails in calm seas, when extra, dependable speed was needed to get the ship out of danger, or when a speedy trip meant more money.

The Greeks used galleys, or war ships, only partially powered by rudimentary sails. Such craft were essentially floating battering rams that relied on reinforced bows and sturdy construction. Oar power was supplied by slaves who synchronized their stroke through the beat of a drum. Such ships were classed according to the number of tiers, or levels of oars each used: hence a bireme had two decks of rowers; a trireme, three.

The Romans perfected rowing as a dependable and swift form of marine propulsion with their versions of the Greek bireme and trireme. The crews of galleys were generally, as had been the case with the Phoenicians and Greeks, slaves and criminals, chained to their thwart.

The earliest citation of amateur oarsmen—sailors who rowed for pleasure or the sake of display—can be found in Homer's *Odyssey* in the description of the islanders who greeted Ulysses on the occasion of his return to Ithaca. The first recorded rowing competition is cited by Virgil in the *Aeneid*, who described a rowing race held as part of the funeral games organized by Aeneas in honor of his deceased father Anchises.

The waiting crews are crowned with poplar wreaths;

Their naked shoulders glisten, moist with
    oil.
Ranged in a row, their arms stretched to
    the oars,
All tense the starting signal they await.
Together at the trumpet's thrilling blast
Their bent arms churn the water into foam;
The sea gapes open by the oars up-torn;
With shouts and cheers of eager partisans
The woodlands ring, the sheltered beach
    rolls up
The sound, the hills re-echo with the din.

As Greek culture is credited with creating the first organized athletic culture, it can be assumed that boat races were included in the Panathenaic and Isthmian festivals, the competitors being fishermen and crews from galleys.

After the Romans, the technology of rowing remained unchanged for many centuries, the only innovation being the number of oars shipped aboard a boat and what stroke or style was used. Oars are distinguished from paddles by the fact that oars pivot between thole pins or oarlocks, a simple improvement that doubles an oar's power; it also affords the rower much more control over the oar and thus more control over the craft. If we consider the boat or the water as the weight to be moved then an oar is a basic lever, and the oarlock or thole pin is the fixed fulcrum.

As ship design evolved, more attention was paid to sail than to rowing. Naval architects looked for new and stronger ways to increase a ship's speed and stability, allowing fishermen and coastal sailors to concentrate on improvements to the small skiffs and gigs that they used mostly for fishing and the carrying of passengers from shore to ship. Yet galleys, once the luxury liners and battleships of the ancient world, continued to be rowed in the Mediterranean until the eighteenth century.

Competition among rowers was as inevitable as a race between two horsemen traveling on the same road. Annual religious fetes, particularly in Spain, France, and Italy, usually featured a race among the village fishermen. With such perishable cargoes as fish, the amount of time it took to get from the fishing ground to market could mean a big difference in a fisherman's pocket. The obvious place speed could be increased was in the design of the boat. Yet since most fishermen couldn't or wouldn't learn how to swim, and thus needed a stable platform to fish from, their craft tended to be wide and heavy and difficult to row.

True speed became more of an issue among sailors who carried passengers for hire. Before the construction of bridges, such sailors, known as watermen or water taxis, depended on light, narrow craft to speed their cargoes across rivers that divided cities. They also transported people and goods to and from ships anchored away from the docks. Business and tips went to the fastest oarsmen, who constantly proved themselves against the competition.

Although rowing was invented in the Fertile Crescent and honed on the Mediterranean, it was in

A college rowing team in the late 19th century.

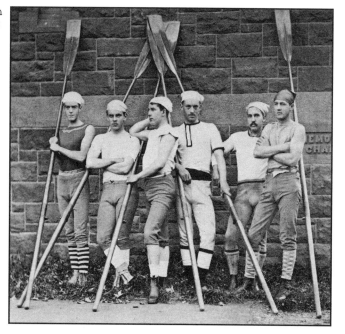

which the growth of London and England's eminence as a maritime nation stemmed. Before roads were constructed, and for a long time afterward, the Thames was the main thoroughfare for commerce and travel. Lavishly decorated barges carried the nobility and gentry that lived along the river from one town to another. The political and financial life of London also relied on the Thames. In 1454, the lord mayor of London, Sir John Norman, "built a noble barge, and was rowed by watermen with silver oars." Until 1856, The lord mayor's procession to Westminster was an annual event accompanied by all the pomp and circumstance the city could muster (although probably without the silver oars).

As London grew from its origins as a Roman fort to a leading world capital, so did activity on the Thames. Parliment, in an effort to control the sprawling maritime industries, passed statutes that described watermen as those who earned their livings "by the trade of rowing." By the time of Queen Anne's reign in 1702-1714, more than ten thousand Londoners earned their living on the Thames; a considerable majority of them were oarsmen aboard barges, lighters, and small boats called cocks or gigs.

Competition among watermen probably occurred every day as cargoes and passengers were raced from one bank of the Thames to the other. The first recorded rowing event, and the longest on-going athletic event, is the Doggett Coat and Badge. In 1715, Thomas Doggett, an Irish comedian, endowed a race between the apprentice watermen of the Thames in gratitude for their years of service in

England that it was perfected and glorified to a level that no other nation has been able to duplicate in richness and glory.

Starting with Caesar invading Brittania aboard biremes, then with the Viking raids, England, the island nation, embraced rowing like no other country.

William of Malmesbury wrote that Edgar the Peaceful was rowed down the River Dee in 1080 by provincial kings, with Edgar at the helm, acting as coxswain. Just as the Nile was the heartstream of Egyptian culture, the River Thames was the highway around ferrying him from one side of the river and back again.

The first invitation to the Doggett Coat and Badge read:

> **This being the day of His Majestie's (George I), happy accession to the throne there will be given by Mr. Doggett an orange colour livery with a badge representing liberty to be rowed by six watermen that are out of their time within the past year. They are to row from London Bridge to Chelsea. It will be continued annually on the same day forever.**

And to this day the Doggett Coat and Badge has been raced, with the only interruptions caused by the two world wars. Today the race is run by the Fishmongers' Company, charged with the responsibility by Doggett's will. Today the prize is competed for in racing sculls instead of the heavy barges used in Doggett's time.

Sixty years later, in 1775, the first regatta took place on the Thames. Crews from the Royal Fleet, shipping companies, and professional watermen competed for purses and the acclaim of the royal family. Rowing quickly became a spectacle for the masses and a sport open to any member of society—worker, nobleman, or soldier—competing against each other in full view of a holiday crowd lined along the river's banks.

Rowing left the working world in 1811, when some students at Eton took to the river in the *Monarch*, a ten-oar barge that was soon followed by three eight-oared boats. Since the first formal race records only began in 1817, students in the years before that may have used their boats solely for recreational excursions along the river; or it may have only been an escape from the school's confines to tour from town to town and find some mild mischief. Informal races, however, must have started the first day the Etonians launched two boats. By 1817, when those same students were undergraduates at Oxford and Cambridge, they organized the Leander Club, now revered in rowing circles as the original club entirely devoted to oarsmanship and small boats.

The first race between Oxford and Cambridge took place in 1829 over a two-mile course from Hambleton Lock to the Henley Bridge, the future site of the famous Henley Regatta. The race gained notice in the sporting press, partly because of a rumored side bet of 500 pounds; but it wasn't raced again until 1836, by which time spectator interest was immense and rowing events were eagerly attended and avidly followed.

The Oxford 1829 eight-oared shell has been preserved and is on display at the Science Museum in London. Commissioned by Balliol College, she is forty-five feet long and weighs 600 pounds (nearly two and half times the weight of a modern eight). The clinker-built shell with a transom stern is a good example of the behemoths that the first oarsmen had to prove themselves in. The oarlocks consisted of pairs of wooden thole pins set into the gunwales and the seats are immovable narrow thwarts.

The introduction of rowing to Oxford may be attributed to William de Rose, an oarsman who learned the sport at Strangford Lough, a deep protected inlet on the Irish Sea twenty miles into Northern Ireland. De Rose exported his talent to the Westminster School and then Christ Church, Oxford, between 1815 and 1820. He is also credited with introducing the first four-oared shell to the Eton, Oxford, and London rowing circles.

In 1944 a farmer bought at an auction a four-oared shell built before 1815 at Strangford Lough. Named the *Royal Oak*, the shell is typical of the four-oared racing gigs fielded by the aristocratic manors of Strangford and Belfast and very likely similar to the shells used by William de Rose. According to the farmer, who launched the *Royal Oak* and found her seaworthy despite her 110-year stay in a local barn, she was raced by a crew of fisherwomen.

In 1839 the Henley Royal Regatta was first raced on the now famous 1 mile, 550 yard course, that (like the first Oxford-Cambridge race) finishes at the town bridge. The course was selected because Henley enjoys one of the most scenic stretches of the Thames— and more important to the oarsmen who row on it, one of the straightest. The oldest race still raced today, the Grand Challenge Cup for eight-oared crews, is as prestigious a race as any Olympic championship, attracting the best collegiate and national crews in the world every first week of July.

For many years there have been eight events open to amateur oarsmen. They are: the Grand Challenge for eights, founded in 1839; the Stewards Cup for fours without coxswain, founded in 1841; the Ladies' for collegiate eights, founded in 1845; the Diamond Sculls for single scullers, first raced in 1844; the Visitors and Wyfolds for fours-without, both first held in 1847; the Thames Cup, for junior varsity and school eights, raced since 1868; and the Goblets, an event for pairs without coxswain, competed for since 1850.

Modern Henley events include the Princess Elizabeth Cup for prep school eights; the Doubles, for double sculls; and the Prince Philip, instituted in 1963 for fours with coxswain. The distance of the Henley course, 1 mile and 550 yards, is unique when compared to the present international standard of 2,000 meters. Yet like the length of modern marathon races (26 miles, 385 yards, the distance between Marathon and Athens) the length of the Henley course is still used as a standard of sorts, with crews racing and setting times that can be compared to those set on the original course by some of the best crews in history. Henley is the ultimate destination for many American crews, who from 1839 to 1939, entered seventy crews and came home with 13 victories. From the end of World War II to 1979, 336 American boats have raced at Henley, winning a total of 44 times.

America's debt to British rowing is deep and far ranging, encompassing everything from the invention of the swiveling oarlock and outriggers, to coaches and styles. Before the arrival of the Europeans, Native Americans relied on canoes and paddles for transportation through the wilderness; coastal tribes also constructed large craft used for coastal trips and fishing expeditions.

Colonization introduced the oar to American waters, with the colonists depending heavily in the early years on the heavy ships' boats they brought across the Atlantic. Diaries and chronicles of the first explorers and the Plymouth Bay Company cite hundreds of instances where rowed boats were used to gather supplies, hunt game, and catch fish. Because the first settlers founded their encampments on river banks and harborsides, the craft of shipbuilding was one of the first to assert itself in this country. Thus small boats were constructed in large numbers, especially in ports such as Boston, New York, and Philadelphia.

Races between crews occurred as early as 1762, when two Philadelphia sporting clubs raced four- and six-oared barges on the Schuylkill River. In 1811 and 1823, the ferrymen of the Whitehall Landing at Manhattan's Battery defeated rival crews from Long Island and Staten Island in races held on the Hudson River. In 1824 those same Whitehall watermen beat a crew fielded by a visiting British frigate, the *Hussar*. The captain of the *Hussar* offered a purse of $1,000, which was undoubtedly surpassed by the amount of bets taken on shore by the large crowds attracted to the spectacle of America's first international race.

Regattas and rowing clubs cropped up on the rivers and harbors of the Eastern Seaboard from 1810 to 1850, years in which American oarsmen

looked to England for the latest in shell design and efficient rowing styles. In the spring of 1843, a student at Yale College purchased a used Whitehall boat and brought it to New Haven, where the country's first collegiate rowing club was formed; it led to the first race against Harvard on New Hampshire's Lake Winnipesaukee in 1842.

Unlike England, where private rowing clubs and college crews are often synonomous, American rowing developed a schism in 1872, when the National Association of Amateur Oarsmen (NAAO) was founded by the college crews in reaction to the increasing influence of professionals in the clubs.

For a strong man who could handle a small boat and oar, professional rowing was a far more lucrative and pleasant occupation than unloading barges or taxiing passengers from ship to shore. As professional sponsors came up with purses ranging from $50 to $1,000 in American races and from 500 to 2,000 pounds in international races, rowing rapidly achieved a status with the sporting public comparable to modern professional sports. Consequently the press began to follow the events with breathless interest.

England's contribution to professional rowing was a constant stream of improved boats, better oars, and expert coaches. English coaches were usually amateur men of independent means, offering their time and advice to their alma maters for no consideration other than the chance to continue rowing and winning in the name of the old school ties. Amateur competition was open only to oarsmen from a public school, college, or club—no prizes were awarded and no sponsors hung banners from the bridges—closing the sport to those who couldn't afford to train every day, race in the latest scull, or attend a school as expensive as Eton or Oxford.

English teams regularly crossed the Atlantic, shipping their shells with them to challenge the best America had to offer. Rowing fans flocked to any race that matched an American against an English-man. Many English coaches and oarsmen were persuaded to stay and coach. As demand in America increased, some of the best shell builders followed, in particular the Pococks of Seattle, Washington, who settled there and went on to build nearly every shell used by an American crew between 1930 and 1970.

Canada's contribution to professional rowing is exemplified by one man: Edward Hanlan of Toronto. Hanlan, born on an island, the son of a waterman, was champion of the world during the golden age of rowing, beating the best scullers of Canada, England, Australia, and the United States through the 1870s and 1880s. His leading rival was Charles Courtney, an American amateur who turned professional in 1877. Courtney was older and heavier than Hanlan, and won eighty-eight races over the course of his career.

A race between the two at Lachine, Ontario, ended with Hanlan winning a 5-mile-turn-in-the-middle race by a mere boat length. Early races favored a turn midway through the race, usually around a moored boat, stake, or buoy so that spectators could witness the start and finish. Entangled oars at the stake, especially in races with six or eight crews starting together, turned many crews to the straightaway courses.

A Hanlan-Courtney rematch, the second of three races, was for a $6,000 purse on New York's Lake Chautauqua. The purse was courtesy of Hops Bitters, a patent medicine manufacturer. It was never awarded because someone hacked Courtney's boat in half the night before the race. Courtney refused the offer of another boat, outraging the bettors who had to be content with watching Hanlan row the course unchallenged. Hops Bitters withheld the purse on the grounds that no race was rowed. The final race, held a year later, suffered a similar fate when Courtney dropped out again. The failure of the Courtney-Hanlan series set back professional rowing, marring the sport's reputation forever; fans began to suspect that "sharp tricks" and behind-the-boathouse deals were bilking them of true sport.

Rather than squelch rowing-for-money, the creation of the NAAO in 1872 served to usher in the halcyon days of professional sculling. The sporting press of the day, such as *Leslie's Illustrated News* and the *Police Gazette*, were rowing's best boosters, and even the New York *Times* devoted an entire front page to Columbia's victory in the 1874 collegiate rowing championships.

Because rowing was an easy sport to watch, especially from trains that ran along the banks of most urban rivers, the public flocked to races in enormous numbers. About twenty-five thousand enthusiastic college students, rowing fans, and gamblers overran Saratoga in 1874 for the college championship. The press glorified rowing and covered it so intently that collegiate captains and professional scullers became heroes who challenged the popularity of the best pugilists.

The earliest American professionals were the Biglin brothers, the Ward brothers of Philadelphia, and James Hamill of Pittsburgh, who raced club members and each other for money and prizes before the Civil War.

In 1876, at the Centennial Exposition in Philadelphia, rowing and sailing were the only sporting events. The professional scullers who raced at the exposition included the best Americans: Hanlan, who was just then emerging as Canada's top sculler; and a sculler from London named Higgins. Hanlan, then twenty-one years old, beat the talented field of international scullers, embarking on a career that carried him around the world and to acclamation as the champion of the world until he lost it in 1884 to the Australian champion, William Beach.

Hanlan continued to race professionally until 1897. Like many of his competitors, he coached a college crew, at Columbia. But he never achieved the same fame and recognition as a coach as he had enjoyed as a sculler. Many professionals earned their livings not only by racing for prize money, but by coaching for a club during the summer, a college during the spring, raffling a boat away after a race, and repairing or constructing shells during the winter.

Many professionals went on to become some of the best remembered college coaches. Charles "Pop" Courtney coached Cornell's crews from 1885 to 1919, 101 of them had winning seasons. Michael Davis, a sculler who also built sculls and invented new equipment, coached Yale. Ellis Ward, the fourth member of the famous Ward brothers, became coach of the University of Pennsylvania heavyweight crew in 1879. J. A. "Jim" Ten Eyck joined Syracuse in 1903, coaching until 1938. He won his first Intercollegiate Rowing

Columbia crew practices indoors in 1926. A record 95 students showed up to try out.

Association championship in his second year.

Many professionals turned in their oars for a coach's megaphone at the turn of the century, bringing to American crews a wealth of experience and a tradition that resulted in American dominance of international rowing from 1915 to 1960.

Organized college competition originated with the Harvard and Yale race in 1852 at Lake Winnipesaukee in New Hampshire. For the next nineteen years, the race was rowed on several "neutral" courses including the Connecticut River at Springfield, Lake Quinsigamond in Worcester, and Saratoga Springs, in New York state. In the 1870s, the year after the formation of the NAAO, Harvard invited other collegiate teams to join them in the founding of the Rowing Association of American Colleges. The association's first races were raced in 1875 at Saratoga, with a fleet of thirteen boats assembled at the starting line in 1875 for the 3-mile race. The crews raced in six-oared shells without a coxswain, a situation that made collisions inevitable. Yale, which broke an oar in one overcrowded race, quit the association on the grounds its races were too crowded for good rowing, and invited Harvard to a match race in Springfield. Harvard resigned from the association the following year, and for another one hundred years, neither school competed in the collegiate championships, instead racing against each other in what was to become one of the country's leading athletic-social events.

The remaining members of the association, regrouped as the Intercollegiate Rowing Association, or IRA, raced at the end of every season on the Hudson River in Poughkeepsie.

Olympic competition for oarsmen was first offered in 1900 at the second Olympic Games in Paris. The American eight, a crew from the Vesper Boat Club in Philadelphia, won the first gold medal in the history of the event. Four years later, in St. Louis, American crews won the gold, silver, and bronze medals in the following events: pair without coxswain, single sculls, pair with coxswain, four without, double. Vesper again won the gold in the eights. From 1920 to 1956 American crews won the eights without interruption. Every one of those crews, with the exception of the first two Vesper crews, was the American collegiate champion. Today, selection camps sponsored by the U.S. Olympic Committee form boats composed of the best oarsmen in the country. Yet few of those all-star crews have seen the success of such famous eights as the Naval Academy, Yale, and the universities of California and Washington.

Although rowing started on the East Coast, it migrated west by 1899, finding a home in Seattle with the University of Washington and the boatbuilding Pocock family. The Huskies of the University of Washington achieved early fame after only a few years rowing on Lake Washington. Their acclaim lay in the contributions of their coach, Hiram Conibear. Conibear is credited with adapting the English orthodox style of rowing to American conditions, creating a hybrid stroke that proved fa ter and more effective than any other secret style invented by the professional coaches.

Conibear, a football trainer, took the job of coach in 1907 and over ten years, until his death at the age of forty-six, developed a style of coaching and rowing that had a lasting effect on American rowing. Former members of his crews spread across the country, reteaching his discoveries to nearly every college crew.

By the beginning of World War I, rowing was one of the most popular sports in the country. Prep schools built boathouses and shipped shells filled with novice adolescents down virtually every river and lake of New England. After they left school, men missed the life of pulling an oar and formed boat clubs in locations as unlikely as Iowa. Oarsmen garnered more respect on college campuses than football or baseball players. Their coaches were colorful reminders of a rough and tumble world of fixed races and unpolished spectators. A day in a shell on a river was a delightful escape from the pressures of the cities and industries. Mill workers, shop clerks, college students, and dandies all joined each other on the river, slipping their sweethearts aboard to share a seat.

The grandeur of the sport is every bit as beguiling and addictive today. From its origins in antiquity, chronicled in the writings of the Greeks and Romans, to its modern perfection of synthetic materials and empirical training methods, rowing has distinguished itself in the history of athletics as a sport for all, owing its progress to the labor of workingmen, its perfection to amateurs, and its allure to the inexplicable beauty of gliding, unfettered, in a small boat on open water.

CHAPTER 3
SCULLS, SHELLS, AND OARS

A visit to a boathouse is the most beautiful introduction to rowing a person can receive.

Sixty-foot long shells varnished to gleam like amber rest upside down on racks stacked from the floor to the ceiling. Shining in the darkness, sculls hang in slings rigged to the rafters, and sets of oars, blades striped with the school's or club's colors, nest together by the enormous bay doors. Outside, through the tall bay doors and down a ramp, is a long floating dock.

During a practice, when several crews are launching shells, a boathouse is a noisy place. Rowers stretch their leg muscles on the floor while the riggers adjust the pitch of an oar, replace an oarlock's gate or patch a torn section of decking. Each boat's coxswain checks his tiller ropes and plugs in his megaphone and electric stroke timer. And over on the wall, the coach slides names written on tongue depressors into a slotted board, seating his boats for the afternoon.

The order to pull the shell from its rack is given by the head coxswain and the crew reaches underneath and grabs onto the gunwale, carefully lifting it up and out to their shoulders.

The coxswain guides the crew down the ramp, keeping one hand on the shell's bow to prevent it from swinging into the door frames. As the crew steps onto the floating dock, they sink up to their ankles lifting the boat high over their heads and swinging it out and down with a slight smack onto the water.

Half of the rowers go back to the boathouse for the oars, while the others hold the shell off the dock. Grease is spread or sprayed on the nylon leathers and buttons of the oars before being slipped into oarlocks.

In the boat the rowers face astern, and at the coxswain's command, put their left feet onto the slides and grab the oar handles. As one they push away from the dock with their right legs and together sit down on their sliding seats.

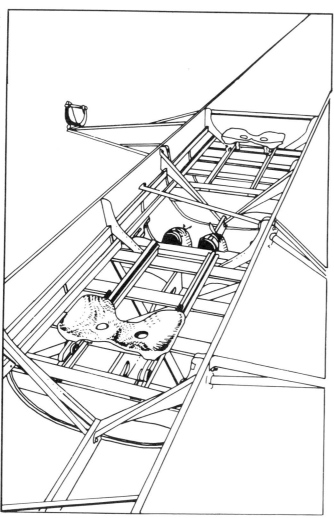

A detail of a wooden shell's construction, showing slide, stretchers, rigger, keelson and stringers.

A few strokes are taken to clear the docks before the rowers adjust the length of the footstretchers and tie themselves in. Sweatshirts are shucked and stowed while the coxswain puts on his megaphone and waits for the coach to join them in his launch.

Beginning with the bowman, the crew members count down, telling the cox that they are ready to row. The command, "Ready all?" is given and the rowers roll forward on their sliding seats, oars dipped in the water, ready for the coach to arrive in his launch, the team manager at the wheel.

One of the most difficult obstacles for any novice to overcome is the terminology associated with the sport. Slides, stretchers, starboard and port, bow and stern quickly identify themselves as seats, shoes, right side and left side, and front and back. As in yachting, where a rope can be a halyard or line, rode, painter, or sheet, rowing has its own unique glossary.

To the rower, a boat is a shell, an appropriate enough name given the fragility of the thin planking and the long, slender hull. A boat is the people who row the shell. There is no varsity, but a first boat, second boat, third boat, and so on—the first being the fastest and therefore the premier boat of the team, the second, the second best, and on down the line.

Shells, like sailboats, are divided into classes. The largest shell used is called an eight, the smallest a single scull. Two-man shells are called doubles, or pairs if each rower uses two oars (sculling) instead of one. Four-man shells are fours, unless they're sculled and called quads. Save for the single, there are no odd-numbered shells. Such a configuration would be impossible to steer in the case of rowing, and are never built for scullers.

In pairs, doubles, fours, and quads, the coxswain usually sits astern of the stroke (the rower who sets the pace for the rest of the boat) or rides in the bow with his back to the bowman. Most coxswains sit in the stern, where they can watch the rowers, correct faults in their style and exhort them with more authority. Bow seated coxswains lie inside the boat with only their head and shoulders appearing above deck, steering with a tiller cabled astern to the rudder. The advantage of a forward-seated cox is the view of the course, enabling him to keep the boat exactly centered in its lane and to gauge the progress of the competition. Such boats are usually raced in elite and international competitions for quads and fours, the high quality of the rowers obviating the need of a coxswain's critical eye.

A 27-foot long racing single is about 1 foot wide in the middle and weighs between 25 to 35 pounds. An eight weighs less than any two rowers, yet is 60 feet long.

Until 1975 nearly all shells were built from wood, except for a few varnished paper sculls in the late nineteenth century. Wooden shells are harder to maintain and heavier than a shell constructed out of carbon fiber, Kevlar, or fiber glass. Yet while synthetic shells have gained universal acceptance because of their weight and durability, most Olympic and world class shells are still built of wood.

Shells are expensive, with custom racing shells costing more than $5,000 for a single and nearly $15,000 for an eight. Wherries, or training sculls, are generally less expensive because they follow a less radical design and can be built with heavier hardware. They are usually clinker-built; the hull planking is laid with an overlap of one strake, or plank, over another, much like clapboard siding in house construction. Thus training boats are much heavier than racing shells, but they are extremely stable and durable. Schools rely on the small shells to teach new rowers the fundamentals of balance and feathering. Occasional and recreational rowers generally row wherries for pleasure trips and when carrying passengers for a row up the river to a favorite picnic ground.

The array of shells found in an average boathouse run the gamut from the best synthetics that leading-edge technology has to offer to well-preserved and treasured reminders of the exacting craftsmanship of wooden shell builders. Fifty-year-old relics that once may have had a season of glory at the hands of a first boat, are hauled out and given to the new crews for another spring thrashing. Club boathouses generally have more sculling shells than sweeps—or shells where each rower uses one oar, instead of two—because members tend to row on their own schedules and maintain their own singles for morning and late afternoon rows. Collegiate and prep school boathouses have more team shells: fours, eights, and pairs. Because most collegiate competition is in eights, a school with a large and popular program of men's heavyweight and lightweight and women's crew will have up to twenty eights under the same roof. Prep schools are divided between eights and fours. The general rule of thumb is eights for schools with an enrollment of at least a thousand and fours for those under five hundred students.

Because crew is such a communal sport, with all members sharing the responsibility of rowing and caring for the shells, it might be taken for granted that the rowers themselves repair and tune their craft. That is often the case in many rowing clubs; however, coaches and professional craftsmen called riggers handle the chore at the prep school, collegiate, and national team levels. In the off-season, riggers (in rowing, the metal framing that holds an oarlock is also called a rigger) sand and varnish the hulls of every shell and scull until they gleam like glass. Shells are regularly damaged in random collisions with floating debris, docks, and other shells. Oars snap when overzealous rowers slam their weight against them (the custom was once to give the offending rower the broken oar to hang over his mantle, but it is a practice that is disappearing with the invasion of inflexible, colorless, and virtually unbreakable composite oars). Riggers bend and oarlocks are knocked out of alignment.

Boathouses that see a lot of use usually have a full workshop attached to one side of the building. There the rigger and his assistants are constantly making minor and major repairs, revarnishing shells, and adjusting the rig to the coaches' specifications. Many riggers are former builders or builders' assis-

tants, capable of building a shell themselves if the occasion should call for it.

The art of shell building originated in England, where the earliest craft were heavy barges and cutters constructed for a working life in the navy and merchant marine. As rowing was adopted by the country's universities and schools, builders who started their shops by building stout craft designed for trade turned their talents to the construction of light, streamlined boats that were constantly being altered and rebuilt in the quest for less weight and more speed. The affluence of the rowers (or their fathers) and their backers in the English club and college circuit provided incentive for a clever builder to experiment with his designs.

Rowing owes much to English builders and inventors. The rise of the four- and eight-oared shells is attributed to British crews and builders. The outrigger, which placed the oarlocks or thole pins on metal frames attached to the side of the boats, allowed British builders to reduce the width of the hull while increasing the fulcrum and therefore the power of an oar.

The most important technological advance in rowing—and America's major contribution to the sport—was the sliding seat. Before its introduction, in a six-oared shell on the Hudson River in 1870, rowers used only their arms and backs to pull their oars, sitting rigid on fixed thwarts. The sliding seat married leg power to the short, choppy stroke required to row a barge, increasing shell speed considerably

Before movable seats, rowers wore leather-bottomed shorts and greased their thwarts so they could slide on the narrow seats. One Yale legend holds that the rowers of that school smeared oatmeal from the college dining hall on their seats for lubrication.

Soon after sliding seats were introduced, the swiveling oarlock allowed a rower to swing his oar a greater distance in and out of the water. English rowers continued to use thole pins for a number of years, believing the fixed pins afforded more power at the beginning and end of the stroke.

By 1870, the dawn of rowing's renaissance, shell design (as opposed to materials used) had reached a point that has remained fundamentally unchanged to the present. (Only the six-oared shell, the most popular boat among college crews in the late nineteenth century, is no longer built or rowed.)

There have been attempts, all unsuccessful, to adopt a set of standard specifications for each class of shell, but competitive pressure has thwarted them. Builders continue to experiment with departures from accepted design standards in their constant search for speed. Unlike yachting, which has instituted rigid one-design classes, rowing has never adhered to a tight set of rules where shell design is concerned. Yet a shell's speed depends on the strength and form of the people rowing it. A few pounds saved here and there make little difference if any over a race course when compared to the vast amounts of training and preparation that have to take place to produce a winning crew.

A typical wooden shell is constructed of thin

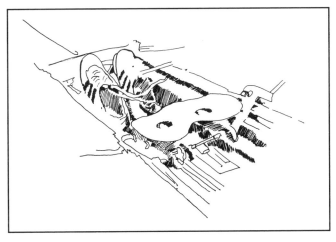

A sliding seat and set of stretchers in a single scull.

Honduras mahogany planks bent and nailed over an oak framework. Seat supports, footstretchers, and ribs are usually oak or spruce steamed into pliancy and riveted together with the planking tacked over it. Fittings are generally stainless steel, chosen because it doesn't corrode. Fastenings (the rivets and nails) are usually bronze. Riggers are nearly always fashioned out of stainless steel, molybdenum or magnesium—all lighter materials than the iron used in the nineteenth and early twentieth centuries.

Varnish, not paint, is used to preserve the wood from water's ill effects, with as many as eight hand-rubbed coats applied to develop a rich shine over the deep brown mahogany. Fiber glass can be tinted to nearly any color on the palette, but white is almost always used.

The most notable American builder of wooden

shells is still the Pocock family. The Pocock boat-house, on the shores of Lake Washington, is where most of the American rowing fleet was built between 1920 and 1970.

The Pococks deserve a large part of the credit for introducing and establishing crew on the West Coast after their beginnings at the University of Washington. Every year for the past fifty, a truck towing a trailer laden with shells of every type drives across country, delivering shells to expectant crews across the nation, including Eastern teams. Pocock shells are renowned for their durability and are usually used in prep schools, where rowers are hard on their equipment, and for the training of novice rowers on the collegiate level.

In addition to the Pocock's of Seattle, there is the Garofalo family's boat works in Worcester, Massachusetts, and Graham King's in Woodstock, Vermont. King's shells, considered among the fastest in the world, are also prized for their beauty.

Michael Vespoli is at the other end of the spectrum, working in the latest synthetics. He is the former captain of the Georgetown crew, a former Olympic rower and a former freshman coach at Yale. Vespoli's shop on Columbus Avenue in Hamden, Connecticut, not far from New Haven, turns out a full line of fast, state-of-the-art shells. Van Dusen Engineering in Winchester, Massachusetts, is renowned for their fast sculls, used by the best American scullers in international competition.

Although synthetic shells don't delight the eyes the way their wooden counterparts do, they are extremely light and, in theory, faster. Rowing them, with composite, or synthetic oars with wooden handles, takes away much of the beauty of the sport for some rowers. But for a crew intent on winning, their use can give a psychological boost akin to a bicyclist or swimmer shaving their arms and legs before an important meet. Today, most college varsities and national crews race with composite oars. Ironically, however, at the highest level of competition, after years of innovation and evaluation of synthetics, there has been a definite return to the beauty and integrity of wood.

SHELL TYPES

SINGLE SCULLS

In all sports, the most dramatic contests are head-to-head, one-on-one, rower against rower. In rowing, the sculler is the undisputed star, one person rowing against another, with no one to blame for defeat or praise in victory but himself or herself.

It is something of a contradiction in crew, the consummate team sport, that the most prestigious and graceful events belong to the single sculler. Observing the combination of athlete and shell gliding with the ease of a skater over ice, it is hard to imagine the agony of the effort and the total concentration required to move the needle-thin scull through the water at high speed.

Many rowers will agree that sculling is a sport for loners who relish the more quixotic elements of the sport. Few colleges coach sculling, concentrating their resources on a group of rowers in the same shell. The economies of concentrating several bodies in the same boat are obvious. Coaching and supporting a full time sculler is a luxury that few colleges or prep schools can afford. Hence there are virtually no sculling races at the collegiate level, and most scullers are former rowers who turn to sculling after graduation, when the emphasis is no longer on teamwork and the driving force is no longer the coach. Many scullers prefer the sport's solitary beauty to the hustle of team rowing. That beauty is a reflection of the scull itself—the most fragile in the entire sport—a craft so small and fine that it seems to vanish beneath the form of the sculler.

Twenty-two feet long and less than two feet wide at the widest point, single sculls have no rudder, only a small skeg similar to a surfboard fin. They are steered through the oars, by applying power to one while easing off the other to negotiate a river's curves. Because the sculler, like all rowers, faces backward and has no coxswain to look out for obstacles or keep the scull in its assigned lane, the lone rower must constantly look over his shoulder to see where he is going.

The oars used by a sculler are called sculls as opposed to sweeps, which are used by rowers in eights, fours, and pairs. Lighter and shorter than sweeps, sculls are narrow enough for a single hand to grip and control them with ease.

Single sculls were raced late in the history of competitive rowing, appearing only in the 1850s as a novelty then known as needles, but becoming the most competitive class after the Civil War when professional rowers made them the most popular rowing event followed by the public.

DOUBLES, QUADS, AND OCTETS

Double, or two-man sculls, were originally intended to be used as training and teaching aids. A coach or experienced sculler would stroke the boat while the student sculler sat in the bow and imitated his mentor's style and pace. Doubles and pairs were used by rowing clubs as a congenial way to share the company of a friend during an afternoon of recreational rowing. Professional scullers began racing them, usually as a team, and doubles crewed by brothers were common in the 1870s and 1880s.

Although considered a less prestigious craft than the single scull, the double is a faster boat and far easier to row hard because of the added stability of another set of oars. Their construction is nearly identical to that of a pair, or two-oared shell. Some are coxed, with the coxswain riding either in a slot in the bow or astern of the stroke.

Quads, or four-man sculls, are very common in Europe, where rowing clubs emphasize sculling over rowing. A fast boat, some are coxed but by far, most are uncoxed. Coxed boats are generally designated as quad-with or pair-with (that is, quad with cox and two with cox). Uncoxed boats are known as ''straight'' boats but not referred to as a straight quad or straight pair; rather, they are known as a quad, a pair, or a double. The exception is a straight four.

Straight boats are equipped with a rudder, a necessity given the inevitable discrepancy in strength between the rowers rowing on the starboard and port sides. The bowman, the rower sitting at the front of the shell, steers with one foot, which is mounted on a swivel at the heel with two tiller ropes connected to the toe running back to the rudder stock at the stern.

Octets are extremely rare boats and only a few exist, and even fewer ever rowed. Most are clustered in Europe and England, with only a handful in the United States. Because there is little demand and no recognized international class, builders are not building them and octets are only rowed on special occasions.

Lithographs from the 1880s show examples of ten and twelve-oared shells. Those engravings usually place the shells—sometimes referred to as galleys or centipedes—in the background, as spectators to a race of six-man shells. Some historians say ten- and twelve-oared shells were nothing more than the fancy of an uninformed and fanciful artist. Yet some were built and rowed as an oddity at regattas by club crews. Even some sixteen-oared barges, massive floating platforms, are still maintained by large college crews to train at once two eight's worth of beginning rowers.

PAIRS, FOURS, SIXES, AND EIGHTS

The most ubiquitous shells now rowed and raced are the so-called sweep boats: pairs, fours, and eights. Sweep rowing—one oar to every rower—is the form of rowing that nearly all scholastic rowers learn first. The force of one person applying all of his strength to a single oar is considerable; multiplied eight times, it can propel a featherweight shell at speeds over 15 miles per hour.

The first competitive rowers at Oxford University rowed a shell that would stagger the average modern college crew.

An eight-oared barge used in the first Oxford-Cambridge Boat Race has been preserved and is on display in an English museum. The dimensions of the shell give a sense of how difficult it must have been to row during the sport's early days. Forty-six feet long overall, the Oxford boat weighs 672 pounds. A modern eight, about 66 feet long, weighs about 250 pounds. The rowers rowing the 1829 barge each had 28 inches of room to move around in, a sliding seat in a modern racing eight requires more than 50. Rowing such a boat, on fixed thwarts, with long heavy oars swinging in thole pins must have been a back-breaking labor, especially over long reaches of the Thames in the cold, early spring.

If sculling is a display of grace and style, sweep rowing—two hands using one oar as opposed to sculling's one hand to one oar—is strength concentrated into a single 12-foot shaft. But rowing a sweep is much more than each rower simply heaving with all his might. Successful rowing hinges on balance. In an eight-person shell, one rower's idiosyncrasy will be felt by the other seven rowers. If one oar is too high, then the boat will roll down to one side, destroying the efficiency of the boat, sending water

Note the large "barn-door" rudder on the stern of this eight-man shell. Such rudders were used until the early 1970s when advances in shell design allowed builders to reduce the size down to a small rectangle mounted beneath the shell's hull.

An eight on the slings in a boathouse, showing the slides, stretchers, stringers, and riggers of a typical wooden shell.

over the side, and slowing down the speed.

With the blade of his oar square (perpendicular to the water) a rower has about 6 inches of play in the handle to keep the oar in or out of the water.

Balancing a shell in the water is called "setting-up," a difficult job for eight rowers sitting in a round-bottomed hull with a two-foot beam.

The first goal of any beginners' boat is to learn how to balance the shell. It is a difficult skill to master and one that must be practiced until it becomes a habit, even when all eight rowers are at full power and pulling a stroke every second and a half. Leaning to one side or the other is not allowed, and balance must be achieved through the oars, their height or depth determined by each rower's hands. Should one side of the shell be lower than the other,

the oars on that side will strike the water first. The boat's timing will fall apart and the run of the shell will be checked as a result.

COMPONENTS: SLIDES, RIGGERS, STRETCHERS, AND OARS

The art of shell construction is to marry strength and grace. A heavyweight crew—nearly a ton of muscle and wood—imposes a heavy combination of stress and torque on a shell's hull. Instead of battling the stress with a heavy keelson (the long, longitudinal piece of wood that runs the length of the shell from bow to stern) and stout ribs, a shell is braced by its slides (the frameworks that support the seats and footstretchers), a network of light steel cross-tubing, and a series of light ribs tied into a small oak keelson. Every element of a shell, from the thin skin of cedar to the riggers, contributes to the overall strength of the craft.

The designs of most sculls, doubles, fours, and eights have remained essentially unchanged since the turn of the century, although slides and stretchers have evolved to a considerable degree of technical sophistication.

The first slides were brass rods that ran through holes drilled into a block on the bottom of the seat. The next development were four pairs of wheels that straddled a wooden runner. The modern slide rolls on silent nylon wheels, mounted on ball bearings, gliding inside of two parallel stainless steel tracks.

Riggers have dropped in weight and increased in complexity since the 1850s, when heavy iron braces were first used to move the pivot point, or fulcrum, of the oar outboard and away from the rowers. The English continued to use their immovable thole pins until the 1920s, when they adopted the swinging oarlock. Advances in the science of metallurgy have created stronger and lighter riggers made of stainless steel, aluminum, and magnesium to replace the ponderous rigs of the past.

Riggers are attached to the reinforced gunwales of the shell by bolts anchored in ribs. The pitch, or angle of the rigger and oarlock, can be adjusted with washers or shims placed between the rigger and hull plates.

Stretchers are what a rower places his feet in to push off of at the catch or start of the stroke, and then pull himself back with. They are adjustable, being bolted through a series of holes drilled into the stringers that run down the inside of the hull on the port and starboard sides.

The taller the rower, the farther astern in the holes he sets the stretchers, fastening them tight with wingbolts. As the first racing barges of the nineteenth century didn't have slides, but immovable thwarts, rowers braced their feet inside of leather loops fastened to the floorboards. The earliest version of the modern footstretcher was two boards, laced leather straps over the instep, and steel heel cups that allowed the ankle to flex freely.

Modern stretchers are usually two running shoes that are cut in half and fastened back together by a Velcro strap. If a shell should capsize and turn turtle, a rower can rip his feet out of the shoes with a jolt and thus free himself. Should a rower be unable to get his feet out of the stretchers, he can still pull himself forward and grab onto the crossbar in front of him, pulling his head up into the hull, where an airspace can always be found. He can then collect his thoughts before unlacing his feet and bobbing to the surface.

Stretchers, slides, and riggers are integral parts of a shell but a well-equipped team will usually have spare stretchers to accommodate different foot sizes, and replacement parts of anything that should wear out or break.

Rowers tend to form personal attachments to their oars, much as a baseball player has a favorite bat. Each oar is numbered and kept in an original set, as each set usually is shaped from the same piece of wood and has the same degree of flexibility and weight. On most crews, every rower has his own oar for the entire racing season, caring for it by not letting the blade become chipped and keeping it in shape by greasing the button. The button is a collar—made of nylon today, leather in the past—where the oar pivots in the oarlock.

The first oars used in racing were standard cutter oars used in the navy and merchant marine. The shafts were long and heavy, the blades flat, narrow, and long. As barges and naval gigs were replaced with shells built especially for racing, oars were

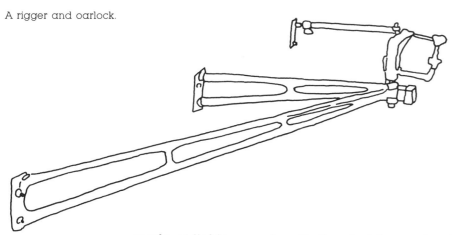

A rigger and oarlock.

made of lighter woods, with the shaft tapered outboard to the blade.

Blade design evolved from the flat to the sweep blade, a long, cupped blade that curved inward, giving the oar a better "bite" of the water. In the 1950s, European crews began using the tulip blade; very broad, round, and short, it looks something like the flower blossom. Today tulips are still used by nearly every crew, and sweep blades have, for the most part, been retired or hung over mantles.

The oar handle of a sweep oar is between 12 and 18 inches long and is unvarnished, roughened wood that can be roughened more with a few scrapes of a saw to guarantee the hands won't slip off when wet or sweaty. The handles of a set of sculling oars, or sculls, are somewhat wider than a large hand and are usually covered with rubber grips. The diameter of the handles is smaller than

that of a sweep oar so each hand will have a firmer grasp.

The specifications of racing oars are 12 feet, 6 pounds for a sweep and 9 feet, 4 pounds, for sculls. Most oars are still made of wood, despite the growing popularity of composite, or hollow synthetic oars. The light weight of composites allow a rower to maintain precise control of his oar, especially near the end of a race after taking 250 strokes at full power. Yet many rowers, even at the elite peaks, continue to row with wood because they feel wood is more responsive and controllable than synthetics.

Rowers are responsible for their seat and all the equipment they use including their oars, footstretchers, and slides. It is up to each rower to keep all moving parts clean and well lubricated and to warn the coach or rigger about any problems or strange noises. A shell receives the most attention the day before a race, when the coach usually calls a light practice and returns the crews to the dock early, where they clean and oil the shell. Nothing is more frustrating to a crew that invests hundred of hours of training for one six-minute race, than losing because of a broken oarlock or a jammed seat.

To a rower a shell builder's shop can feel almost like a sacred place, especially if it is a traditional shop where wood is still used. The smell of cedar sawdust, the whine of a saw, windows fogged with dust, and steam rising from a steambox all combine to make a rigger's bay or a builder's shop special. The sight of a shell being framed on its mounts, a skeleton of spruce and oak, is a lesson in the miracle of shell design—that delicate balance of weight and strength that seems too clever to be true.

A modern shop where synthetics are used, carbon fiber or fiber glass, is certainly impressive, albeit far less piquant. Computer-assisted design work stations, sophisticated test equipment, and a staff with backgrounds in jet engine turbine blade design or aerodynamics can make a state-of-the-art shop a very confusing place for the uninitiated. The latest in technology and design techniques are impressive to behold, and their success is indisputable. It would appear logical that the character of rowing would be changed completely by such innovations as eight-man shells that weigh under two hundred pounds, composite oars that feel like orchestra conductor's batons, seats that whisper in their tracks, coxswain's stations outfitted with stroke counters, digital watches, and electric P.A. systems. Even though it has been propelled out of an age of rich woods and heavy steel to one of fine tolerances and antiseptic precision, rowing remains rowing—it remains the act of moving a small boat efficiently through the water using nothing but human power; it remains an act that can be described in the most technical or the most lyrical terms.

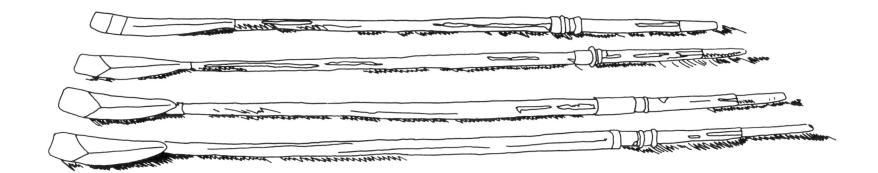

CHAPTER 4
HOW A
CREW WORKS

Watching a shell glide by is one of the gentlest sights in all sport; the boat almost seems to be a natural part of the river or lake. To the casual onlooker it appears to be an effortless sport, one that anyone could do if given the chance. Rowers swing fluidly back and forth, seeming to do little more than flick their oars into the water and pull them out again.

What looks like eight people moving in easy synchronization is the product of years of practice and coaching. An experienced eye would look for the slightest flaw in the boat's stroke, noting every errant splash and check where the casual observer would see only a long sleek craft moving quickly through the water. Put that self-assured onlooker on the sliding seat of a shell, and he will find that the deceptively easy-looking exercise becomes a struggle to keep afloat.

Rowing consists of the same sequence of moves repeated over and over: catch, drive, finish, recovery. Catch, drive, finish, recovery. It is a sequence that can never be varied, only improved.

An eight-man shell pushes off from the dock for a race.

THE CATCH

The catch is considered the start of the stroke simply because the first stroke a boat takes begins with all blades square and submerged. Although all the elements of a stroke are important, the catch is especially critical to the speed of a shell. Each oar has to enter the water at precisely the right angle, with the same speed and timing as the other oars in the shell; otherwise, an under-squared oar (one that is slanted downward) will knife beneath the surface and be torn from the hapless rower's grasp, causing him to "catch a crab."

Crabs, the bane of rowing, the ultimate *faux pas*, are so called because a victim's oar shoots under-water like a crabber's net after a hapless crustacean. A crab will stop a shell dead in the water. The worst form of crab is one that a rower tries to control. Hanging onto the handle of an oar with the combined force of an eight-man shell behind it will more often than not rip the rower out of his seat and throw him over the side into the water. An experienced rower will usually give the stroke up for lost, lie back, and let the oar careen over his head. Then he can lean over and pull it back into position. However a crab is handled, the net impact on the crew is utter chaos.

THE DRIVE

If the oar enters the water at the perfect angle, then the rower pushes backward, toward the bow, flattening his legs with his arms fully outstretched and pulling the oar toward him. Care must be taken not to "shoot the slide," that is, push the seat too quickly toward the bow. Yet if the seat moves too slowly, the leg muscles won't be used to their fullest potential. At the moment the oar catches the water, the rower jams back with his legs, opening the forward angle of his torso backward in a smooth arc.

THE FINISH

At the end of the stroke, or the finish, the oar is turned slightly as the hands are pushed down into the lap, allowing the pressure of the water to push the oar gently to the surface where it continues to be turned until the blade is parallel to the surface.

The practice over, a crew lifts its shell from the water, lowers it onto their shoulders, and carries it into the boathouse.

THE RECOVERY

Then the rower begins the recovery, pushing his hands away from his body and following them toward the stern, moving gently so his body weight

won't check the shell's forward run. The recovery requires perfect balance as the oars are out of the water and there is nothing to stabilize the shell except the weight of the oars and the coordination of the rowers. When the oars are in the water, the shell is "anchored" in the water by the oar blades. The coxswain only steers with the rudder when the oars are in the water, because a turn during the recovery will cause the boat to lean to one side and throw off the timing of the rowers.

The seating of a crew is up to the coach, who determines which rowers row best on which side and in which seat. In the past, the practice for selecting sides was simply to divide the rowers into starboard and port. If a rower rowed port the first time he entered a shell, he usually rowed port for the remainder of his rowing career unless a coach needed his talents on the opposite side...an event comparable to learning how to write with your other hand. Despite this, being right-handed or left-handed has no bearing on which side a rower will row best.

As a result of this practice, rowers who could row both port and starboard were prized by their coaches and sometimes could gain a seat in a better boat on the strength of their ambidextrous talent. Most rowers today are taught to row both sides from the start of their careers and are frequently switched back and forth several times in the same practice.

In an eight-man shell, the first seats a coach will fill is the stroke pair, otherwise known as the seven and eight men. The stroke sits farthest astern, facing the coxswain and the most formidable task for a sweep rower. A stroke has to be the most precise, the most determined, and the most controlled rower in the boat. When the coxswain increases or decreases the stroke rate, it is the stroke who has to shift his speed smoothly and precisely to the called rate, leading his boatmates in the transition. Behind the stroke sits the seven-man, who follows the stroke and mimics every move and change of pace.

"The seven and eight oars are the lead dancers of the boat," says Dick Erickson, coach of the University of Washington heavyweight men's crew. "I look for rhythm, strength and continuity to fill those seats because the rest of the boat is going to follow them. A stroke is an elusive quality but whenever you get a group of rowers together, that person will always stand out."

The next four rowers are usually the tallest and heaviest members of the boat. Known nautically as the "waist" of the boat, the middle set of four rowers is more popularly known as the "engine room." Because a shell is widest midway between the bow and stern, it is also more stable there; thus the rowers who occupy the 6,5,4, and 3 seats are selected for their strength and endurance.

If the stroke pair's job is to set the timing of the stroke, and the engine room's task is to provide the power, then the bow pair balances the shell, stop-ping it from rocking from port to starboard. They are often the lightest members of the boat and display the most finesse with their style and bladework. In long races on curving rivers, a coxswain is often unable to turn the shell quickly through the turns while honoring the confines of his assigned lane. Then the bow pair are called on, the rower on the outside of the turn pulling especially hard while the other member of the pair rows a bit more lightly. At the starting line of a race, the bow pair keep the boat straight by pulling or backing their oars.

The orthodox seating arrangement of fours and eights is to alternate port and starboard oars evenly from the stroke up to the bowman. Such a spacing requires that each side be evenly matched in strength; otherwise the coxswain will have to steer constantly to one side to keep the boat on a straight course. In the past, nearly every shell was rigged in the ortho-dox pattern because switching the riggers from one side to another was nearly impossible. For the past twenty years, beginning in Europe, different rigging configurations have been used to balance the strength between the port and starboard sides.

Such rigs are rare and can be difficult for a novice crew to use efficiently. Erickson said their use is most prevalent in boats where one side is outpulling the other and the steering suffers as a consequence.

"If you happen to have four starboard guys who happen to be on the average bigger than your port guys, then if they row in a standard rig they'll have a mechanical advantage and cause the boat to veer. Doubling up the two and three man on the same side, will put more strength on that particular side in the bow, where their position will put more pressure on the bow to turn against the stronger side."

The coxswain's command "Ready all?" results in all eight rowers rolling toward the stern on their slides and setting their blades in the water, ready for the first stroke. At the start of a race or exercise, the crew could roll half or three-quarters of the way down their slides before setting their blades in the water, making a short chop of a stroke to break the shell free of the water and starting it moving for the next quick jab or full stroke.

The command, "Row!" results in just that: the first strokes, expended at a slow pace. When a crew is slowly moving along without expending much effort, the rowers just barely setting their blades in the water and pulling them gently through to the finish, they *paddle* at a rate of 20 to 25 strokes per minute. Like a horse walks, trots, canters, and gallops, a crew paddles and rows at quarter, half, three-quarter and full power. The fastest speeds occur during a *sprint*, when the cadence can reach 40 to 45 strokes a minute.

If the coxswain wishes the rowers to stop rowing, he simply calls out, "Way enough!"

The practice of a typical prep school or collegiate crew usually begins with some light drills and exercises to warm up the rowers' muscles. Tense rowers have a difficult time setting up a shell, so time and care is spent at the beginning of the practice to work on timing and balance.

After a half-mile of drill work, with the rowers practicing such exercises as stopping their hands midway through the recovery, pausing at the catch and balancing in place without taking a stroke, the coach will start a routine of short spurts of hard rowing called *pieces*. Pieces are used to train the crew and build their endurance. They also enable the coach to compare rowers and determine who can move a boat fastest during a defined period of time.

Pieces are usually rowed at a racing cadence, which varies from 30 to 38 strokes per minute. The coach, riding nearby in a power launch, calls out to the coxswains to pull their boats even with each other and work up to full power at a moderate cadence. Within ten strokes each coxswain builds his crew up from a paddle to full power.

In practices with more than one shell participating (the rule rather than the exception in scholastic rowing), the crews will naturally tend to race each other during the timed pieces, adding to their effort and familiarizing them with the sensation of racing alongside another shell.

Most practices consist of timed pieces and end with a long piece or a time trial over a racing course. Coaches vary the length of the pieces, having their crews row "pyramids"—that is, pieces that gradually increase from one minute to six or eight minutes and then back down again with corresponding rests in between where the rowers recover, catch their breath, and paddle along working on flaws in their bladework. Other practices may consist of nothing but four-minute pieces with four-minute paddles separating them. The length of a practice and the amount of hard rowing accomplished varies according to the time of year and the day of the week.

In the fall, crews usually work on style; new rowers learn the basics of rowing and veterans brush away summer's cobwebs. Because the only races in the fall are usually head regattas—long distance races of 1 to 3 miles modeled after Boston's annual Head of the Charles—crews work on endurance over time rather than the short sprint style of racing practiced in the spring. By late November, when rivers and lakes begin to ice over, the crews leave the water and stay inside for the rest of the winter, working on aerobic training, ergometers (rowing machines), and indoor moving water tanks.

Spring training is usually the most intensive period of a crew's annual rowing schedule. Collegiate and scholastic championships are held in the late spring, and match racing takes up most weekends beginning in early April and continuing until the second week of May. Therefore, spring practices entail harder work—sometimes double practices, one in the early morning before classes and again in the mid-afternoon—and fierce intrateam competition as rowers try to gain a seat on the first, or varsity, boat.

Most rowers take the summer off from rowing, save the cream of the collegiate and scholastic teams; they continue to train for national and international championships and the Henley Royal Regatta. A competitive collegiate rower usually rows year round for the four years he is in college and often after graduation, training for a seat on the national boat or an Olympic shell.

Critics frequently observe that rowers practice an inordinate amount, proportionate to the very short time spent racing. Simple calculations show that for about every three hundred strokes pulled in a practice, an rower will pull one in a race. However it should be noted that excellence in all sports that involve the repetition of a single motion, such as golf, bicycling, and swimming, are distinguished by the constant practice and refinement of that motion.

A great deal of concentration and practice is needed to perform any motion well under duress. A tennis player's serve will falter after several hard sets, an archer's aim will wander after he holds back a bowstring for several minutes, and a rower's bladework will become sloppy near the end of a race, when he is usually called on to sprint and when every stroke counts. In a sport where the margin between winner and loser is sometimes measured in tenths of a second, there is very little room for strokes that are less than perfect. An oar that drives too deep, or enters the water before or after the rest of the crew's, will throw the timing and balance of the entire shell to the wind. The result will be a loss in speed and, in extreme cases, a crab, which will stop a boat altogether.

The typical 2,000-meter race happens this way: the crews launch their shells at the boathouse and paddle upstream, parallel to the race course, practicing drills and doing 10- and 20-stroke full-power pieces

A winning coxswain takes his traditional post-victory dip, the one time the crew is allowed to exact its revenge.

to warm up and divert their minds from the task ahead. Equipment is checked for any flaws, and extra clothing is handed off to a launch to cut every bit of excess weight from the shell.

When the judges return to the starting line from the finish of the previous race, the crews pull up to the starting floats—either a floating dock or anchored rowboats. The coxswains back the shells down to the docks until the starters can grab onto the sterns.

The coxswains then ask their bow pair to pull or back their oars until the shells' bows are perfectly aligned and aimed down the center of the race course lane. While the bows are being pointed and until every member of the crew is ready, the coxswains keep a hand raised in the air, a signal to the judges that the crew isn't ready. One coxswain will shout to another, "Shirts?," setting the traditional bet of all rowers, a wager that has probably led to the cliché: "He lost his shirt."

When the coxswains are satisfied that their boats are ready, the rowers roll up to the catch and bury their blades in the water, poised for the first stroke. The coxswains then drop their hands and the starters call out:

"Rowers, are you ready?"

And if there is no signal from the coxes to delay the start, the starter says:

"Ready all? Row!"

The first stroke is a short stroke, either a half or quarter stroke to break the shell out of the water and give it momentum. In rapid succession the crew takes two three-quarter length strokes or a combina-tion of quarter- and half-strokes, extending their reach to its full extent within five.

The first 10 to 20 strokes are full-powered and rowed at a high cadence, usually over 40 strokes a minute.

The most important stroke of the race occurs after the first 20 high-cadence starting strokes. Called the "settle," it is the stroke where the crew settles from its starting pace down to the racing pace it will maintain for the next six minutes. The crew all knows when the settle will occur and is forewarned by the coxswain, who tells them, "Settle in three strokes to a thirty-six." The coxswain then counts down the strokes and on the last one, the stroke pair slow their recovery on the next stroke to the exact racing rate. If any member of the crew is too slow or fast on the settle, the entire boat will feel the effect and lose whatever speed it built up through the starting sequence.

After the settle, the rowers begin taking long, hard, and determined strokes, never looking out of the boat to see where the competition is, concentrating on style and effort while the coxswain steers and gauges his shell's progress against the competition.

The coxswain is the boat's throttle in a race. If the other crew is gaining, then the coxswain will call a "drive," a sequence of 10 or sometimes 20 strokes where the crew makes an extra effort to concentrate on their bladework and pull harder. The effect of a "drive" is to calm the rowers and force them to concentrate on the task of moving the shell and forget, for a moment, the fact that another crew is racing just as hard in the other lane.

The coxswain keeps the crew informed of their progress, telling them if they are moving ahead of the other shell or losing ground. Progress is measured by seats, hence a cox will say something like, "I have their stroke!" or "I have their bowman!," indicating that his seat is directly opposite a specific seat in the opponent's shell. Rowers are forbidden to look out of the shell because of the effect that simply turning their head can have on the balance of the entire shell, their individual stroke, and morale. A rower is always aware of the general position of the competition in the corners of his eyes, but it is up to the coxswain to divert his attention from the race and onto his oar.

The middle of a race (between 500 and 1500 meters, the middle two minutes of the race in an eight-man shell) is a matter of hard, steady rowing. The crew, after settling out of its start, usually remains at a cadence somewhere in the middle 30s, driving hard in 10 stroke sequences whenever the coxswain feels the boat speed slipping, or to match a drive called by the competition.

The last quarter of the race is known as the *sprint*. Depending on the crew's relative position to the other shells on the course, the coxswain usually brings the stroke up from a racing cadence to a pace in the low 40s, shifting the speed up in three strokes just as it was brought down at the settle after the start.

The sprint is the true test of a crew's abilities and physical conditioning. If the race is close at the 1500-meter mark, then a rower has to find one more minute's worth of strength that will mean the difference between winning or losing. Pulling his oar through the water every second and a half, with every remaining bit of energy behind it, can cause a rower to collapse at the finish. He may vomit and faint; his muscles burn and his vision blurs with the intensity of a torture that never seems to have an end. Yet a championship crew will make it all look easy and graceful.

The rowers stop rowing when the coxswain is sure the boat is completely over the finish line. After a few moments of exhilaration and celebration, or dejected exhaustion, the crew paddles back to the boathouse.

After the shells are taken out of the water and carried back to the boathouse or boat trailer, the losing rowers seek out the victors and give them their shirts.

Races vary. Scholastic rowers sometimes race a half-mile course while the longest race in rowing is a Swiss competition that is a 90-mile test of endurance raced in fours-with. The first rowing races were rowed around a turning point so the spectators could watch both the start and finish. Regattas, when several crews were on the course at the same time, adopted straight courses—at first between two prominent landmarks, such as two bridges.

Modern racing is generally done on a 2,000-meter course. The Henley Royal Regatta course is 1 mile, 550 yards long, a distance copied by many American crews as a benchmark. The Harvard-Yale Regatta is 4 miles long, a distance unrivaled in American collegiate rowing, yet one that was ubiquitous until the 1950s for collegiate rowing championships. Women's races are usually over a 1,000- or 1,500- meter course, although 2,000 meters has been established for the 1988 Olympic Games.

An eight will make speeds of up to 15 miles per hour during a short sprint, averaging 10 to 12 miles per hour during the body of a race. While those speeds may not seem remarkable, they are exhilarating to experience, especially when a crew has swing. Swing is the nirvana of rowing, a transcendent state when the boat is perfectly balanced and every stroke seems easier than the last. Every rower is perfectly attuned to his teammates, moving at precisely the same speed, their oars entering and exiting the water as one. It is a difficult experience to describe, yet one that is unforgettable for those who have known it. There is no other aspect of crew so addictive as the feeling of being in a shell that swings. Accomplished crews can feel it every day. Some rowers may feel it only a few times, but work for it every time they climb aboard.

Some crews can have undefeated racing seasons and be content. Other rowers are happy simply paddling, perhaps rowing hard when they feel like racing an imaginary opponent, but most of the time simply enjoying the sensation of sliding through the water in a fragile craft propelled by nothing more than the strength of their own bodies and the skill of their hands.

HOW TO ROW

No book or set of diagrams can teach a person to row well. Climbing aboard a shell or scull with this or any other rowing book in your lap will result in bad rowing, a wet book, and a wet rower.

If you are a novice and are serious about learning how to launch, rig, and row a shell or scull then seek out an experienced rower or coach. If you aren't a member of a rowing club, then call your local newspaper or write to the United States Rowing Association and ask for the nearest community rowing club in your area. Despite rowing's reputation as an exclusive sport, opportunities for any person to row have always existed, and today rowing clubs can be found nearly any place with convenient access to calm water. Some of these clubs offer their facilities for the teaching of rowing. Elsewhere, rowing and sculling schools offer a week or two of concentrated instruction. Many private clubs, particularly the older urban barge clubs and navies, have long waiting lists and memberships that are passed on with the family name. Some colleges and less exclusive rowing clubs, however, open their doors in the summer when students and permanent members are on vacation, offering classes and the chance to row an eight-man shell. In many cities, the rowing equivalent of racquet clubs and health spas are becoming popular and profitable. For a fee, these clubs rent recreational singles and doubles by the hour. Included in the memberships are such amenities as locker room, ergometers, weights, and Nautilus machines.

Unless you live in a bone dry desert, you should be able to find some experienced rowers who are willing to take you out on the water and teach you the basics of rowing. Simply going down to the water and striking up a conversation with someone who seems to know what he or she are doing may result in an offer to climb aboard and try a few pulls on the oars. If you are serious enough to seek out rowing and research the opportunities, then you are well on your way to better health, the society of other rowers, and the sublime pleasures of the sport.

Once you've acquired a boat, oars, water, the desire to learn, and the ability to swim, then the rest is up to practice, time, and more practice.

Time and practice are the two most important ingredients to successful rowing. The first few experiences on the water can be frightening and disorienting. You will be sitting on a tippy, frail-looking boat, your seat only inches above the water, the oars impossibly long and skittish. What once looked like so much fun, now feels like juggling while peddling a unicycle across a tightrope. Any movement and the shell seems to go berserk. Itchy nose? You don't dare remove a hand from an oar. What looked so easy from the safety of dry land is now a matter of panicked survival.

The cure to a case of the beginner's jitters? In most cases: simply tip over. If you're unfortunate enough to be floating away from the dock for the first time in a racing single, then you don't even have to try to tip over—you will anyway. I constantly tip over when I push off from the dock for my morning row. The only damage that comes from the dunking is my pride and a few laughs from inside the boathouse bays. Just go ahead, take a hard stroke, and hang on. If you wear glasses, then make sure they're secured to your head by a strap or piece of string between the temple pieces. If it's early in the spring or late in the fall, then you shouldn't be on the water by yourself. Don't set off from the dock unless you are sitting in at least a pair or double with an experienced rower next to you. If you must try it for yourself, then postpone those images of yourself flashing along in a six-thousand dollar racing scull and settle for an old wherry, broad comp (looks like a racing single, but is nearly twice as wide), or recreational shell.

A flip in cold water is dangerous, especially for people in less than tip-top shape, because of the effects of hypothermia, which can numb a person senseless in a matter of minutes. If your boat does flip, then make sure your feet are out of the stretcher, slide the oars until they are running parallel to the hull, and flip it back over. If the dock is only a few yards away, then swim the entire rig back to the float and climb back aboard there. If you are in the middle of a river, then wait for help while kicking toward the nearest bank. *Do not attempt to reboard a racing shell after capsizing!* The washbox, or thin construction that surrounds the section of the shell where the rower sits, will crack off, and any effort to pull yourself aboard will probably ruin the shell forever.

A better introduction to rowing is in the stern seat of a double, with a more experienced person, coach, or shell salesman in the bow to literally look over your shoulder and keep the boat on an even keel. You'll enjoy your first experience even more if you can to get a seat in an eight, either in the company of other beginners or intermixed with some veterans.

In Europe, nearly all beginning rowers are started off as scullers rather than sweep rowers because it is believed that the most important thing to learn early on is how to set up or balance a shell. Racing sculls are used because of their sensitivity and the fact that they are unforgiving. In America, where opportunities to row are more limited than on the Continent, sweep shells (eights and fours) are favored because they concentrate students, boats, launches, and

Rowing massive sixteen-man barges such as this one at the University of Washington, Seattle, is how many rowers remember their first time on the water behind an oar.

coaches together in an economical way.

The time it takes a beginner to master rowing varies according to the rower's age, prior experience with boats, and the ratio of rowers to coaches. At the collegiate level, where most freshmen rowers have never rowed before, it generally takes two to three months of daily practice before a shell composed entirely of novices can row alone and avoid serious problems or flaws. For a person starting the sport after college, then the learning process shouldn't take much longer than three months, especially since most adult novices start out in a stable ocean shell, which is much more forgiving of those mistakes that would flip a delicate racing boat.

Novices should ask questions, no matter how stupid or naive they may seem, because it is the obvious questions that need to be answered first. Questions are the only way to learn, and many times experienced rowers take certain fundamentals for granted as they teach or explain.

The first question a beginning rower usually asks is: "How do you see where you are going?"

True, more sarcastic comments have been made about rowers moving backward toward their destination than any rower cares to hear again, but it is a logical question, especially when it is perfectly possible to row a boat so the rower is facing forward: in a racing shell that is known as rowing backward. But the answer is simple: if you row in a shell with one oar to each rower, then there is usually a coxswain sitting in the stern keeping an eye open for hazards and steering around the curves in the river.

If you scull, or row in a straight four or pair without cox, then you simply have to turn around every now and then to see where the shell is pointing.

The next chapter will go into more detail on the basics of sculling. The discussion here will focus on sweep, or one-oar, multirower rowing.

What I've attempted to do is break down the components of a stroke the way a coach would, as he rides in a launch alongside a shell, and calls out criticisms and suggestions on every detail of every rower's style. A coach is invaluable when a novice tries to learn how to row well, because no one can see what he is doing wrong, while he is doing it, unless he can find a way to have himself filmed in the act and then analyze it afterward.

As the famous wooden shell builder, the late George Pocock, wrote, "There are ten actions that have to be performed simultaneously in an eight-oared boat. If you miss any one of them, the whole crew is out of balance—the least thing will put it out. You've got to have your hands all on one plane, you've got to catch right at the same time, you've got to pull through, you've got to slide, you've got to drive your legs down, you've got to turn a wrist—all at exactly the same time. It's a beautiful thing to watch when it's done right."

Some have described rowing with seven other oarsman as the working in a state of total trust. When one person is rowing poorly, overexcited and rushing and flailing, then the other seven suffer. When all eight find perfection, then they achieve swing.

The first thing a novice needs to learn about

rowing is *feathering* (also known as bladework), the trick of holding and rotating an oar. Scullers (those who row with an oar in each hand) also feather, but in a manner slightly different from that of a rower, one who rows with one large oar.

A sweep, or rowing oar, is grasped with both hands, the hands spread a little less than a shoulder's width apart. The grasp is light, with most of the pressure carried in the fingerpads and not by clenching around with the thumbs and palms. Grasp is the most important part of feathering, because the hands have to roll the oar from a *squared* position—when the blade is perpendicular to the water and ready to bite in—to *flat*, when the blade is parallel to the water and sliding forward during the recovery.

Next to be mastered are the various components of the stroke, or the cycle of movements that put the oar in the water, pull it through the water, take it out of the water, and then slide it through the air back to the starting position.

The start, or beginning of the stroke, is called *the catch*, because the curved blade of the oar snaps crisply into the water, catching and setting itself to start the next step, *the drive*.

The drive encompasses the entire time the blade is buried in the water. The rower doesn't try to pull the blade through the water but instead places it firmly in one point and then uses the oar as lever to pull the boat along. At the end of the drive, when the oar is angled back toward the stern, the stroke moves into *the finish*. The finish requires the most

The Catch: At the catch or beginning of the stroke, the hands swing over the side of the shell with the outside shoulder slightly cocked towards the oar. The hands move sharply upwards, dropping the blade crisply into the water. The eyes focus on the horizon and the chest touches the knees.

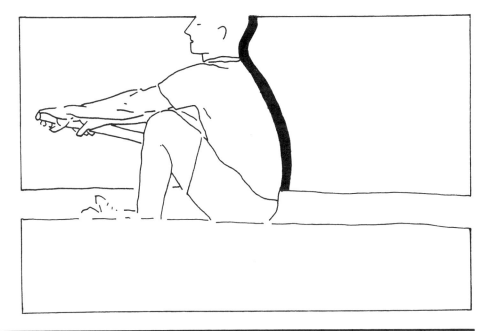

The Drive: The legs flatten out, the arms remain straight, and the back begins to open, or rise up.

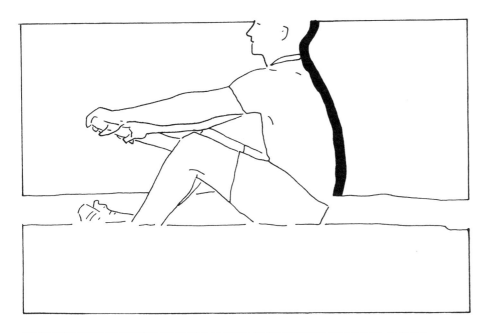

concentration as the blade must be angled enough to push itself out of the water and into the air where it is pushed back toward the bow of the shell through *the recovery.*

The recovery is the most important piece of the stroke because it takes up half the cycle, all of it with the oars out of the water, a mere six inches off the water. A rower tries his best to keep the oar from hitting, or skipping off the waves, as each touch of the blade will cause the narrow shell to rock over in that direction, making the stroke choppy, instead of fluid.

Within each of the stroke's four phases—the catch, drive, finish, and recovery—the body and hands are constantly changing position. Control of the hands is one of the most difficult aspects of rowing. Using the hands to maintain the proper height and atitude of the oar takes an enormous amount of concentration, even for experienced rowers. This is especially tough during a race when hand movements are accelerated and hampered by the pressure of the oar.

Feathering takes place with a roll of both wrists, the heels of the hands dropping away from the body, the fingers rolling the handle around in a clockwise and then counterclockwise direction. Learning this wrist motion can be the hardest part of learning how to row, a trick that takes anywhere from an hour to a month to master but one that can become second nature.

The hands turn the oar twice in a stroke. The first time is when the blade is squared and placed in the water at the catch. Most coaches tell their rowers to start **"rolling the hands over the ankles,"** the hands rolling clockwise in a gradual motion until the blade is perfectly square at the catch, when the arms and hands are raised up and the blade is dropped neatly into the water.

The hands don't roll during the drive; rather, the wrists lock and the fingers clench the oar as the legs and back rip the blade through the water to the finish.

At the finish, the hands roll the blade counter-clockwise when the handle nearly touches the rower's abdomen at a level close to the navel. It is crucial that the oar smoothly release from the water without *checking* (slowing-down) the shell's forward run. Whereas the catch is a gradual roll of the hands, the finish, or release, is a much more emphatic motion; the blade tilts enough so the force of the rushing water will push it out, easily preventing the shell from rolling over to one side. In the worst scenario, the handle catches in the rower's gut and wrenches him right out of the shell with a crab.

During the recovery from the finish back to the catch, the hands are said to lead the body down the slide, moving out of the lap, across the thighs and knees before the seat begins to roll.

After the hands, the next movement to be mastered is the *slide*, or control of the rolling seat. When all the parts of the stroke work in concert, then the sensation of rolling back and forth on the slide is a nearly addictive pleasure. It can be felt even near the end of a long, hard-fought race when the body

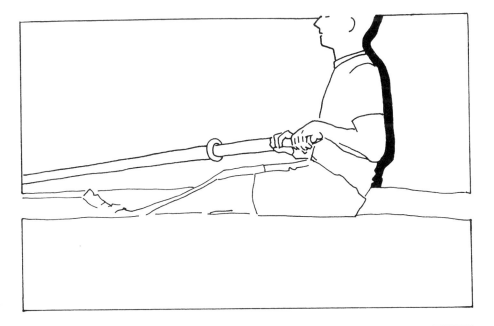

The Finish: When the legs are fully extended, the elbows break and finish the stroke by pulling the oar handle into the lap. As the handle nears the rower's abdomen, the hands feather it out of the water and smoothly push it forward into the recovery.

The Recovery: The recovery, the point in the rowing cycle when the shell is most unstable, demands perfect balance and composition. The hands lead the body down the slide, the oar shield six inches off of the water, and as the handle passes over the ankles, the hands begin to feather the oar into a squared position and raise it up into a sharp catch.

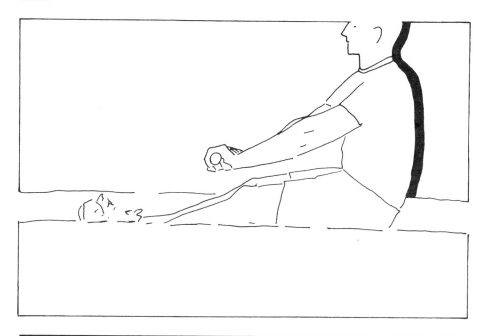

is rebelling and most rowers feel pushed beyond the limits of endurance.

The rower must be careful to sit squarely on the seat because if he drives hard while sitting skewed, the wheels can jam and cause a minor disaster. Even worse, the seat can jump the track and become completely derailed, a condition that is difficult to fix quickly, particularly when a rower is under the pressure of a race.

The reason slidework is so important is the effect the crew's rolling weight has on the run, or forward motion of the shell. Remember, nothing is driving a shell forward when the oars are out of the water except the kinetic energy released by the last drive. During the recovery, when precise and smooth slidework is most important, the crew must take pains not to rush the slide, or move too quickly into the catch, because their combined mass will check and counteract the shell's momentum and cause it to slow down, making the next catch much harder.

At the catch, the seats should stop and reverse direction almost without a pause. The hands should roll the oar square beginning at the ankles. When the body and arms are stretched out to their fullest, the seat should stop moving, the hands and arms should drop the oar in the water and the legs should drive back on the stretchers. All of this takes place in a fraction of a second, the seat and oar never stopping for even a moment.

During the drive, the rower should keep his arms straight and begin to open up his back from a forward lean to the upright position as the legs push him back with the oar. If the back doesn't work as a stiff hinge, focusing the power of the legs, then the rower will "shoot his slide" (also known as "shooting the bum"). Much of his leg power will be wasted, the arms merely hanging onto the oar while the legs shoot the seat toward the bow too quickly.

Throughout the entire stroke, the head should be held upright, eyes focused a little bit above the horizon. Controlling one's head will force control into the back and slide. An upright head also keeps the windpipe open, feeding more oxygen to the lungs and making hard rowing much more efficient. During a race (in a coxed shell), there is no reason for a rower to look out of the boat.

Several fundamentals to sweep rowing should always be obeyed. They are:

TIMING

Keeping in perfect time with the other rower or rowers in a sweep shell is harder than it looks. Many rowers achieve it by keeping an eye on the oar in front of them, using it as a cue to keep their own oar perfectly synchronized. If the timing of even one oar in an eight-oared shell is off, then the entire boat will suffer. It is the coxswain's job to keep the rowers in time, calling out to those who are early or late with their blades.

HARD CATCH

Some styles earlier in this century favored a soft catch where the blade eased into the water before the full force of the leg drive was applied. By current thinking such an approach is wrong because it loses the most effective point of the stroke. A hard catch is accomplished by raising the forearms crisply up about 6 inches when the rower is rolled all the way up his slide and is compressed into the stretchers. The motion that drops the oar into the water, when done correctly, should result in a small back splash.

SLOW HANDS

The hands should lead the body out of the finish and into the recovery. If the rower rushes them away from his body, the run of the shell will be checked. An indication of this failing is small spacing between the puddles, or whorls left in the water at the finish from the last stroke. During the recovery the hands should finish, then move out of the lap at a speed that won't vary at any point to the catch.

KEEP OVER THE KEEL

Many rowers lean from one side to the other to compensate for a flaw in their stroke. Leaning is not the way to balance a boat and can lead to bad habits that are difficult to break. Some early rowing styles encouraged an exaggerated lean away from the oar handles, the thinking being that the further outboard, or away from the rigger, that the rower placed himself, the greater the leverage he'd have on the oar. The unnatural strain of such a stroke, and its tiring effects, led to a return to centered rowing. A coxswain in a shell where all the rowers are perfectly centered over the keel should be able to see only one head, one torso, and two sets of hands.

NEVER LOOK OUT OF THE SHELL

Coxswains look around and steer; rowers row and nothing else. It is of no concern to a rower where his opponents are during a race; the coxswain will tell him that. Turning the head from one side to another will upset the balance of the boat. Looking around also means the rower isn't looking at the rower in front of him, checking the timing and staying aware of any increase of decrease in the rate, or strokes per minute.

DON'T RUSH THE SLIDE

In the excitement of a race, many rowers want to rush their oar in and out of the water, thinking that the more strokes they take, the faster the boat will go. Rushing and flailing back and forth on the slide leads to nothing but a disorganized, sloppy boat where no one is effective and tempers will certainly flare. One rushed slide can be felt by everyone in the boat, the break in momentum passed along and affecting each slide's speed. As the rower concentrates on the principle of slow hands (see above) to lead him out of the finish, he should also keep his seat moving at the same controlled rate.

HAVE FUN

Most competitive rowers will laugh outright at this piece of advice, but it isn't written anywhere that rowing has to be a chore that leads only to enlightenment and a strong body. Competition should be enjoyable. While talking in a racing shell is forbidden, except for the coxswain's constant chatter, rowing should be an enjoyable experience for everyone in the shell. Many rowers, dissatisfied with the unyielding strictures of rowing in shell with other rowers, find bliss rowing alone in a single shell. Other rowers need the company of others to share the pain and pleasure of what is a unique and special sport.

In later chapters, there will be much discussion of rowing styles and how they evolved through time as new technology such as sliding seats and swinging oarlocks were invented. Today, as was true a hundred years ago, there is no standard rowing style, especially on the competitive level, where coaches try to develop their own variations on the standard theme described above to accommodate the physiques and idiosyncrasies of a specific crew and make them faster than their competition.

J. Fletcher Chace, a varsity rower at Harvard in the 1930s, described the remarkable differences in styles taught by the coaches of that time.

> **(In prep school) we rowed in the style of Ed Leader: reaching as far as possible out of the boat and then laying back and squeezing out each stoke against our often bloody chests. All this probably gave us six inches more in the water and had a minimal effect due to the acute angle of the oar at the finish of the stroke. It bounced the boat when we used our over developed stomach muscles and took too much out of the rowers. Trying to raise the beat while whipping our torsos in great awkward arcs eventually increased rushing the slides and checking the boat's run.**

The exaggerated "torso whipping" so vividly described by Chace was a direct descendant of the orthodox English style, one developed out of necessity in the old, fixed-seat barges first rowed on the Thames before the advent of the sliding seat. Even after the invention of the slide, coaches were slow to take full advantage of the potential power contained in the rowers' legs. The use of the legs before the invention of the slide was regarded as a vaguely unsportsmanlike trick. In fact, the legs contain the strongest muscle groups in the body, and their anatomy gives them a leverage that when harnessed can move nearly three times the weight of the entire body.

The first sliding seats in the 1880s moved only a few inches and gradually increased in range to their present limit of about 24 inches. Old habits die hard, however, and it took several decades for collegiate coaches to understand how to completely adapt the upper body swing of the English style to the seats.

Much has been made of rowing styles and their effect on a shell's speed, especially in the golden age of the sport when professional scullers dared to experiment with every aspect of the stroke in their drive for more speed and money. When those scullers retired and went on to coach college crews, they imparted the secrets of their style to their crews. Some, such as Ellis Ward of the University of Pennsylvania, went to the extreme of whispering directions to his crew through a carefully directed megaphone to safeguard his trade secrets.

The rowing styles that underwent major changes around the turn of the century resulted in a style that changed the emphasis on stout men with barrel chests and mighty arms, to tall, thin, lanky types with the reach and strength to exploit the potential of swiveling oars and sliding seats. Training emphasis shifted from the arms and backs and moved down to the legs.

Modern styles are all fundamentally the same. A

rower who has mastered the basics of rowing hard with precise blade and slidework will have no trouble adapting to a new coach's preferred style. As in any sport, there are infinite refinements; just as golfers talk about their grips and backswings, serious rowers avidly discuss the subtle points of varying the speed of their hands during the recovery and the length of their reach.

At the turn of the century, Steven Fairbairn, an Australian sculler and coach, founded a school of rowing that held as its basic tenet that power, not nice form, was what made a fast crew. An outspoken critic of the formal English orthodoxy, according to rowing historian Thomas C. Mendenhall III, Fairbairn taught, "Drive at your blade and let your body and slide take care of themselves." Those words of advice have metamorphosed to the modern style. Yet today's technique is hardly as simple as just lunging against an oar and waiting for the style and fine points to fall into place on their own. Rowing is a sport that demands continual repetition of the same cycle of movements, a cycle that is demanding and offers very little room for error, especially at the competitive levels, where races are decided by a margin of hundredths of seconds and a missed stroke by one member of the crew can mean the difference between winning or losing a shirt.

Although a rower doesn't have to surround himself with the mountain of equipment that a hockey or football player needs, there are a few special requirements.

Clothing should provide warmth for late and early season rowing, but be easy to remove as the rower warms up and starts to break a sweat. Shorts should be tight fitting, almost like bicycling tights. There are special shorts available for rowing, double-knit wool or cotton with a drawstring waist and tight cuffs around the thigh so no loose folds of cloth will dangle down and jam the wheels of the seat. Men usually wear an athletic supporter or jockey shorts under their rowing shorts, women a pair of briefs. The shorts should be kept clean and dry to avoid the common problem of rashes and boils.

Worn on the upperbody are usually T-shirts, turtleneck pullovers, or polo shirts that have short tails and are fairly tight. Oar handles have a tendency to tangle in the folds of a loose shirt, spawning crabs and missed strokes; so the tighter the shirt, the better, as long as it is loose enough not to impede the athlete's movements.

Shoes are unneeded, except for walking around the boathouse and for carrying the shell down to the dock. Many rowers wear simple beach sandals, storing them on the bottom of the shell under their slide or feet. Sweat socks are a necessity, especially in older shells that use leather insteps and metal heel cups instead of modern running shoes for stretchers. In the older equipment, the feet constantly move around, sometimes chafing and raising blisters. Modern shells equipped with running shoes are far more comfortable, but socks still should be worn both for warmth and out of consideration for the next person to occupy the same seat.

The graceful appearance and fluid speed of a racing shell exacts a steep price from its rowers.

Don't row in tennis whites or your best, high fashion sports clothes. Rowing may look clean and graceful, but it can be a very dirty sport. The grease that is smeared on oarlocks and oars will inevitably find its way onto shirts and shorts. That's why the attire of a rower in ordinary practice leans toward ripped shirts and mended shorts.

In the early days of rowing sport, when barge clubs and navies were a refuge for the wealthy and socially prominent of America's Eastern cities, ornate uniforms of silk, with satin sashes and jaunty caps were *de rigeur*. College rowers relaxed the stiff formality of early rowing fashion; photographs of crews from around the turn of the century demonstrate a remarkable similarity to modern rowers. The only exception is modern T-shirts more often than not proclaim a message.

During the 1960s and 1970s, when men's hair was worn long, rowers wore sweatbands or hats to keep their hair out of the eyes. Since a cardinal rule of rowing is never, ever take a hand off an oar in a moving shell, even for a second (exceptions are made when paddling at a very slow rate for experienced rowers), anything a rower can do before climbing aboard that might distract him should be repaired, taped, scratched, or cut beforehand. Hence the popularity of the crew cut with rowers, that apotheosis of style that leaves enough hair on a head to keep the bearer on this side of baldness, but one that does away with the need for comb and towel.

The last personal aspect of rowing that should be mentioned is blisters and callouses. Every rower gets blisters sooner or later (usually sooner). Only a few days after first putting an oar's roughened handle in his hands, his hands will degenerate into a mass of torn skin and red, raw patches.

Blisters are the natural result of friction between the hand and handle. As the oar is feathered over and over, the inside of the thumb and the top of the palm where the fingers join the hand take most of the pressure and pain. The first blisters are little fluid-filled sacs that inevitably pop and rip apart. Adhesive tape should never be wrapped over popped blisters as the adhesive can roll into the open wounds and cause infections. Gauze pads will also roll into a thin, useless tube, and gloves will only prolong the inevitable, dull the hands' sense of the oar, and earn their wearer the sobriquet of one who can't take the pain.

Pain is useful because it informs the body that something is injuring it. Rowing in pain is not good because it can breed a hatred of the sport faster than a bad coach or a leaky shell. Telling a newcomer to the sport that his blisters will, in time, evolve into nice, tough callouses isn't much of a consolation when immediate relief is needed. There are as many approaches to blister maintainance as there are to rowing styles.

Most boathouses and trainer's rooms have the necessary tools to keep callouses strong and blisters away. Rubbing alcohol, alum, gauze, tape, and emery boards are the usual blister tools, with some rowers using their own salves and ointments (lanolin, Corn Husker's Lotion, baby rash medicine) to keep their hands in shape. Within two or three weeks, most blisters will disappear entirely and the rowers can forget about the pain in their hands and concentrate on the task of balancing the boat and building their power.

If you are new to rowing don't let the complex equipment and emphasis on perfect timing and bladework discourage you. No rower is expected to pull a perfect stroke at first, and many of the best rowers carry imperfect strokes with them for their entire lives. Rowing should be a simple pleasure that is enjoyable and beneficial to one's health and peace of mind—not a precise chore that demands 100 percent of one's concentration.

C H A P T E R 6

SCULLING

"The art of sculling is like any other art. It is perfected only with constant practice so that each movement is graceful and is done correctly without thinking about it. It takes a lot of thinking about, before this can be accomplished, however."

George Pocock *Notes on the Sculling Stroke as Performed by Professional Scullers on the Thames River, England*

There is a great deal of confusion among most people as to the usage and definition of rowing, sculling, and crew. The last is sometimes used as a verb—a grievous mistake that will mark the user as a rank beginner or ignorant critic. One may crew on an America's Cup 12-meter yacht, but one rows *on the crew.*

Rowing is defined as the act of propelling a boat with oars set in oarlocks or thole pins mounted either on riggers mounted on the hull, or set in the gunwale. The use of oarlocks or pins is the factor that differentiates rowing from paddling, where both hands grasp and move the paddle without using a fulcrum.

To a yachtsman, sculling means moving a small craft, such as a dinghy, punt, or skiff, with one oar set into a notch in the transom or stern board. By moving the oar back and forth in a figure-eight, the dinghy moves forward—often very quickly. To a rower, however, sculling is the act of rowing a boat with two oars. A sailor would simply call it rowing, but sculling is derived from the Middle English *sculle*, or *skulle*, which, loosely translated means "paddling."

The reason most oarsmen spend most of their competitive days in a shell in the company of others is simple economics, eights give a college team more mileage for their money, so to speak, opening up more seats for more oarsmen under the direction of fewer coaches (and hence fewer motor launches and drivers).

But the freedom of sculling is undoubtedly appealing! One rower in one boat, racing himself down the river, conscious that every foot of progress gained is earned at the expense of his work and his alone. Yet such freedom is usually denied to the journeyman oarsman for the same reasons that colleges train and race aboard eights: sculls are rare.

There are usually a few sculls in the boathouse, usually ancient specimens abused on weekend jaunts by everyone from the dilettante chemistry professor to a novice graduate student who wants to complete his education with a shaky, usually terrifying and wet paddle down the sylvan river of academia. There may also be those gleaming works of art owned by a coach or a serious contender for the Olympic team. These fine specimens hang from the ceiling, hoisted aloft in a sling secured to a block and tackle and are too delicate to be used by anyone other than their owners.

And then there are wherries—heavy, beamy, lapstraked craft that don't even rate a rack, but sit on the boathouse floor, their age determined like the rings of a tree trunk by the layers of peeling varnish. Wherries are for the feeble, for people with dates to impress, for people who don't mind stopping every hundred hard strokes to bail out the river flowing through the planks.

Serious scullers tend to be older than the average oarsman. They usually are devoted graduates or persons of means who want to keep rowing and can afford the expense of their own scull and the space to stow it in. Hence sculling is very popular at rowing clubs, where the members come and go as they please and have the wherewithal to own their own boat to be used at their own leisure.

Competitive scullers also tend to be older than college students, for it is only a person free from the constraints of team participation who can cut loose and row on his own with the self-control and dedica-tion that single sculling demands.

Sculling is a very difficult art to master, let alone compete and win in. Where a 60-foot eight is a difficult craft to balance perfectly, a single scull is a near impossibility. Both oars must strike and exit the water at exactly the same moment, the oarsman must never, even for a moment, take his mind off of the oars and balance of the shell. One mistake, one lapse in concentration, and he will flip into the water in the span of a heartbeat.

First off, examine the construction of a scull. A typi-cal wooden racing scull (with a price tag as high as $5,000 for a custom European design) is between 24 and 27 feet long and anywhere from 10.5 to 12 inches wide at the waterline. The weight of a scull, complete with riggers, slide, and stretchers, is be-tween 25 and 36 pounds—little more than a racing bicycle!

The slide and stretchers are essentially the same as those found in an eight- or four-oared shell, the only difference being that one of the stretchers often has a stopwatch mounted on it so a solitary sculler can train and time himself if a coach isn't accompa-nying him during the row.

There is no rudder on a scull, simply a skeg, which is a small fin similar those built onto surf-boards. The purpose of the skeg is to keep the boat on a precise track, keeping it stable if the sculler is rowing in a crosswind. Steering is accomplished with the oars. Pulling hard on one oar and easing off on the other will cause the scull to turn, the speed of the turn depending on the degree of power and easing the sculler applies to the oars.

The oars, or more precisely, the sculls, are between 9 feet, 5 inches., and 9 feet 10 inches. The blades are between 18 and 24 inches long, their design a close copy of the tulip shape used for sweep oars. The handles are much shorter than sweep oars and covered with rubber grips. When both sculls are run out through the oarlocks, the handles overlap, a situation that confuses many first-time scullers who can't decide how to pull the oars in through the drive without jamming them together. The solution lies in the riggers, which can be adjusted so the left handles always passes over the right without upsetting the balance of the shell.

A scull, like a full shell, looks very fragile but in fact is just as strong as an eight, just sleeker and narrower. Red cedar or spanish cedar is used for the planking, with the ribs and keelson made from sturdy New York or Pennsylvania ash. The decks are covered with canvas, silk, or plastic, stretched taut and then sealed with a thinned coat of varnish. The seat is a laminate of cedar and white pine, mounted on a steel slide on rubber or nylon wheels.

Such modern materials as Kevlar—the carbon fiber cloth invented to strengthen truck tires and bullet-proof vests—are used in scull construction just as they have been used for a number of years in eights and fours. Fiber glass is still used, especially in recreational sculls, but has lost much of its popularity among competitive scullers, the majority of whom prefer wood, followed by the new high-tech com-

The Catch: The beginning of the stroke, or catch, begins when the rower rolls forward on his or her side and buries both blades in the water in a squared position. The head is held upright, focusing on the horizon, the arms are extended fully forward and the chest touches the knees. At the instant the rower reaches this position, the drive begins.

The Drive: Following the catch, the rower drives back with his or her legs, and begins to straighten the back, pushing back and flattening down the knees without breaking his or her elbows.

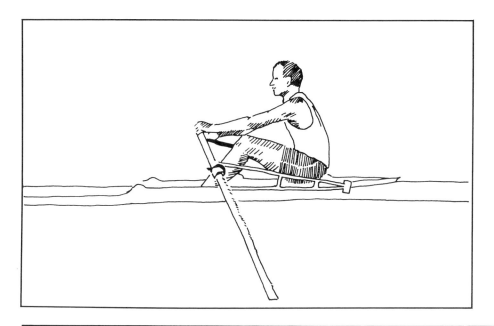

posite construction such as Kevlar or carbon fiber.

The riggers of a scull resemble a right triangle, buttressed with additional braces, the entire construction made of lightweight metals such as molybdinum or magnesium. Further advances in the use of synthetic materials have resulted in racing sculls with carbon fiber riggers, a light and deceptively strong application that is becoming as popular as oars and shells made from the same materials.

Learning how to scull demands only the ability to swim and good, old-fashioned patience. Some American teams start their novices off in sculls for the same reasons the Europeans do, as a way of developing basic skills. One such team is the Durham Boat Club in Durham, New Hampshire, home to the University of New Hampshire crew.

Jim Dreher, coach of the Durham Boat Club and founder of the UNH crew, said Durham's emphasis on sculling has paid off with some prestigious victories.

Dreher said the German rowing federation limits competition between junior oarsmen (sixteen years old and younger) to training sculls, or skiffs as they are known in Europe. "Most oarsmen learn in training singles because they want unstable boats to help the novices develop the basic skills and feel the instant feedback only a scull can give," Dreher said of the Germans.

Another reason Dreher cited for the dominant position sculling occupies in European rowing is the close relationship between clubs and scholastic teams. England is a perfect example of clubs such as Leander providing space, boats, and financial backing to university crews, while American rowing has always been divided into two different worlds—with clubs and schools generally operating independent of each other.

Dreher said, "In Europe and in Canada and Australia, rowing is, for the most part, club supported. We (the Durham Boat Club) are one of the few that operate that way in this country. Durham sponsors the Oyster River high school crew, as well as providing space for the UNH crew. Eights are very rare in Europe. When people are learning to row for the first time, sculling is a much more natural movement to learn. Where sculling is balanced and symmetrical, in sweep rowing you are pulling on just one side and twisting your back in the same direction over and over again."

Dreher's emphasis on sculling has worked well for him and his crews. "We won the quad (four scullers in one boat) in the Scholastic Nationals as well as the junior doubles. We won the double at the Canadian Henley. We won the four at the Head of the Charles, beating Navy and Yale with a crew of juniors rowing against twenty-year-olds."

Although most of America's English coaches were professional scullers first and foremost, in America they worked with eights and fours. A few of these coaches would hire themselves out to clubmen or donate spare time on weekends to a collegiate oarsman who wanted to learn the secrets of sculling; but by and large, the most successful American

The Finish: Three-quarters of the way through the drive, the elbows break and the arms smoothly take over from the legs. The back is slightly curved, the head remains upright, and the hands begin to feather the sculls so the blades will smoothly exit the water and the grips end up in the lap. In a smooth motion, the hands, without stopping, move the sculls out of the lap into the recovery.

The Recovery: During the recovery, the hands lead the rest of the body forward on the slide, the body moves gently forward without rushing, and the blades, feathered parallel to the water, should move above the surface without striking. At the end of the recovery, the hands begin to square the blades and drop them into the water for the catch.

scullers have taught themselves how to scull.

Sculling is a sport for self-motivated loners, people who can set their alarm clock for 5 a.m. and drag themselves out of bed and down to the boathouse. Working out requires the dedication of a long-distance runner: it is so easy to slack off on a few strokes, or stop and rest for a few extra minutes when there isn't a coach standing in a launch a few feet away, megaphone and stopwatch in his hands.

Brad Lewis, gold medalist with Paul Enquist in the 1984 Olympic doubles, trained alone in Southern California, racing himself from landmark to landmark, becoming completely absorbed in the business of training without the company of another sculler to challenge or pace him. Lewis went so far as to invent a device, attached to one rigger, that measured his speed by forcing water through a tube. Learning to scull on one's own is not that difficult. What is difficult is learning to scull the right way without developing all sorts of bad habits.

Other elite scullers pack up their shell and belongings and move to a rowing center like Washington, D.C., Philadelphia, or Seattle to train under the eye of a coach. There they rely on the philanthropy of others, living a hand-to-mouth existence in the quest for faster rowing.

Launching a scull is a one-man operation. The first thing to carry down to the dock are the oars, as it is very inconvenient to launch and then sprint back up the dock to the boathouse for them while the scull bobs unattended away from the float. A single scull is carried over the head, with the hands holding onto the riggers where they bolt into the splash boards. Care should be taken to make sure the bow and stern don't knock into the racks or doorway of the boathouse. At the water's edge, the shell is rolled down and gently laid onto the surface. Then both oars are run out through their oarlocks, the gates are locked down, drain plugs and inspection ports closed, and without further ado, sculling can begin.

Moving away from the dock takes some practice. Facing the stern of the scull, slide the seat into the bow and place your left foot on the slide. Hold both oar handles in the left hand, crouch down to lower your center of gravity, and push away with your right foot in an emphatic, smooth motion. The boat will glide sideways away from the dock and as the inboard rigger clears the edge of the float, slowly sit down onto the seat. Don't worry about slipping your feet into the stretchers yet; think instead about getting the inboard oar blade clear of the dock and shell a few boat lengths away so other rowers may launch or land their shells. If a strong wind is blowing onto the dock and impeding the scull's outward glide, then just pull in the inboard oar and place the blade gently against the dock and use it to force the shell off far enough to set the blade in the water. Take a few strokes with your arms to pull the boat away from the dock, just far enough to give you time to adjust the length of the slide and get settled into the boat.

Adjust the slide by loosening the stretcher bolts and tighten them so that when the legs are straight down, the back wheels of the seat don't touch the stops, or end of the slide, but are within a half-inch of them. Don't lace the stretcher boots too tightly if this is one of your first times out, because if you flip, you want to be able to get your feet out quickly so you can swim clear of the shell.

With the oar blades flat on the water providing balance (don't try to lift them clear until you are sure you can maintain an even keel without their assistance), roll slowly forward to the catch position. The body should lean forward at about a 30-degree angle, the arms fully stretched out and spread out over the water. With your hands holding the handles, thumbs over the ends, roll the blades square and bury them in the water. Both knees should be inside of the arms at all times.

With the arms straight and the wrists flat, start the leg drive, keeping the body leaning forward until the seat has moved halfway up the slide, when the body should start swinging upright. The arms begin to break at the elbows, the speed of the upswing and arms timed to end exactly at the end of the slide.

At the finish, the body should be leaning back, toward the bow at the same 30-degree angle used at the catch. The hands, left over right, make a final squeeze into the middle of the abdomen, turning during the squeeze so the force of the water against the back of the blades will pop them to the surface without checking the speed of the boat.

At the finish of the stroke, when the handles are in the rower's lap and the scull blades are clear of the surface and feathered flat, the recovery begins, the hands and arms moving away from the body in a quick, but controlled motion that keeps both blades at the same height above the water. Novices should keep the blades on the surface, and let them skip on top of it during the recovery to provide an extra measure of balance. When the arms are fully extended, then the body follows, sitting upright and at the same time moving slowly down the slide toward the catch. Just as the slide must move slowly in a sweep shell—a pair, four, or eight—to preserve the run of the shell while the oars are out of the water, a sculler should take particular care not to rush back to the catch.

Some coaches recommend a slight pause at the catch. The reason is that the scull will still be moving quickly and that movement should be allowed to peak before another drive is started. George Pocock wrote that pausing at the catch also holds the weight of the sculler toward the stern of the shell, lifting the bow out of the water and making the hull design more efficient as it moves through the water.

The hands should not clench the oar handles, as too tight a grip will tire the arms and possibly cause cramps in the forearms. Instead, the hands should act like hooks around the handles, holding on with the fingers and not squeezing around them with the palms.

Another secret to efficient sculling is to avoid pulling the body down the slide during the recovery with one's feet. Doing so checks the run of the shell and often results in a rushed slide. The momentum generated by the hands and arms moving out of the bow at the finish should provide enough forward motion to lead the body and slide up into the catch.

To turn a scull around 180 degrees—a common manuever when a sculler runs out of water or wants to turn around and return to the boathouse—the shell should first be stopped dead in the water. Stopping is accomplished by finishing a stroke and then moving the arms away from the body. When the oars are perpendicular to the sides of the shell, the blades can be slightly turned and dug into the water, turning to a fully squared position and braking as the boat begins to slow.

Once the boat is completely stopped, one oar pulls and the other pushes in short choppy strokes. Gradually, the bow will swing around to the desired direction. Backing up a scull is done by simply pushing instead of pulling the oars, the slide stationary, the arms doing all of the work. Care should be taken not to push too hard on the oars, as the riggers are constructed for maximum strength for pulling.

Other than the number of oars, the most discernible difference between sculling and sweep rowing is the effect of the body's weight on the stability and performance of the scull. The hull of a scull is designed to float on a specific water line or level, and anything a sculler does to change that water line can either hurt or improve the shell's overall hydrodynamics. Concentration is needed to keep all the body's weight moving in a horizontal plane, as an

up-and-down motion will cause the hull to plunge and rise out of the water, a defect called hobby-horsing.

The best way to gauge if a scull is being rowed efficiently is to watch the water as it rolls out from beneath the stern. If the stern bobs with every stroke, sinking as the legs begin to drive, and rising at the finish, then some of the sculler's energy is being wasted on moving the boat up and down rather than forward.

Also, listen to the boat. The sculler must depend on his own senses to judge how efficiently he is moving the scull and how his form is affecting its performance. Sound is one of the best indications of how well a scull is moving. Splashes will signify bad rowing, especially on calm water where there are no waves to blame. A rhythm should be established, so the sound of the wheels under the seat, the oars squaring and feathering in the oarlocks, and the sculler's deep breathing are all coordinated.

Finally, breathing is the metronome of rowing. Some oarsmen attempt to inhale during the recovery and exhale during the drive, yet as the rating increases from a racing cadence of 30 to 38 strokes-per-minute to a 40 to 45 strokes-per-minute sprint, it is difficult to maintain an even pattern of breathing. Other oarsmen silently count while rowing, breaking the stroke down into defined segments and then counting them off. Breathing rhythm is extremely important for very obvious reasons, yet it is something that is easy to forget for a few strokes during a stressful period in a race, especially during the first minute after the start.

While single sculling is the most popular form of two oared rowing, double and quad or four-manned sculling is also strong, especially in rowing clubs where most of the members are avid scullers. The construction of doubles and quads is basically the same design for the pairs and fours used in sweep rowing. In fact some crews on a tight budget simply rig a pair with sets of sculling riggers (the oarsmen often being none the wiser). On the elite level, quads and pairs are rarer and are used by oarsmen for training practice for international events. Some of these boats, specialized as they are, have survived for more than a decade of hard competition. That is a long life for any racing shell, considering that the average college varsity crew races in a new shell every year.

Sculling in the company of others is a mixture of sweep rowing's emphasis on perfect timing and the rigid self-control of single rowing. Few colleges and only some clubs row quads, and pairs are usually found in the clubs. The reason quad and pair rowing is relatively unknown compared to single sculling and sweep rowing is that although they are events raced on the international level, there are few American races that feature them, and most elite oarsmen gravitate to them only after being eliminated from the single.

Recreational rowing has spawned a new interest

in sculling, especially singles, but most recreational shell builders include a pair in their fleets, a very popular design as it is a sociable way to exercise and a fine way to teach a novice how to scull.

It would be nearly impossible to convince a modern sports fan of the important place sculling once occupied as a professional sport. Rowing today seems to be a sport completely lacking in the unexpected thrills (and perhaps occasional violence) of the most popular professional team sports.

Yet it was not always so; like prizefighting and basketball today, sculling was once viewed as a ladder out of the slums by young men who saw no alternative means of rising from poverty. For the lucky and talented few, the rewards of sculling were widespread fame, large purses, and the luxury of a corporate sponsor.

Professional scullers in the late nineteenth century were some of the most famous professional athletes.

Professional sculling was, along with prizefighting, one of the first sports where its participants competed for purses. In the second half of the nineteenth century, those prizes were big for their time, some reaching up to $5,000 for the victors of races. Many a poor boy with a strong back and an affinity for the water, built or borrowed a scull, or needle as they were sometimes called, and spent his days brushing up against the college crews and legendary professionals to see if he had the potential to earn his living with an oar.

Scullers covered the waters of industrial America like water bugs. Every young man who lived near the water wanted one, and most built their own, or bought raffle tickets at the big face-offs between professionals for a chance to win one of the competitors' sculls after the racing was finished. Brothers like the Biglins of Philadelphia, the Cooks and the Courtneys, trained and raced together, creating avid followers who would journey from one end of the eastern seaboard to the other to watch them compete. A number of those races have gone down in rowing legend.

There was the infamous race between Michael Davis of Portland, Maine, and Patrick "Patsy" Reagan of Boston in 1878 on Silver Lake, a long, narrow body of water about thirty miles south of Boston near Plymouth. The Portland-Boston rowing rivalry was a fierce one; Michael Davis even brought a law suit against a competing boat club for allegedly copying some of his inventions on the club shells. Davis had beaten one Boston sculler, George Faulkner, before thirty thousand spectators on the Charles River. He challenged any Boston sculler to a 4-mile race for a total purse of $2,000, each side to put up $1,000. Boston's pride rested with Reagan, a working man who was acknowledged by all as the best sculler on the Charles River.

A race was set, the purse put up, and a location picked. The Old Colony Railroad, interested in promoting Silver Lake as a resort, scheduled a special twenty-two-car excursion train for the race. By the evening of October 7, betting was enthusiastic in Beantown, with the hometown crowds betting the

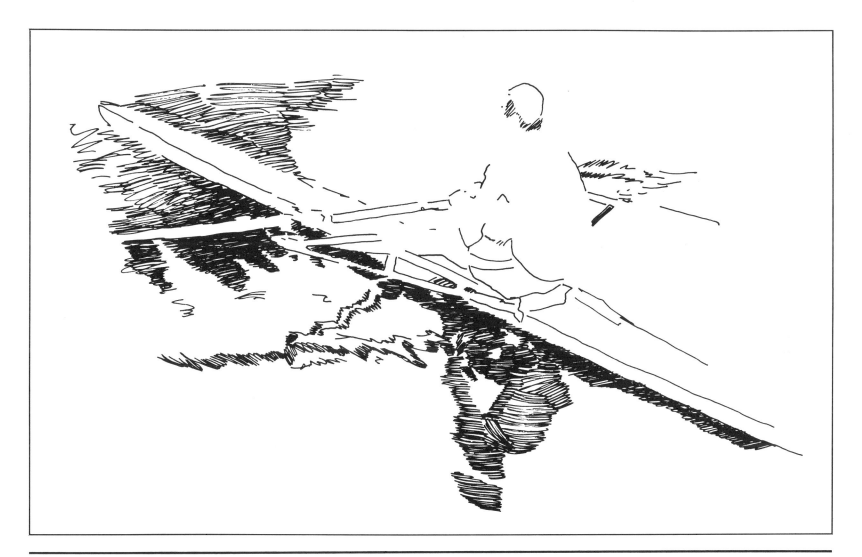

odds up to three to one in favor of Reagan.

The next day, the train departed South Station packed to the ceilings with more than a thousand passengers. The race began, an hour and a half late, at 4:30 p.m., when the scullers took to the water and paddled out to the starting line of the mile race.

It was 2 miles to a turning stake; races with turns were then popular, since they afforded better views for the spectators. After much delay, the race was started. Reagan made a poor rounding, emerging at the beginning of the home stretch at a clear disadvantage.

Davis crossed the line in record time for the course: 28 minutes, 6¾ seconds. Reagan was a distant nine lengths back, clearly exhausted when he crossed the finish line to the stunned silence of the Boston crowd.

An immediate cry went out, "All bets off!" as the outraged Reagan supporters refused to believe their man could be so roundly defeated. Fights broke out, bookies brandished pistols, and Reagan became too distraught to attend the prize ceremony with Davis. He and his scull were spirited away to the excursion train by his consoling entourage.

The $2,000 prize was awarded to Davis, and the train was quickly loaded for the return trip to Boston. The train crew began to nervously eye their pocketwatches while their departure was delayed later and later. It wasn't until well after six before they finally pulled away from the lake and headed back to the city.

The train ride back was a hectic one. The Portland and Boston fans fought with each other, arguing from car to car that Reagan had been fouled by Davis as he turned the stake. Meanwhile, Davis had repaired to a nearby town with his seconds for a champagne party. Reagan, however, was a broken man, emotionally and financially; he and his family had wagered every cent they owned on the race.

During the train ride, the passengers learned the news that Patsy Reagan's loss had left him bankrupt. So a hat was passed and both sides contributed to it.

Ahead, in Wollaston, near Quincy, a freight train had been broken apart to place another car inside the string. One of the switches on the excursion train's track was opened while the cars were shuttled around. That switch led to New England's greatest train disaster.

The excursion train barreled down the track, through the open switch and derailed, the engines piling together with a catastrophic crash. The engineer of the freight train, seeing what had happened, disengaged his engine from the remaining freight cars and roared off to the Quincy station to seek help. The unconnected cars rolled down into the wreckage, adding to the horrifying calamity.

Patsy Reagan was lifted from the wreckage and laid on the side of the track bed, dying and unable to speak. The last rites were given and he was covered with a blanket, as the uninjured went about the gruesome task of pulling bodies out of the splintered wreckage.

Nineteen people were killed that evening and

more than 190 were injured. Patsy Reagan's funeral attracted more than six thousand mourners.

Another great race from the era of professional sculling took place on the Hudson River in the 1890s between Jim Ten Eyck, crew coach at Syracuse University for thirty-five years, and a prominent German sculler lured abroad by the promise of a large purse. The race, certainly one of the longest ever held, started at the Battery on lower Manhattan and finished under the New York Central railway bridge in Albany, 150 miles up the Hudson.

Ten Eyck was by far the better sculler, and at Poughkeepsie, the halfway mark, he was far ahead of his opponent. Ten Eyck stopped at a dock in Poughkeepsie to rest. His father, who had been following in a launch, came alongside and offered his son a swig of brandy to restore his strength. Instead, the firewater sickened the exhausted oarsman, who was forced to climb back into his scull when his opponent pulled into view downriver.

Ten Eyck rowed on for a mile, sickened and weak, before pulling ashore and asking a railroad worker to fetch him a drink of spring water. Restored by the water, Ten Eyck was able to complete the race and finish more than an hour ahead of his opponent with an elapsed time of twenty-two hours.

Ten Eyck was bedridden for two days afterward, was unable to walk erect and lost all the skin on the palms of his hands. Teddy Roosevelt invited Ten Eyck to the White House to hear Ten Eyck's first-hand account of the marathon. Ten Eyck's shell now hangs in the National Museum in Washington.

By the 1920s, talented amateurs, like the Kellys of Philadelphia, were becoming the popular heroes of the sport. In their time, the Kellys captured the public's attention, rowing to Olympic and Henley victories with an ease and good humor that belied the hours of dedication and years of accumulated experience that went into their success.

John B. Kelly. Sr. was the founder of the sculling dynasty (and the father of Grace Kelly, the film actress who later became the princess of Monaco). John Kelly was the most famous oarsman of the 1920s and 1930s, a man who exemplified the city of Philadelphia's place as the rowing capital of America. In 1920, rowing for the renowned Vesper Boat Club, Kelly won the gold medal in the singles at Antwerp. That same year, with his cousin Paul Costello behind him in the bow seat, Kelly also won the gold medal in the double sculls—repeating the victory four years later in Paris.

Kelly gained the most attention of his rowing career when the stewards of the Royal Henley Regatta banned him from competing because he was not a "gentleman" (although he eventually became a millionaire, he originally earned his living as a bricklayer). The snobbish standards of the British created a stigma that did more than any Ivy League crew or patrician rowing clubs to brand crew as a pastime for the leisure class.

The Kelly name entered the American rowing hall of fame again through the extraordinary career of John Kelly's son, John, Jr. In 1947 and 1949, Jack Kelly won the Diamond Sculls at Henley, avenging his father in a way that captivated both the American and English public, as he rowed through English snobbishness and class attitudes to a victory that seemed to cleanse the tarnished memory of many professional scullers bounced from their sport by the sanctimony of academia and the elite.

While the romance of rowing today may fall short of yesterday's color, scullers are still gaining attention as the standard bearers of rowing, the elite individuals who seem improbable heroes as they charge down race courses on tiny, 25-pound wooden needles, their seats only inches above the water.

Today's scullers are the heroes of competitive rowing. They are the rowers the press write about, the solitary competitors that are somehow easier to get excited about than a boisterous eight-oared shell. Rowers such as Christopher "Tiff" Wood, graduate of the famed Harvard "Rude and Smooth" crew of the early 1970s, Gregg Stone of the same crew, Jim Dietz, who represented the United States for years in Olympic compeition, Pertii Kaarpinen, the indominable Finnish sculler, John Biglow, the American sculler in the 1984 Olympic Games, and many others have gained more attention in the press than scullers have since the heyday of Jack Kelly.

But the true excitement of sculling isn't its lore, nor its element of fame, but the enjoyment that thousands of people get from the sport, rowing their own races against themselves, day after day.

CHAPTER 7

OFF-THE-WATER
WORKOUTS

Until an enterprising rower invents a way to mount a shell on skates the way sailors have with iceboats, rowing in northern climates comes to a frozen stop during the winter. Race courses sheet over with ice and snow drifts across rivers, harbors, and lakes, forcing the rower to forsake his sport and seek a substitute.

Cold-weather rowing is fraught with danger to both a rower and his equipment. Even the thinnest sliver of ice can easily slash through the fragile hull of a wooden shell. Icicles hang from oars and hands turn purple. Such rows make for legends to be retold when the freshmen complain and uncomprehending bystanders question the sanity of those rowing their way to a certain case of pneumonia.

Yet ice is not the only reason crews leave the water in the winter. Even though teams in California, Texas, Arkansas, Lousiana, and Florida could row 365 days a year, many do not for the simple reason that too much of a good thing can breed boredom. A month, even a week, away from a boat and the water can give a rower an opportunity to enjoy other diversions and work on elements of physical training that an oar cannot provide.

Most crews turn their backs on rowing in late November and head for the boathouse or gymnasium for a winter of indoor workouts. Fifty years ago, rowing was mostly a spring and summer sport. The winter was spent relaxing or on another sport. Terms such as *aerobic, anerobic, circuit training*, and *ergometers* didn't exist in the rowing lexicon. There were rowing machines in those days, but they were inefficient contraptions scorned by most rowers. So coaches and riggers repaired and varnished the shells, coxswains watched their weight, and the rest of the crew blithely went about life with no thought of rowing until spring's first balmy days.

That outlook on the sport changed in the late 1950s when a West German high school coach named Karl Adam decided that fast rowing wasn't simply a matter of a smooth stroke and polished technique, but that good physical conditioning and continuity were just as important. In those relatively unsophisticated days, physical conditioning was synonymous with wind, or the ability to run, swim, or row a long distance without collapsing into a wheezing heap. Adam looked for ways he could extend a rower's wind and thus brought to rowing the concept of aerobic and anerobic training.

Adam's initial success led to the founding of the world's first year-round rowing center. In Ratzeburg, a lakeside town near Hamburg in West Germany, Adam pushed his crews through a winter routine of running and weight lifting, a program designed to expand their lungs, improve their cardiovascular systems, and tone their muscles. Films of the previous season's races were reviewed and critiqued as crews stayed together as a team for an entire year.

In the early 1960s, Adam's technique proved its efficacy as West German crews began to win and win big in Olympic and other international competition. American rowers, once the most successful in the world, were finishing in the wake of the Germans and other Europeans. German crews were powering their way to victory rather than finessing it, as had been the philosophy of the orthodox English school of rowing. Adam was pleased to share his methods with others. His Ratzeburg rowing clinics became a mecca for coaches, and by 1970 there wasn't an elite team left in the world that didn't follow Adam's practice of off-the-water training.

The heart of Adam's training philosophy applies to any endurance sport: expand the athlete's aerobic capacity and he or she will run faster for a longer time. Aerobic training is not dancing in leotards to the sound of music, although the basic goals are fundamentally the same. Aerobic training attempts to extend the time athletes can exert themselves using oxygen for fuel. The aerobic state lasts only as long as the athlete's cardiovascular system can take in enough oxygen and then transport it efficiently through the blood stream to his or her muscles. When oxygen levels dip to a certain point, the body automatically shifts gears, so to speak, and enters the anerobic state—an inefficient condition where the body literally turns upon itself and begins breaking down sugar in its search for fuel. A body working in the anerobic state produces lactic acid; the result is an overall stiffening of the muscles and the inability to continue working. Rowers feel it when their bodies scream for a rest, causing their shell to lose its speed.

The ultimate goal of off-the-water training is to postpone, for as long as possible, the transition from the aerobic to anerobic state. Vast amounts of exercise are needed to push the cardiovascular system to a high level of performance. So much work is needed that the credo of Walter "Buzz" Congram, coach of the Northeastern University heavyweight crew in Boston, is: "It takes twice as long to get into shape than it does to get out."

In the past two decades a plethora of technology has been developed to help rowers extend the time their bodies may remain in the aerobic state. Running and swimming are both excellent, accessible, and basic ways to build endurance and strength.

Home rowing machines also provide a good workout; but most are poorly made, cannot withstand the pressure of an intense session, and fall short of accurately simulating the true action of a stroke.

For rowers living in areas where snow covers the ground most of the winter, perhaps the best substitute for rowing is cross-country skiing. Peter Gardner, coach of the Dartmouth heavyweight crew in Hanover, New Hampshire, and Randy Jablonic, coach of the University of Wisconsin heavyweight crew, rely on cross-country skiing as the backbone of their winter training programs. The leg motion of cross-country skiing is comparable to that used in rowing, and more importantly, skiing also uses the arms to a greater extent than running. Skiing stresses a polished technique during hard work, a combination that rowing depends on for effectivenes. Many northern college teams organize skiing trips during Christmas breaks as a way to continue training and to build camaraderie among team members. Some college rowing teams, such as Wisconsin's, are so competitive on skis that their members sometimes win races against athletes who consider skiing their best sport.

Another good source of aerobic exercise is bicycling. In the winter, when icy conditions can make a foray onto the streets aboard a bike a suicidal risk, a stationary bike or a roller-mounted ten speed can give the legs a great workout. The only drawback of indoor bicycling is that the arms and upper body are somewhat ignored.

Give any coach his choice of machines to provide a rower with the best possible workout and he will select an ergometer. Ergometers are true rowing machines that have been in use for less than twenty years. The first ergometers, or "ergs," were developed at Stanford University in the early 1960s. They were expensive, loud, and nearly impossible to move without a forklift. By 1970 the Gamut ergometer began to appear in boathouses and is still in use today as one of the better quantitative measurements of a rower's condition and progress. A more specialized ergometer was developed in Sweden and is used in Olympic selection camps and by sports physiologists. Furthermore, a newer version of the ergometer, inexpensive and convenient enough for most people, has come onto the market: the Concept II.

Ergometers differ from home rowing machines in important respects. A true ergometer consists of a rolling seat, or slide; a flywheel, or revolving drum with a resistance mechanism; a lap counter, or odometer to measure distance; and an oar handle attached to a cable or chain to spin the flywheel. On the Gamut machines, the rower's weight is calculated to set the pressure of the brake against the flywheel. When the rower begins rowing he starts a large darkroom-type timer mounted on the head of the machine. With the clock running, the rower does his best to spin the flywheel as rapidly as possible, each revolution being noted on a counter. A tachometer is mounted next to the clock to tell the rower how effective and powerful his stroke is. For the next five to twenty minutes the rower slides back and forth, driving his legs down and hauling back

At the beginning, or catch, of the stroke, Charles Clapp's head is held erect, eyes focused on the ergometer's tachometer. This is the instant where the body has stopped moving forward and is poised to drive backward. Clapp's abdomen is flat against the top.

The leg drive begins as the knees push down and the back begins to rise perpendicular to the floor. Clapp keeps his arms rigid and straight with his shoulders taking most of the pressure of the stroke.

Now three-quarters of the way through the leg drive, Clapp's back is leaning past perpendicular, his legs are flat and his arms are pulling in the oar handle to finish the stroke.

THE BOOK OF ROWING

At the finish of the stroke, Clapp tucks his elbows to his side and pulls the handle into his stomach.

the mock oar handle, his body working exactly as if it were rowing in an actual shell.

The uses of an ergometer are many and lend themselves to a variety of physical goals. A rower may use an ergometer for an extended period of time and row for distance, pacing himself and using the machine for an aerobic workout; or he may use it for short spurts of concentrated effort, sprinting against the clock and raising his pulse rate over and over.

For coaches, an ergometer is a valuable instrument for measuring a rower's improvement in comparison to past workouts or against the performance of other team members. Most colleges set aside one practice session a week—usually a Saturday morning—for test rows on ergometers. Such rows test not only the rower's physical condition, but also his attitude and desire to compete. The final score is irrefutable and the source of much anxiety around the boathouse on "erg" days. Coaches often become quite adept at predicting the scores of their rowers.

In Olympic selection camps, the more sophisticated Swedish ergometer is used in the early days of the camp to winnow out less competitive athletes. Instead of driving the flywheel with a handle attached to a cable or chain, the Swedish ergometers consist of a handle and a long bar that drives the wheel. In some colleges, up to eight rowers will face off on eight machines and row as if they were sculling against each other in a true race.

The rowing machine was once standard equipment in any gym of the late nineteenth and early twentieth centuries. Heavy, black iron machines, they were used to strengthen legs, backs, and arms by simulating sculling. Ridiculed in cartoons and films, the first rowing machines were associated with red-faced, cigar puffing tycoons trying to stave off a case of gout.

Photos of the *Titanic's* gymnasium show a set of rowing machines as examples of the ship's well equipped accommodations. Teams had used them since the 1850s, when they were introduced to English oarsmen as the next best thing to being in a shell. Over the years the design of the machines evolved into the modern ergometer, a specialized, high-tech machine that is used by physiologists as a precise measurement of an athlete's physical capacity.

The surge in demand over the last decade for convenient, safe methods of exercise has spawned a boom in the home rowing machine business. Where many bedrooms of the 1960s had a stationary bicycle parked, unused, in a closet, rowing machines are replacing them and being used.

A home rowing machine can range from a true ergometer for serious exercise of a rower's off-water workouts, to a simple metal frame with a sliding seat and two handles affixed to two hydraulic cylinders.

The price of a rowing machine, at the high end, can float somewhere over $600 dollars for an ergometer. Many schools replace their set of ergometers every two years or so due to the punishment they receive from their crews; yet for a couple hundred dollars and some maintenance, a bargain hunter can procure one of the best exercise tools bar none.

Those on a more modest budget and with small quarters, should consider a hydraulic home rowing machine. The most fancy have timers, counters, and digital pulse meters. The most basic cost in the neighborhood of $100 to $150. Over a million were sold in 1985.

Accomplishing an efficient workout on a home machine is a matter of devoting the time to raise the heartbeat for a sufficient length of time to improve the cardiovascular system. Many machines can be used for weight training, allowing a rower to work on curls, or even, with the machine up ended and the athlete lying on the floor, allow him or her to work on bench presses and the chest muscles.

While the feel of a hydraulic machine is a far cry from the fluid action of a true ergometer, they are effective and inexpensive devices that work on the same key muscles for rowing.

In the Ivy League, coached practices on the water end by agreement on the Saturday before Thanksgiving and resume only when the spring thaw opens up the water again. During the winter, Ivy League and other rowers across the country rely on indoor rowing tanks to simulate floating workouts aboard shells.

Tank rowing is a luxury enjoyed by several colleges and prep schools across the United States. Some colleges, especially those in the North, have several tanks that can accommodate up to sixteen rowers at once. Although such tanks don't allow the rowers to practice setting up or balancing a shell, they do provide a realistic setting in which to practice bladework and style.

Tanks work by having water pumped through a continuous loop down a shallow pool and then down through a conduit into an impeller, which forces it back up into the other end of the pool; the coach sets the rate of the flow by adjusting the speed of the impeller with a throttle. While most modern tanks are moving-water types, others are nothing more than a stationary pool of water that can only be rowed in using oars with hollowed-out blades.

Tanks are often used to teach rowing to novices. Experienced rowers will sometimes spend an entire afternoon practice in a tank, working to build endurance and to polish their style. Yet, according to most coaches, the primary purpose of a tank session is the exercise it provides. Tanks give no sense of swing or the balance of shell, so their use, in the end, is to keep rowers acquainted with their oars and the sequence of a stroke. Mirrors are mounted along the sides of tanks so the rowers can watch themselves and catch any stylistic flaws pointed out by their coaches.

Although pushing the anerobic threshold higher and higher is one of the goals of off-the-water training, building muscle strength is equally important. While rowing itself builds and tones muscles, a crew must leave its shell and enter a weight room to make rapid and lasting progress.

Thanks to the advent of the ergometer, rowing is now a year-round sport.

THE BOOK OF ROWING

Free weights, or barbells, are the best way to build muscle strength. Unlike most weight-lifting programs that impose a slow progression to increasingly heavier weights, the object of weight training for rowing is to lift as much weight as possible, as many times as possible, in the shortest amount of time. Rowing, which values the leg and back muscles over the arms, is best served by focusing on exercises that emphasize those specific muscle groups. The object of rowing is not to pull an oar as hard as possible over a short period of time, but to pull it consistently hard over an extended one. By contrast, football players exert themselves in short bursts of activity with longer periods of rest in between plays; thus their physiques and conditioning demand more heavy muscle and bulk. Rowers are constantly working, pulling their oars as hard as possible from the start of a race to the finish. Muscle-bound rowers have a difficult time controlling their oars. When their bodies are extended to their fullest reach—such as at the catch of a stroke—it is difficult for an overmuscled person to subtly control the speed, angle, and height of his oar.

Like swimmers, bicyclists, and cross-country skiers, rowers try to control their style for the most effective speed. The balance between hard work and finesse is a fine line in rowing. Some crews thrash their way down a race course lashing their oars into the water as quickly as they can; the result is an unbalanced, inefficient boat that detracts from every oar's effectiveness.

A rowing weight program starts with high amounts of weight lifted a relatively low number of times and gradually increases to low weights lifted many times by the end of the season. For example, a late winter workout might find a rower lifting a barbell 25 times in 45 seconds, resting for 15 seconds, and then lifting 25 more times and so for 10 minutes.

Flexibility, control, and precision throughout the lifts are more valuable than lifting an enormous amount of steel once. Thus such "macho" weight exercises as bench presses and curls are virtually banned by most coaches. Rowers are identified by broad shoulders, enormous thighs, and lean forearms and calves. Barrel chests and ballooned biceps are ineffective in a shell.

Weight sessions for rowers center on such exercises as the squat thrust and the clean and jerk. Squat thrusts develop the thighs, calves, and lower back. The barbell is placed across the shoulders along the back of the neck and is lifted by standing up and lowered by crouching back down. Care should be taken to keep the thighs parallel to the ground on the squat, and the head should always be kept up.

Clean and jerks are done by grasping the barbell from a crouch and then standing up, the arms hanging down, the shoulders and back supporting the weight. The exercise is completed by hunching the shoulders back and then jerking the weight up to a position below the chin.

Circuit training combines light weight lifting (40 pounds maximum) and aerobic training in a series, or circuit, of exercises. As with the heavier squats and cleans, the object of circuit training is to complete as many repetitions of each exercise as possible within a set amount of time. The exercises, a combination of calisthenics and traditional weight sets, are done in repetitions of ten or more. Working through the exercises nonstop over the course of half an hour or more is guaranteed to raise the pulse and respiration rate while also forcing the muscles to work to their fullest potential.

Nautilus machines are used by some college teams for circuit training and can be found in nearly any well-equipped health spa or gym. These gyms often have better equipment than many schools and feature stationary bicycles, cross-country skiing simulators, and, increasingly, ergometers.

Most off-the-water workouts end with a session of running stairs. Football stadiums, office buildings, dormitories...anyplace with a long flight of steps may be used. At Harvard, where the crew runs in the football stadium, such a workout is affectionately known as the "tour de stade." At Yale, where the Payne-Whitney gymnasium has 18 flights of stairs, the oarsmen start at the bottom, and run to the top, running back down to the second floor and back to the roof, down the third, and so on.

Stairs are one of the oldest and best off-the-water workouts, and a steep hill can provide a great substitute. There is a new machine that duplicates the sensation of running stairs—a stair-treadmill in essence—that can be set for any speed or distance.

Athletes should keep detailed records of their off-water training; noting their ergometer scores, body weight, and other empirical data. Basal or resting pulse rates may be charted as an indication of fatigue. They should be taken first thing in the morning before the athlete has risen from his bed. A low basal pulse denotes a rested body, a high rate indicates fatigue. Rowers in excellent condition average basal heart rates of 38 to 42 beats per minute.

If a rower is so lucky as to live in an area where there is open water throughout the winter months, then of course there is no better practice for rowing than rowing itself. Many Olympic and elite oarsmen make a special effort to spend the entire winter close to rowable water. Most Northern colleges head south in March in spend their spring vacations practicing at Florida colleges. Coaches usually select their boats for the racing season during those Southern sojourns, and competition is fierce among teammates.

In areas where the water is open, but cold temperatures prevail, care should be taken not to row alone in the event that the boat should swamp or tip over. Hypothermia, especially to a person who has been exerting himself, is a deadly threat. Wet suits are impractical and can cause very painful chafing.

Prep and high school crews ordinarily don't participate in any organized winter practices. The size of the school, the degree of competition with rival schools, and the demands that more traditional sports place on small school enrollments have precluded winter workouts on the junior level.

David Swift, assistant coach of the Phillips Exeter Academy crew, feels it is best that young rowers take a few months off from rowing and do whatever

Although this tank is usually used for moving-water practices, this women's team is rowing with hollow-blade oars in stationary water. Such a workout is used for purely physical training with little attention paid to the finepoints of style. Note the mirror to the left of the far oarswoman.

appeals to them during the winter. He noted that some New England prep schools, especially St. Paul's in Concord, New Hampshire, dominate prep school rowing despite the handicap of getting open water in late April, a scant week before the racing season opens. Other prep schools follow the lead of colleges and organize practices during March vacations, either traveling to colleges to make use of their facilities or heading south for a week's worth of precious water workouts.

Many prep schools own at least one ergometer. Swift said some of the most serious rowers at Exeter get together once a week to race each other on the machines when they can find time away from their formal winter sport.

Rowing clubs remain active during the winter,

organizing squash tournaments and making their facilities available for general workouts. Most clubs have an ergometer or two for the use of their members.

Rowers who aren't affiliated with a team or club either are fortunate enough to live near open water, or simply follow the example set by Northern colleges and make do with running, skiing, and weight training. Novices who wish to learn the sport and soak up some sunshine at the same time, can spend a few weeks at Southern or Caribbean rowing clinics such as the one run by Peter Sparhawk, former coach of the Princeton crew, in Tampa, Florida.

By the end of the winter, even the most devoted rower begins to suffer from a severe case of claustrophobia and starts to yearn for spring to melt the ice that keeps him from his natural element…a shell, an oar, and water on which to use them. In the end, winter's dedicated workouts, the countless flights of stairs and flailing ergometer pieces pay off when the shells are back into the starting floats and the rowers hear the words:

"Are you ready? Then ready all. Row!"

CHAPTER 8
COACHING

Coaching a crew is an honor that few rowers ever know and one that only the most dedicated aspire to. For to coach a crew is to know rowing under a microscope. A coach needs to know each rower's strengths and weaknesses and how to correct them quickly before moving onto another problem. He has to be a wily diplomat, cadging donations out of institutions and alumni for new equipment and better shells. He has to be a doctor, able to diagnose the physical and mental ills of his charges, heal them, advise them, and keep them focused on the team, the next race, the next piece of hard rowing.

The task of a coach, simply put, is to teach good rowing and to produce fast boats. Tactics are of no concern; at least not to the extent that a football coach cares about them; instead the training, strength and speed of his rowers are everything.

Rowers spend an inordinate amount of time analyzing their coach. Will he order us to turn around and head for the boathouse now or later? Will he seat me in this boat or that boat for tomorrow morning's workout? Was he impressed when I passed out after yesterday's ergometer piece? Do you think he wants to hear about my problems with exams?

Rowing coaches are, like any group of people, impossible to stereotype. For every taciturn pillar of stone, there is a flamboyant person destined to go down in team mythology as a colorful, eccentric wit. What can be said is they do basically the same job: they ride in a launch and watch rowers row, commenting on their style and telling them to row hard or soft.

Collegiate and national team coaches usually come from the elite of rowing's fraternity. They are former Olympians, national team rowers, or, in the case of club or scholastic rowing, simply available volunteers impressed into service at the last minute. Coaches are the "names" of rowing. Most college rowers know the names of the coaches of all the teams on the spring racing schedule. Coaches of national and Olympic teams are better known; and some, over time, have even attained the status of legend.

Some coaches would argue that the toughest crew coaching job is the lowest: teaching rank novices the very basics of the sport and building a foundation of skills that the more presitigous coaches can then work with. Other coaches would agree that keeping a crew competitive with the latest advances in sports medicine and equipment-tuning techniques makes coaching a full-time job that demands the skills of a spy, the patience of a saint, and the knowledge of a physician and engineer.

Today's coaches are paid for their work. The era of the gentleman "adviser" to teams is over. With coaching a full-time job, one open only to those individuals who have devoted years of their lives to competition and volunteer coaching assignments, the concept of a truly amateur coach is outdated.

In rowing's early days, the American philosophy of coaching differed sharply from the English attitude that only complete and true amateurs should accompany and advise a crew. Americans, hungry for the latest in equipment and techniques, welcomed professional scullers and boatbuilders in their boathouses. They wanted coaches who could teach the latest tactics and moves and thus ensure victory.

Professional coaches dominated American rowing in the latter half of the nineteenth century, dividing their time between racing for purses and sculling alongside a college six- or eight-oared shell, shouting out advice and encouragement while training for the next race and guaranteeing themselves a steady income when the racing season was over. Many of the most famous professionals—James Ten Eyck, Ned Hanlan, John Kennedy, James Wray, Michael Davis, and George Faulkner—found the greatest success of their careers as college coaches. But the movement toward amateurism was beginning to push professional oarsmen out of regattas and the emphasis was being placed on competition between collegians and club oarsmen; therefore, it was only a matter of time before some colleges banned professionals from coaching undergraduates.

A professional coach, in the early days of American collegiate rowing, was a coach who made or had made his living as a competitive sculler. Because the formation of the first amateur rowing associations forbade the participation of professionals in club and collegiate boats, races, and regattas, the amateur teams found themselves at a loss for qualified coaches who were willing to donate large amounts of time for nothing but the praise and gratitude of the old school. In England just the opposite was true. There amateur rowing was a long tradition founded in the practice of men of means returning to and spending their time in the service of their alma maters.

In America, undergraduates often coached their classmates, and faculty members were pressed into service, but as the fervor of the first amateur wave passed, professional oarsmen began to work their way back into club and college boathouses, working as riggers and boat builders while offering tips and critiques on the side. Gradually, and to the overall benefit of the rowing, paying coaches for their services became acceptable (and in many cases encouraged by zealous boosters) within the rigid strictures of scholastic rowing. Coaches who

Duncan Spaeth, Princeton coach, shouting instructions to his crew on the Harlem River, in preparation for the Child's Cup Regatta in 1925.

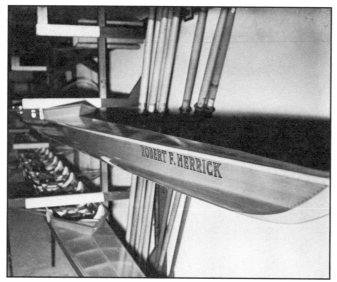

The Robert F. Herrick, a Harvard shell named in honor of the college's famous coach of the early 1900s.

had learned and practiced the sport as amateurs were hired on as fulltime coaches. Some replaced the professional scullers recruited as consultants to club and college crews, other supplemented the advice of the sharp pros, handling the nuts and bolts training work while the professional worked on the fine tuning.

The first amateur American coach to distinguish himself in the English tradition was Robert Cook, a Yale rower who spent some time in England, rowing with the Oxford, Cambridge, London, and upper Thames River crews. Bob Cook returned to row at Yale, eventually being elected captain by his teammates. As captain he rowed as a member of the varsity boat, coaching from his seat.

After he graduated, Cook stayed on as a coach in New Haven, to help rowing attain formal recognition by the college administration. He also embarked on a career as a journalist and editor.

Cook dominated Yale rowing from 1872 to 1896, bringing a standard of pure amateurism and competency that no college team had known before. As a newspaper publisher in Philadelphia, Cook often coached the team from a distance, relaying his wishes to the captain and traveling to New Haven and New London for races and important practices.

The best proof of Cook's effect on Yale rowing is his record against Harvard during his nineteen-year tenure as coach of the team: out of nineteen contests, fourteen victories. Most historians of the sport trace his influence on American rowing to his experiences rowing with English crews. When a sophomore and captain of the Yale crew, Cook wrote, "Reading descriptions and conversing with one or two English varsity men had given me a faint idea of what their stroke was. I felt convinced that Yale had to go to school in rowing and learn her alphabet."

Cook married the formal English style developed in fixed-seat barges to the American technological advances of the sliding seat and swiveling oarlock. Yet even Cook's successful experiments and the subsequent improvements and revisions introduced by imported English coaches weren't enough to make American crews competitive with the English.

Twenty years after Cook made his mark on Yale, Harvard also gained an amateur coach who would leave a lasting mark on the way rowing was taught, coached, and rowed at the school for the next fifty years. Robert Herrick, a graduate of Harvard and an accomplished rower, was a successful lawyer and devoted member of the Union Boat Club. A colorful man who sported heavy fur coats to ward off the chill of the Charles River, Herrick provided most of the direction and instruction followed by the Harvard varsity crews in the years after 1915.

Herrick had succeeded James Wray, a professional sculler who coached the crews from 1905 to 1915. Wray's tenure as coach had left the Harvard crew in less than top form. Francis Peabody, Harvard 1880, wrote in the *Harvard Graduate Magazine* in December 1915: "Up to the season of 1914, Wray apparently took his victories modestly and his defeats in a good sportsmanlike spirit, but after the Cornell race of that year, when Harvard was defeated by less than two lengths, and again after the Yale race, he made an undeserved attack in the press on his own his crew and especially on that excellent stroke, Lund."

Herrick took over for Wray reluctantly, and only after supporters of Harvard rowing pleaded with him to step in and salvage the demoralized program. Herrick, already deeply involved with his law practice and many business holdings, agreed, and for the next ten years rejuvenated Harvard rowing both in spirit and practice. When Herrick's law practice demanded his full attention, he shared his coaching duties with William Haines, the "full-time" coach who managed the boathouse and ran the

crews through their morning and occasional afternoon workouts. Haines, an English sculler, had coached at the Union Boat Club for a number of years before joining Herrick upriver at Harvard. Upon arriving, Herrick immediately pulled together the Harvard crew, teaching them a stroke that was smoother and more efficient than anything practiced up to then—a stroke that valued fluidity over raw power.

Meanwhile, Harvard's archrival Yale was in the capable hands of Guy Nickalls, an English amateur lured to America by wealthy Yale alumni who were raising the stakes. Nickalls was in charge of an enormous rowing program that at one time boasted twenty-one complete eight-man crews. Nickalls was well aware of Herrick's reputation and described Herrick to his crews as "a formidable rival."

Indeed, Herrick's crews beat Nickall's in 1915. The year marked the beginning of a golden age of rowing for Harvard and the start of a decline for Yale that culminated with Nickall's leaving in 1921 after calling that year's crew "gutless" following a poorly rowed defeat.

While Nickalls and Herrick battled for supremacy in American rowing, a quiet revolution was taking place thirty-five hundred miles away in Seattle, where a complete novice was experimenting with the physics and mechanics of rowing and forming a new philosophy of the sport that would fundamentally change the way oarsmen sat in their boats, moved their bodies, and pulled their oars.

Hiram Conibear came to the University of Wash-

Hiram Conibear.

rowed mostly for the sake of the exercise and recreation, competition being rare and a long distance away.

Conibear was fascinated with the mechanics of rowing and the interplay of an athlete's body with an oar. With no Eastern competition to set an example, Conibear developed his own approach to the business of creating a rowing style. With a book on the English rowing style and the experience of a summer spent rowing at Chautauqua, New York, under the eye of one of Bob Cook's disciples, Conibear created a style that was similar to the fluidity of Herrick's stroke. But it was much more efficient and would eventually spread across the country and dominate American rowing.

Conibear broke down the elements of rowing by using a biology laboratory's skeleton to examine how a body moved through a stroke, discovering which positions yielded the most leverage and power and when, in the cycle of the stroke, the body would be applying force and when it wouldn't.

The most significant discovery Conibear made in the course of his studies was how to keep a shell gliding forward when the oars were out of the water during the recovery. Conibear equated the movement of a shell through the water with that of a spinning bicycle wheel: once enough energy had been applied to it to get it moving, a slight slap of the hand on the tire was enough to keep it moving along. The slap of the hand, or the stroke of the oars, had to propel the wheel, or shell, quickly, wasting no time on the tire, or in the water that could

ington from Chicago, where he had been a trainer for the White Sox baseball team and Alonzo Stagg's University of Chicago football team. Conibear was lured to Seattle, then the center of the raw Pacific Northwest, to train the football team. As we have already noted in Chapter 2, by 1907, he was coaching the university's crew team, an informal group that potentially check and slow its speed.

The present Washington coach, Dick Erickson, says Conibear was able to create the first truly successful American rowing style by adapting the orthodox English style to American physiques. "Hiram adapted the style to the tall, rangy athletes that were available," Erickson said. "Conibear really maximized the efficiency of the leg drive, and with tall rangy people he added a force and strength to the rowing that had never been seen before. When Washington started winning then other schools started hiring Washington graduates to coach their crews. Conibear, more than any one else, established the West Coast as a rowing force."

In 1913 Conibear startled the Eastern rowing establishment when his varsity placed third in the Intercollegiate Rowing Association Championships at Poughkeepsie, New York. Few oarsmen and coaches on the East Coast were aware that Washington even had a crew, let alone believed it might compete and hold its own against the best of the East.

After Conibear's untimely death in 1917, he was replaced by one of his protégés, Ed Leader, the first coach to come from the ranks of amateur rowing and then make a career as a professional, paid coach. In 1923 Leader was lured East to coach Yale, taking over where Nickalls and a succession of failed coaches had left off.

Two other Washington oarsmen who learned their rowing under Conibear and who went on to coach at other colleges were: Ky Ebright, a coxswain, who coached at the University of California for thirty-five

Al Ulbrickson rowed under Washington's Hiram Conibear and went on to become one of college rowing's most successful coaches.

years; and Rusty Callow, who took over the Washington crew after Leader moved to Yale, then followed Leader's example and traveled to the University of Pennsylvania in 1927, finally moving to the Naval Academy in 1950.

Al Ulbrickson rowed at Washington under Callow and replaced him when he moved to Pennsylvania. Two more Callow students, Stork Stanford and Tom Bolles, became the coaches of Cornell and Harvard, respectively, in 1936.

Bolles brought to Harvard a new style of rowing, a variation on Conibear's basic stroke. J. Fletcher Chace, a rower at Harvard at the time, recalled, "In 1936, a new style of rowing where the rower sat up over his work and used more flexible tactics came to the East from Washington. Harvard got Tom Bolles but Yale was doomed as they kept Ed Leader with his great layback."

Few coaches made drastic revisions to the basic cycle of the stroke, preferring subtle changes in the prevailing style. Layback, the speed that the hands are moved away from the body at the finish; the crispness of the catch, when the leg drive is applied—all were subtly altered every season by different coaches, often in an attempt to correct a crew's collective bad habits.

Coaching in the early days of competitive rowing was a haphazard and difficult job because there were few power boats capable of keeping up with a hard-rowing shell. In England, the practice of bicycling alongside the crew on a river bank towpath was seized upon as the logical solution to the problem. But in America, where rowing was often practiced on lakes, harbors, and rivers with undeveloped banks, the task of correcting the crew and calling out drills often fell to the captain, who of course was sitting in the boat and had no idea what the men behind him were doing.

Teaching rowing was nearly impossible in the early days. The few available rowing machines were crude devices that gave an imprecise rendition of the stroke at best. Instruction was done in wherries, double trainers, and stable, two-seated shells in which a novice and coach could row together. Another solution to the problem were vessels known as "barges," which were huge, cumbersome rectangles with as many as eight oars to a side. Designed for nothing but instruction, those wide, square-bowed monsters were large enough for a coach to walk easily from bow to stern and back again, stopping to watch each one of the sixteen rowers and offer up his suggestions and critiques.

The availability of steam and petroleum-powered launches in the 1870s had as great an effect on coaching and rowing as the invention of the sliding seat and swiveling oarlock. The captain no longer had to function as coach and was allowed to simply pull his oar and keep spirits high and dedication strong by his example. For no longer was a racing shell the fastest craft on the water. The power launch allowed a coach to ride alongside, in pace, never to be left behind again.

The first coaches to embrace all the new technology of rowing had been oarsmen themselves; they were rowers who had learned the basics and fine points of the sport from such men as Thomas Bolles, Rusty Callow, and Jim Rathschmidtt. All the leading figures of the early and mid-1950s, including such modern coaches as Harry Parker of Harvard and Tony Johnson of Yale, could be considered the heirs of the great Washington school of rowing. Men like Parker, Johnson, and Washington's Erickson rose to the heights of American rowing during the early 1960s, an era marked by eight straight Olympic gold medals won by American crews, but they remained students in the new school of international rowing. As Karl Adam's Ratzeburg crews and the Soviets and East Germans began to threaten America's domination of international rowing, it was American oarsmen and coaches who felt the European's strength

Coach M. Abbott getting the Yale crew in condition for the big race with Harvard in 1919.

first hand, who closely observed every nuance of stroke and form, pressing their opponents for some insight into their training methods and regimens, and emerging with a sense of how far America had to go to compete once more on the level of the state-funded Europeans.

W. M. Harahan, an officer of the now-defunct National Association of Amateur Oarsmen, wrote in the editor's preface of the 1961 *Official Rowing Guide*:

If the 1960 rowing year were to be described in two words, most assuredly they would be disappointment and surprise.

The performance of our crews in Rome was not only disappointing but came as a shock to all U.S. rowing environs. Our Olympic Rowing Team, selected in Syracuse, was considered to the be the best U.S. team ever, that is until the results of the XVII Olympiad Regatta were known. Few people would question that our Olympic rowing contingent for the most part, included the best crews available. However, the fact remains that they were simply, but overwhelmingly, outclassed by the Europeans. More important than the uncomfortable loss of prestige is the ominous warning that these same European crews promise to be even better and faster in Tokyo in 1964.

Our task now becomes one of evaluating our system of selecting Olympic crews and revamping the selection process to afford maximum utilization of the available talent. In addition, more extensive participation in international competition is vital if we are to approach Tokyo with crews whose times give reasonable expectations of Olympic success.

Prior to the 1960 Olympics, the American crews were selected at the Interscholastic Rowing Association Regatta in Syracuse, which was in fact the national college championship regatta. It was also a national trial that included club entries, and it was generally believed that the best possible boat would be one that had practiced and raced together for an entire season. There had never been reason to doubt the truth of this assumption, as it had led the United States to eight victories in eight consecutive Olympiads beginning with the Naval Academy's victory in the 1920 Antwerp games and continuing through Yale at Paris in 1924; California at Amsterdam in 1928 and again, four years later in Los Angeles; Washington at Berlin in 1936; California at Henley in 1948; Navy at Helsinki in 1952; and finally, Yale again at Melbourne in 1956.

Since 1956, America has won only one gold medal in the eights, that being won by the Vesper Boat Club in 1964. Vesper and California share the distinction of winning more gold medals in the eight-oared event than any other rowing team in the world. Vesper won the first Olympics in 1900 at Paris, and again, four years later, at St. Louis. California won in 1928, 1932, and 1948 under the direction of coach Ky Ebright.

Yet the Europeans changed the emphasis on "togetherness" in a shell and formed their national boats on the basis of individual performance, drawing from a deep, country-wide pool of available talent that convened at one place for several weeks to vie for a seat. Thus ended collegiate rowing's complete dominance of American rowing. The new American elite became members of the national team, free agents who prepared for national boats after the collegiate racing season was over, banding together at rowing clubs under the direction of college coaches for a few months of hard rowing, and usually working or living close to the boathouse.

Crew coaches enjoy a measure of tenure not shared by most professional and fellow collegiate coaches of other sports. It is not uncommon for a coach to stay with one team for more than a dozen years, carefully recruiting and then nurturing a constant flow of oarsmen into faster and faster boats.

The method and knowledge of a coach is usually ignored by most oarsmen, who arrive at the boathouse every afternoon to change, launch the shell, and start practicing. Yet underlying the daily routine is a coach's careful study and analysis of the performance of the team, boats and individuals. His tactical decisions include how hard to work the boats, which rowers to focus on, and, in the back of his mind, what alumnus or organization, might be cajoled into donating a new shell for the big race.

No one carries the burden of defeat more and enjoys the fruits of victory less than a crew coach. At the end of a losing season, it is the coach the alumni blame, particularly if the crew has been unsuccessful several seasons in a row. Good coaches usually find their rewards not in the bonus checks mailed their way by the pleased alumni, but by the appreciation and even adulation of their oarsmen.

Harvard's Harry Parker, one of the best known names in all rowing, exemplifies the persona of a successful coach. Taciturn, seemingly aloof and distracted, Parker has been able to work magic with Crimson crews for more than two decades. The oarsmen who have rowed in his boats are known to perpetually second guess and analyze Parker's enigmatic mind, searching his face for an expression of approval or criticism.

One rower who rowed under Parker in the early 1970s said this about the man who personifies much of modern American rowing: "He was an enigma for most people at Harvard. He seemed untouchable, yet a few of the best would wrestle with him on the dock and seemed to get along with him better than others. There was a light side to Harry, but when he wanted to assert himself, people would immediately fall into line. We always thought, 'This guy knows what he is doing.'

Harvard coach Harry Parker with his 1973 heavyweight crew at Red Top before the annual Harvard-Yale race.

THE BOOK OF ROWING

He is totally dedicated to good crews. He sees into souls. He looks at you and he knows you."

Parker's success as a coach, like Bob Cook's a century earlier, is best indicated by the college's record against Yale: eighteen consecutive victories from 1963 to 1981.

Two other coaches dominated American rowing in the 1960s and 1970s. On the West Coast it is Dick Erickson, coach of the University of Washington men's varsity who has continued the strong history of Husky excellence in rowing. His exuberant approach to coaching stands as the antithesis of Parker's quiet, almost backhanded style.

Erickson's antics and insights have endeared him to countless oarsmen who have passed through the Conibear Shellhouse on the shore of Lake Washington. His ability to predict ergometer scores, his loud exhortations and temper tantrums in the launch have created a mythology of Erickson stories that is passed on from year to year by each successive crew. One crew presented Erickson with a memento in the form of a piece of his launch's windshield frame with a set of dentures imbedded in it. Other Washington rowers have spoken of his tendency to replace poorly performing rowers and pick up an oar himself out of frustration.

Back on the East Coast was Ted Nash, coach of the University of Pennsylvania heavyweights until 1980. Nash, like Parker, was a graduate of Pennsylvania's rowing program, where he perfected his approach to the sport that forbids a coach from speaking to his crew once a race is underway. He must sit silently in the following launch, stopwatch and stroke counters in his hands, taking mental notes and either smiling if it looks an easy win, or biting his lip if his crew is left far behind in the wake of the other shell.

All of a coach's talents come out during the endless practices. In England, home of towpath coaching, they ride along the race course on their bicycles, calling out advice and urging on their boats throughout the race. In America, a coach talks about the upcoming race very rarely. The day before the race, he will gather the oarsmen together in the locker room and give them some final words of encouragement, reviewing the opponent's record and comparing it to his own crew's. On the morning of the race, when the crew is resting and trying to push the race out of their minds, the coach will address them once again, never a locker-smashing display of emotion, but simple direct words telling them what will be needed on the race course if the crew wants to keep their shirts and come home with their opponents'.

After the shell has been launched and the crew has climbed into the seats and tied into the foot-stretchers, the coach walks along the dock, kneeling beside each rower in turn, giving quiet advice before shaking hands and moving down to the next.

Some oarsmen may come to resent their coaches for pushing them so hard in miserable weather, while doing nothing more than sit in a launch driven by an engine. Others love their coaches for the feeling of strength and confidence they have learned from them. Few rowers can truly understand the love of rowing a coach must feel to dedicate his entire career to rowing. The life of a coach is one that only a few rowers and boatbuilders are called to; it is a job that is usually underpaid and demands far more hours than any other coaching position.

But the rewards are simple. There is the life spent around shells; young people striving for excellence; an office that is a launch afloat on a river and the wonder of watching eight or four rowers pull themselves across a finish line before their opponents, exulting in a victory that is most definitely theirs but also their coach's.

CHAPTER 9
COLLEGIATE
ROWING

There was a time when football was still being defined from rugby. Baseball was called nines or rounders, and cricket was popular but only in the British Empire. Basketball had not yet been invented and soccer was in its formative stages of development. Rowing was the most popular sport in the world.

As an example of college rowing's immense popularity, one need only point to page one of the *New York Times* after Columbia University won the 1871 intercollegiate rowing championships in Saratoga Springs. Occupying an entire front page, the news that Manhattan's native sons had bested the powers from Cambridge and New Haven was deemed of sufficient interest to push the news of the rest of the country and world inside.

Most major newspapers had a full time rowing correspondent, a man who chronicled every detail of the sport, his byline appearing daily during the racing season, accompanied by lavish spreads of engravings or photographs of the crews on the water

and their coaches and captains. Cartoonists drew each crew in caricature, adding in obscure puns and inside jokes that only a true devotée of the sport could understand.

Skimming through any of the popular journals of the late nineteenth century such as the *Police Gazette, Field and Stream, Rudder,* and *Frank Leslie's Illustrated Weekly* offers more evidence of the important place collegiate athletics occupied in the popular culture of the times. Great races between traditional rivals were reported as avidly and in as much minute detail as today's Super Bowl or World Series. Sporting journalists speculated endlessly in their columns about this or that college star's injuries, his home life, his diet.

In the late twentieth century, sports are mega events that millions share in via their television sets. But college athletics, except for football and basketball, are virtually ignored by the media and hence the public. Even college versions of such mainstream sports as baseball are mostly ignored by the television networks and given only cursory coverage by newspapers (cable-television sports channels have somewhat redressed the balance—but mostly because they have so many hours of air time to fill.)

In any event, one Boston sports columnist, Austen Lake, wrote in 1960:

> **There they go, tugging in perfect unison to the "yo-ho-ho" of some undersized bully who is their only passenger. They never screw their necks around to see where they're going or to exchange any folksy chatter or make wolf whistles at the shoreside girls. They just sit stiffly mute, glaring at each other's backbones, seeing spots dance before their eyes and thinking blank thoughts like ugh-ugh.**
>
> **I am unable to understand why eight-oared rowing requires nine months just to teach college kids to breath in uniform gasps while performing glorified pick and shovel work. And where's the fun in a sport which won't let you whoop "atta boy!" or scratch an itch or hiccup lest you upset the ship, which is frail as a concert fiddle and costs more than a Cadillac.**

Collegiate rowing began with the fateful decision of a Yale junior to purchase a used Whitehall skiff for less than $30 and ship it to New Haven where it served as the seed for collegiate rowing in this country. Oxford and Cambridge had been going at it on the Thames for a couple of decades before that,

pulling their barges against each other and banishing the workingmen from the glory of competition. English rowing should accept much of the blame for rowing's deserved image as a patrician sport, open only to amateurs who could afford to row for sheer pleasure. Yet American clubs and the Ivy League are as much to blame for championing the often unfair definition of "true amateurism."

The early days of collegiate rowing in England and America were informal ones. Rival colleges raced infrequently and most oarsmen rowed for the recreation and prestige. Rowing clubs, brought into existence about the time that competitive rowing started both in America and in England, did much to encourage collegiate rowing. Boats and boathouses were shared, club oarsmen coached the colleges, and upon graduation, most college oarsmen were invited to join the local navy or barge club.

An obstacle to frequent races was the distances most teams had to travel to meet another crew. In England, where Oxford and Cambridge share the same river, it was a simple matter to just row up or down the river and meet a rival on a neutral stretch. In America, where the Ivy League colleges were spread as far apart as Pennsylvania and New Hampshire, match racing was nearly impossible, certainly before the advent of railroads.

As transportation improved and railroads linked the major cities of the East Coast, collegiate oarsmen were finally able to challenge other colleges and find a way to transport themselves, their oars, and their shells. If arranging for shell transportation was

The Yale freshman team at New London, Connecticut, 1919.

too complicated, then most colleges were more than willing to provide a visiting school with a loaner.

Shells don't travel well—especially wooden ones—and considering the painstaking care that goes into transporting a shell today, one can imagine the stress and hazards a nineteenth-century team faced when attempting to transport its shell a long distance. Dartmouth, for example, traveling by train to an intercollegiate championship in the late nineteenth century, lost a shell in the Hoosic Tunnel in North Adams, Massachusetts, when a cinder shot from the locomotive's smokestack, bounced off the tunnel's ceiling and landed on the flatbed car where the shell was stowed.

Even with railroads simplifying transportation, most nineteenth-century crews were unable to race every spring weekend as is the case today. The first college rowing teams were, in effect, private clubs for undergraduates and received little or no support from the college administration. Anything that would interfere with studies was strictly forbidden, and most competitive rowing

A Cambridge crew bringing in their boat after defeating Oxford in a varsity boat race.

took place in the summer, long after final exams.

The first collegiate match races were between Harvard and Yale on Lake Winnipesaukee in New Hampshire in the 1850s, an experiment that was more a lark that tested college pride than rowing skills. Regattas, organized by various cities as part of their Independence Day celebrations, proved to be a wonderful opportunity for college oarsmen to compete against each other. But match racing was far more exciting, as a one-on-one race was a natural extension of traditional college rivalries, exemplified by Harvard and Yale and of course Oxford and Cambridge, the oldest college rivalry in the world.

Collegiate rowing took off after the turn of the century, spreading away ever westward by land and ship. Seattle, Vancouver, B.C., and San Francisco were the first Western cities to boast of a rowing club, Vancouver taking the lead because of its strong British heritage and the miles of bays and inlets along Puget Sound.

The first colleges in the West to adopt rowing, the University of Washington in Seattle and the University of California in Berkeley, started the sport almost as soon as they were founded. Using shells transported across the continent by train, the first crews, like their Eastern counterparts, were completely independent of the school and relied on student subscriptions and charismatic coaches to finance the fun.

Today, some of the nation's best crews and the world's best oarsmen call the West Coast home. Both California and Washington have Olympic gold medals to their credit, both colleges have done as much

as Harvard and Yale to firmly establish the sport of rowing as an American game.

Although they have already been mentioned, it is impossible to overemphasize the importance of the Pocock Brothers in the history of Western rowing. Born and raised on the Thames at Eton, where their father Aaron was the manager of the prep school's boathouse and coach of its crews, George and Dick Pocock left England in 1911, leaving behind an impressive string of victories on the Thames, including the ultimate rowing honor for Dick: the Doggett Coat and Badge.

They set out for the Pacific Northwest not for the rowing, but on the advice of a drunken acquaintance who told a tale of the fortunes to be made there as loggers. Upon arrival in Vancouver, B.C., the two found work not as shell builders but, for Dick: as a carpenter at a mental institution; for George, as a low paid rigger at the Vancouver Rowing Club on Coal Harbour. Then, when his pockets were empty, he went to work as a common laborer in a lumber camp.

The two brothers found their break when a former Cambridge oarsman arrived in the city and joined the Vancouver Boat Club. He knew of the Pocock name—three generations of English scullers and shell builders—and persuaded the club to commission two single sculls for $200.

The brothers started building in an old shed that floated on a raft of logs. Despite the shed's penchant for sticking in the mud at low tide and refusing to rise with the flood, and its fondness for breaking free of its moorings and sailing across the harbor, it served its purpose. Before long the brothers were turning out enough boats to support themselves.

One morning, while they were sitting in their floating shop working on an order for some lap-strake practice boats ordered by two Canadian boat clubs, the brothers saw a strange sight. Rowing a skiff (if it could barely be called that, George recalled) and catching crabs on every other stroke was a lone man. By the time he reached the shed he was out of breath, but managed to introduce himself. He was Hiram Conibear, who knew little about rowing, but was an expert trainer of athletes. Conibear was working at the University of Washington doing odd jobs within the athletic department, especially as a trainer for the football team.

Rowing had existed at the University of Washington since the spring of 1900 when two prominent Seattle lawyers, E. F. Blaine and his partner Charles T. Denny acquired a boathouse on Lake Washington and two four-oared barges. The first real competition aside from intercollegiate contests was raced in 1903 against the James Bay Boat Club.

One year later, ten women formed the first women's rowing club at the university, using the same boats as the men but competing under different rules. They were judged on the basis of style, boat handling, and how well the coxswain knew the course.

In 1906 the boat club purchased two shells from Cornell University and a year later the shell house was expanded to accommodate them. Conibear

was hired the following year—three years after the sport was made an official addition to the college's athletic offerings.

In his first season as coach, Conibear took a Washington crew south by steamer to San Francisco to compete in the first regatta between Washington, California, and Stanford. However, the arduous trip down the rough Pacific was in vain, for on the day of the race, heavy winds and high waves swamped all three crews. The bad weather continued, forcing postponements until finally the Washington crew was forced to return home.

Stanford traveled to Seattle a month later and rowed the first and only 4-mile race ever held on the Pacific Coast. Washington won. Estimates made at the time by the Seattle newspapers placed more than ten thousand spectators on the shore and in boats alongside the racing shells.

In 1909 California and Stanford dropped rowing because of the fierce competition with other sports for funds—a severe setback for Western rowing. But Washington persevered, racing the University of Wisconsin. It thus became the first Western crew to compete east of the Mississippi. In 1911, California and Stanford resumed rowing, but at Seattle, the women's rowing program was disbanded because it was felt that the sport was too strenuous for the young women's health. More than two hundred women were affected by the unpopular decision.

In 1912, California, Washington, and Stanford raced on the Oakland Estuary (California's home course) with Stanford winning and Washington finishing a close second. Stanford rode that victory all the way East to Poughkeepsie, New York, to become the first Western college to compete in the Intercollegiate Rowing Association regatta. They placed sixth.

Conibear knew that to succeed and make the sport a popular one, he would need good boats and plenty of them. Yet the cost of shipping a new shell from the East or England was prohibitively expensive; and the local shipwrights who were turning out lumber schooners and other assorted utilitarian craft, had no time for a special order of delicate shells.

As the Pococks built their first boats, word arrived in Seattle that a new source of fine shells was close at hand. During a race against the James Bay Boat Club in Victoria, Conibear had his first opportunity to admire up close the Pococks handiwork. Impressed by the quality of their shells, he rode a ferry up to Vancouver, rented a skiff, and gave the Pococks his pitch. He promised the brothers an order for twelve eights, a rent-free workshop, and more orders in the future than they could handle. Overwhelmed by Conibear's offer and heady with their own good fortune, the Pococks sailed south to Seattle, where they toured the relatively raw and unfinished campus with Conibear.

Their workshop was a flimsy structure that was built three years earlier for the Alaska-Yukon-Pacific Exposition. George Pocock recalled in his memoirs, "This building, the Tokyo Tea Room, was put up in 24 hours by volunteer Japanese carpenters, and it looked like it. It was poorly lighted, and we told (Conibear)

A California varsity crew lines up for a photo before a Poughkeepsie Regatta.

so, but he cheerfully waved that criticism aside. Not to worry, he assured us. He would have that taken care of if we decided to accept his offer."

The Pococks returned to Vancouver, mulled over the proposition, and finally decided to accept it.

George Pocock, shown here sighting down the keel of one of his famous cedar shells, went out of his way to equip the rowing programs of the country with the best shells in the world.

They wired Conibear to expect them; and also wired home, inviting their father and sisters to sail over and help them with the new endeavor. With tools and family in tow, the Pococks settled into Seattle only to learn that Conibear's order of a dozen boats had been whittled down to one. They built that boat in Seattle, keeping the Vancouver operation running in the event that Seattle's promises fell through completely. They didn't and in no time that first Pocock eight, the *Rodgers*, was christened and launched.

In 1913, the Husky crew of the University of Washington raced the *Rodgers* against their familiar rivals on the Oakland Estuary. Winning by more than a minute, the crew returned to Seattle where they were greeted by a mob that cheered "On to Poughkeepsie!" Later, Conibear had no problem raising a $4,000 gift from a Mr. Frye, of the Frye Packing Company, to finance the long cross-country trip to New York.

There Washington surprised the Eastern rowing establishment by finishing third behind Syracuse and Cornell in the 4-mile race—a race rowed with several spares (substitutes) onboard instead of the usual crew because some of the oarsmen couldn't afford to take a summer off. The race was also handicapped by a footstretcher that broke at the first mile mark.

Collegiate rowing came of age in the first three decades of the twentieth century. Professional scullers, too old to row competitively and without an audience due to the influence of amateurism, found a home coaching college crews backed by avid alumni set on winning at any cost. Crowds packed trains and small boats to watch races on the Hudson, Housatonic, Thames, and Charles rivers. The press assigned full-time reporters to cover each crew's every move,

A ten-oared shell built by George Pocock and Sons for the University of Washington crew.

publishing photo essays, biographies, and practice times.

At this same time, the country was losing its pioneer raw edge, becoming more cosmopolitan and rowing reflected it. Crews began to travel to the Henley Royal Regatta every year, racing and winning against the best in the world in what were considered the best shells.

But in America, rowing was still a labor of love, especially for the Western crews that had to travel thirty-five hundred miles with their shells to test themselves against the best crews in the East.

Yet crews from across the country endured whatever hardships the railroads, steamers, country inns, and bad restaurants could dispense simply to convene at some placid river for a chance to row hard for a fraction of an hour against another untested crew. In no other sport at the time, with the possible exception of football, were the teams as dedicated in their travels. The crews were perfectly willing to pack up launches, shells, oars, and men in one expensive swing across the land to meet another shell.

Collegiate rowing prospered between the wars, and many teams had to take the unprecedented step of winnowing down the hordes of students eager to try their hand at so glorious a sport as rowing. The captain of an Ivy League crew was ensured a prominent place in campus society and on the sports pages of the local newspapers. Literally hundreds of students would try out for a seat in the crew, and the coaches found themselves confronted with the difficult task of coordinating a dozen eights at once, and trying to give each oarsman some attention during the brief practices.

Most crews had a sixteen-oared barge to consolidate the number of novices into one unsinkable, slow-moving unit that a coach could ride along in and observe the progress at close hand.

The sport reached its height of popularity in the Roaring Twenties. The best crew of the decade came out of Yale in 1924, a crew that included Benjamin Spock, who later became the nation's most famous baby doctor and an antiwar activist in the 1960s. It was coached by Ed Leader, an oarsman who rowed under Conibear and who coached the Washington varsity following Conibear's death.

George Pocock said, "In 1924 it was Ed Leader who coached Yale's gold medal winning crew in Paris. He was...a tough taskmaster. His tactics, I think, were similar to those of an old time sailing ship master who would whack a man over the head with a belaying pin if he did not obey instantly. He didn't go that far, of course, but verbally he could make a man feel less than the dust. He was a perfectionist, and his crews became perfection itself; a thing of beauty to watch, getting a beautiful run on the shell, which seemed to literally ghost along."

In the 1930s, the University of California and the U.S. Naval Academy (both crews coached by Washington graduates) were the best in the country; each represented the United States in the Olympics, where each won a gold medal. Harvard and Yale were still fiercely going at it on the Thames, their rivalry reaching a popular fervor never witnessed before or since in rowing, and matched only recently by the great college football rivalries.

The Great Depression took much of rowing's elitism away; the public could no longer afford to travel to the races, the opulent yachts no longer moored along the race courses, with champagne-sipping dandies and their ladies genteely cheering as their crew powered by. World War II created an interruption that claimed as casualties many great oarsmen, but still the sport made a rapid comeback after the war, making a strong reappearance at the 1948 London Olympics at Henley.

In the 1950s, the sport underwent a transition as the great coaches of the 1920s and 1930s retired and were replaced by their best protégés. Crew seemed to lose some of its allure in the 1950s, as veterans attending college on the G.I. Bill concentrated on completing their educations and getting on with the business of life. Yet American crews continued to win international competitions throughout the decade; the Yale crew won a gold medal at the 1956 Olympic Games in Melbourne, Australia.

Rowing suffered through the tumultuous sixties as student activism and radical attitudes began to turn against the perceived elitism of such sports as rowing. With the loss of public interest the status of being an oarsman on campus diminished. Fewer freshmen crowded into the boathouses each fall, looking for glory at the end of an oar. Their ranks were replaced by a small cadre of dedicated athletes, oarsmen who learned the sport at prep school, or the simply

The notorious "Rude and Smooth"—Harvard's 1975 heavyweight varsity: (left to right, standing) Al Shealy, stroke; Ron Shaw; Dick Cashin; Hovey Kemp; John Brock; Chris Wood; Blair Brooks; Greg Stone; (kneeling) Bruce Larson, coxswain.

curious—large young men deliberately sought out
and recruited by members of the varsity with an eye
for talent. The sport survived.

At schools like Harvard, where crew was part of
the school's very soul, the sport never faltered. Yet at
Yale, where American rowing first invaded the college campus, crew suffered; barely enough oarsmen
turned out to field a full complement of freshmen,
junior, and varsity boats.

The 1960s were difficult times for all American
crews. Coaches began to experiment with the basic
Washington stroke, sending their crews out to the
race courses in foreign shells replaced every year
like the latest fashions. The loss of America's dominance over international rowing by 1960 wasn't necessarily the fault of American coaches, oarsmen,
shells, and technique; rather it resulted from a vast
improvement in the training methods of the Europeans and English.

By 1970 American rowing rediscovered the magic that had allowed it to win time and time again
from 1900 to 1950. Better oarsmen turned out every
year, oarsmen who were simply better genetically
than their predecessors—taller and stronger—oarsmen
who understood what it would take to make a shell
move past the best the world had to offer.

Perhaps the best of the 1970s, Harvard's Rude
and Smooth was the crew that made it into the
pages of *Sports Illustrated*. It was a flamboyant and
incredibly fast crew, one that earned its name after
a dignified alumnus allegedly observed stroke Al
Shealy wave goodbye to a losing crew.

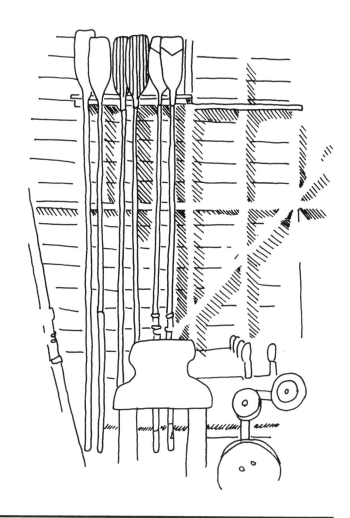

Christopher "Tiff" Wood, a member of that crew and a leading national and Olympic sculler, said: "We were essentially fortunate, not only were we pretty good, we were able to dominate for a few years, and I don't know exactly why. We were lucky in that we didn't have just one good guy, but a collection that made us able to dominate. Four people of my freshman boat—the entire port side—ended up being national team oarsman. It was incredible. No wonder as freshmen we just killed everybody."

The most recent revolution in American rowing occurred in the mid-1970s. This didn't occur on the rivers and lakes of New England and the West Coast, but in the nation's heartland, at the most unlikely universities such as Nebraska, Kansas, Iowa, and Arkansas. There crew was a completely new event, a sport that attracted crowds of twenty people (usually the oarsmen's families), one that scrounged for equipment, space, and recognition, but one that thrived because of its devotées' loyalty.

The story of the University of Nebraska's crew stands as a lesson and example every oarsmen should take to heart—especially those fortunate enough to have alumni wealthy enough to donate a new shell every season, a venerable boathouse lined with trophies, and a bucolic river to paddle down into the sunset.

In 1970 Allan Maybee, a student at Nebraska, decided crew would be a breath of fresh air in Lincoln. He pestered other colleges for equipment to be junked and ended up with an eight that was turned into a four by a car accident. That shell, aptly named the *Genesis*, occupies a place of honor in the Nebraska boathouse—a building appropriated in the middle of the night from the university and protected from repossession by changing the locks.

The Nebraska crew has manged to create its own niche ever since—going so far as to take turns rowing an ergometer on a downtown Lincoln street to raise money in the dead of winter. Although the oarsmen sometimes have to pay their own way, shelling out $500 apiece to support their expensive habit, the sport is thriving despite the formidable obstacles erected by the university and an indifferent public. Nebraska's crowning achievement came in the 1984 Olympics, when Lisa Rohde won a silver medal on the woman's team.

Kansas, Iowa, Texas, Wyoming—places where water, let alone crew, is a rarity—are all home to rowing programs. Those programs may not enjoy a depth of history and tradition, yet they might be considered the essence of rowing: they are places where oarsmen row for the sake of the rowing, not for the glory or the headlines.

In the minds of many fans, collegiate athletics offer far more competitive thrills and honesty than the media-hyped world of professional sports, where money seems to pollute the purity of the contest. The history of sports is bound tightly to the history of collegiate athletics. Nearly every sport now practiced for hire by professionals was founded, played, formed, and perfected by college athletes. Even today, college basketball and football attract national interest, broadcast by network television and providing sports fans with a constant flow of excitement and news.

One hundred years ago, when American athletics underwent a profound change, college athletics became organized under the umbrella of such associations as the Ivy League, the National Committee of Amateur Athletics, and a number of organizations that have since become defunct. Ivy League sports were the best organized athletic events of the late nineteenth century, mostly because the handful of Eastern colleges were among the oldest in the country and had an established base of wealthy alumni who took interest and provided financial backing.

C H A P T E R   10
Y O U T H
R O W I N G

In few youth sports is there as much opportunity to compete on an elite level as there is in rowing. With the exception of gymnastics and swimming, where nearly every competitor is under twenty years old, rowing has a strong national and international network of championships and regattas for young rowers.

Modern rowing directly traces its competitive heritage to the students of Eton and Westminster, two ancient public schools (the English equivalent of an American prep school) which first took up the working-class job of rowing in the late 1700s as a pleasant way to explore the scenic Thames. Students were racing intramurally and staging floating parades in honor of the birthday of King George III around the time of the American Revolution.

Eton College was founded by King Henry VI in the 1440 as the King's College of Our Lady of Eton beside Windsor. The school was intended for one hundred boys from respectable but less than wealthy families, their education paid for by one hundred scholarships. In the sixteenth century, the school was opened to paying students, but to this day the original one hundred scholarships are still awarded, the enrollment having swelled to over a thousand students. Over the centuries, the cream of British society, passed through Eton's hallowed portals and most of them have rowed.

Eton has preserved an enormous number of shells (650) from the late nineteenth century. They include eights, fours, sixes, pairs, doubles, sculls, and wherries — in fact, every class of shell imaginable. All were accumulated after some students first purchased a pulling barge for their own private use, mostly due to the efforts of Dr. Edmund Warre, a headmaster who emphasized rowing as a fine path toward the English ideal of strong minds-strong bodies.

Eton was such an important rowing center that several boatbuilders set up shop on the Thames in the immediate vicinity to provide custom work for wealthy students and groups of students who had banded together and pooled their money for custom racing shells. The school even established its own boat shop to build new shells and to repair the older ones. A full staff of craftsmen built a steady stream of boats for the school crews in the late nineteenth and early twentieth centuries, the same builders serving as riggers, coaches, and trainers for the the horde of students who came down to the river every afternoon for a row. The still-existing boathouses at Eton are ornate structures that house more than the school's collection of shells.

Rowing was so important to Eton that special shells were built for students too wide to fit into a standard boat. Most of the racing boats were christened with militaristic names, such as *Thetis, Dreadnought, Monarch,* and *Brittania.* There were special eight-oared practice shells, built extra wide for stability, as well as ten-oared behemoths trotted out on special occasions. There were fours, doubles, pairs, singles...an amazing collection of boats built by the best builders in England, all rowed constantly, nearly every day of the year, by the avid students. And it was at Eton that many of rowing's sartorial traditions started. Racing shirts were one invention; bright blazers, white ducks, and straw boaters became the fashionable male attire for racing spectators, uniforms brought out of mothballs and stretched into by aging alumni every spring.

The number of rowing clubs and college crews that call the Thames home is astonishing, including the dozens of provincial and coastal clubs that make up the British Amateur Rowing Association. The English love boating with a passion difficult to comprehend until one has seen the Thames filled with punts, sculls, charging eights, and meandering skiffs on a warm June afternoon.

In the springtime, when the universities and public school crews of England are busy training for a three month season of races, the Thames and its tributaries are crowded with crews searching for calm water to practice on, and private reaches to row time trials on without the other team's "spies" catching on.

In America, several prep schools contest for the right to claim the honor of having the first rowing club or team. There are so many conflicting claims—all, it appears with some degree of validity—that one doesn't dare take sides. In the mid-1800s younger students rowed aboard college boats during the summer months, usually in the company of older brothers eager to impress them with the splendor of the sport. Others came together on a single occasion in a borrowed shell to hack their way down the course of an Independence Day Regatta, while others raised the funds, placed an order with a builder and eventually took delivery of a barge around which a crew would be formed.

By 1880, small clubs existed in such prep schools as St. Paul's in Concord, New Hampshire; Phillips Andover in Massachusetts; and Lawrenceville in Princeton, New Jersey. They were dependent on the philanthropy of recent alumni rowing at colleges that had an old barge or two to spare.

At St. Paul's, rowing became so popular after its

founding in 1871 that the students organized two rival clubs within the school to foster competition, a necessity more than a choice because of the formidable transportation problems that had to be overcome in order for a crew to race another school's, not to mention the hard reality that there weren't very many schools to compete with. The Shattuck and Halcyon Clubs were for a long time the source of fierce intrascholastic competition, and they established years of these contests in a rowing program that is renowned to this day. St. Paul's rowers regularly went on to become prized members of the Harvard and Yale crews.

Eights were popular from the beginning at the larger and older prep schools due simply to that boat's importance on the collegiate level. Later, as smaller schools adopted the sport, coxed fours became the boat of choice, as they were easier to transport and coach.

Until 1910, most junior rowing in America was confined to no more than a dozen schools in the Northeast. Inevitably, most of the small schools that were located on or near a river or lake also took up the sport, usually at the urging of alumni who discovered rowing in college and felt deficient when competing against freshmen who had already had four to six years of experience at their prep schools. Schools such as Browne & Nichols, Nobles and Greenough, Belmont Hill, Groton, Brooks, and St. Marks buttressed Boston's reputation as a rowing center in the 1920s and 1930s. In Connecticut, such schools as Salisbury, Gunnery, Pomfret, and Kent picked up

rowing. The sport spread rapidly across New England as more and more prep schools bought boats, built boathouses, and began to recruit recent college graduates as coaches and teachers.

Kent was the first American prep school crew to row at Henley, traveling there in 1927 under the direction of Father Frederick Sill, Kent's headmaster and a leading light of schoolboy rowing. Kent raced an eight in England, a class of boat the school's crews have always excelled in, especially against the freshman boats at Williams, Yale, and Harvard.

One oarsman who learned the sport under Father Sill, said Sill had a start named after him, one that he was fond of using whenever his crews raced college freshmen. As legend has it, Sill would order the two boats to back into the start and then begin issuing commands for the coxswains to get their shells pointed down the course. Sill's typical sequence of starting commands went something like this: "Kent, your hand is down. Princeton, your hand is down. Ready all . . . Princeton back water . . . Row!" and Kent's finest would churn out of the start while Princeton's astonished oarsmen wondered which order to follow. It may have been Sill's way to make up for his oarsmen's age handicap.

Only two years after Kent broke the symbolic ice at Henley, an eight comprising two fours from Browne & Nichols—a day school on the banks of the Charles in Cambridge—followed and won the Thames Challenge Cup.

Prep school rowing, at the typical small school, was practiced under much more spartan conditions

Youth rowing, in private prep schools, high schools, and clubs, is quickly becoming one of the fastest growing sports for adolescents. This four-man shell from the Brooks School practices on Lake Cochienewick in North Andover, Massachusetts.

than those prevailing at the well funded colleges. Many schools rowed their early years without a roof over their head, launched their shells from the water's edge, and stored them during the winter in the basement of the school auditorium. Equipment was patched over and over, coaches rowed with their crews when the launch wouldn't start, and likely candidates for coxswain were bullied into service whether they wanted to steer a wet shell or not.

As the sport became better established and the spirit of competition took over, prep school rowing began to flourish with alumni money and donated shells. Traditional rivalries that had started on the football field carried over to crew, inscribed cups changing hands year after year as the races became ingrained in each school's unique traditions.

The captain of the crew was a big man on campus, an example of awe to the first and second formers in the tenth boat. The oarsmen led a mysterious life of early morning practices and late afternoon rows into the evening hours, running into the dining hall for a late dinner before chapel.

The small traditions of rowing are first taught at the prep school level, where they are revered and flourish like tribal customs. Brooms are still hoisted up the boathouse flagpole when one school's crews sweep another's (a sweep occurs when all of one school's crews beat all of their rival counterparts). Racing shirts are handed out the night before the race and worn to bed for good luck. The crew dines at the coach's house the night before the race and his wife serves the most traditional dish in rowing:

strawberries and cream. White ducks, the school blazer and a striped necktie with crossed oars are donned—a walking spectacle that no other sport practices, a display that lives on at some schools today.

In Europe, the French lycées, German Gymnasiums, and Italian parochial schools have some rowing; however, the strength of youth crew on the Continent is not in its schools but in the club system. This is an extensive network of boathouses that line nearly every navigable river and lake in every country. Skiffs, punts, and canoes were once very popular with Europeans who used them on weekends for recreation or exercise. Serious scullers (and most young European rowers were started off in sculls) used the better clubs to train for local and national regattas, sometimes rowing the course of a river over a summer month, racing every day as the fleet of competitors moved from town to town.

Youth rowing started in Continental Europe after it did in England but before America, growing through a faddish stage that saw hordes of adolescents and adults try the sport before moving onto something new. During the boom years in the latter half of the nineteenth century, countless clubs were founded by villages, guilds, and manors.

In America, the sport that had started off in the prep schools stayed there for more than fifty years, feeding on itself as a sport unique to a privileged world with no need for new blood to keep it going. Before World War II, prep school rowing in New

England had grown to the point where there was a call for a championship to determine the best crews in eights, fours, and singles. The war interrupted plans to institute a regional association; but in 1946, a year after the war when the end of gasoline rationing made it possible to start up the idle coaching launches, several coaches met at the Harvard Club in Boston to lay the groundwork for an annual regatta.

The first was rowed in 1947, but no records were kept. Hence, officially, the regatta is said to have been first rowed in 1948. The 1947 regatta was rowed at Lake Quinsigamond in Worcester, in Central Massachusetts. The lake, so chosen because of its long, wide course, was the scene in 1947 of heats, consolations, and finals for first and second men's fours and finals for first and second eights. Prep school athletic teams are numbered: first means varsity, second junior varsity, leaving those appellations for college level teams.

The winners of the first regatta of the New England Interscholastic Rowing Association were Pomfret in the first coxed fours and Kent in the first eights. From the first regatta to 1970, the fours raced over a ¾ mile course and the eights down a mile. In 1970 the fours raced 1,500 meters; the eights changed a year later to the same distance. Winners of the first eights and fours are awarded the Frederick H. Sill Bowl in memory of Kent's Father Sill. The winners of the second fours is awarded the Howard T. "Ox" Kingsbury Bowl, donated by J. Satterthwaite of Groton and given in honor of the coach at the Brooks School, a legendary Yale oarsman (according to

legend, Kingsbury was so strong that he rowed with an oar six inches shorter than the rest of the crew so he wouldn't turn the shell during races when he put the power on). Winners of the second eights take home the Dixon "Tote" Walker Cup, named for the former Kent coach.

The record for the first eights over a mile is held by Kent, who in 1968 rowed the course at a time of 4:42.6. As of 1983, the record for eights over 1,500 meters was also held by Kent, which rowed the course in 4:21. In the fours, the record over 3/4 mile was set by South Kent's second boat in 1967, a time of 3:51.2. As of 1983, the record for 1,500 meters in the coxed fours belonged to Belmont Hill, who in 1971 rowed the course in 4:25.5.

Girls' crews first rowed in the NEIRA regatta in 1974, the women first rowing a 1,000-meter course and then moving up to the standard 1,500 meters in 1981.

Women's eights from Tabor Academy, Phillips Andover, Kent, Phillips Exeter, Middletown High School, East Lyme High School, Simsbury High School, St. Pauls, Northfield-Mount Hermon, and Shrewsbury High School now compete. Fours compete from the Brooks School, Gunnery, Choate-Rosemary Hall, Middlesex, Winsor, St Mark's, Lyme-Old Lyme High School, Berkshire, Groton, Buckingham, Browne & Nichols, Pomfret, Nobles and Greenough, and Litchfield.

In 1962 sculling was introduced at the NEIRA regatta in response to growing pressure from those dedicated scullers who rowed alone all spring, without the same resources enjoyed by the better organized schools. In 1977 an experiment was tried, and the regatta was held over an entire weekend rather than simply one afternoon. Several classes were added, including a race for men's pairs without coxswain, an open singles event for women and a women's double sculls. The added expense of lodging the multitude of rowers overnight proved too much, however, and in 1978 the regatta returned to a one-day event.

Since the first regatta in 1947, the regatta has grown from being an event for a dozen schools, to one that accommodates about thirty different New England schools and approximately nine hundred oarsmen and oarswomen rowing in several hundred boats.

Outside New England, three other areas are hotbeds for youth rowing. In New Jersey and Washington, D.C., youth rowing has spread out of the prep schools and into public and parochial schools with great enthusiasm and success. In the Seattle area, schools such as Lakeview have turned out great rowers, the best known being the American Olympic single sculler in 1984, John Biglow of Bellevue, Washington.

One of the mysteries of youth rowing in the United States is the fact that most college crews are composed of athletes who never sat in a shell or lifted an oar until they arrived at college, and while it is true that many rowers who learned the sport in high or prep school do very well and go on to lead their college crews to great deeds, the best college oarsmen are not necessarily the experienced ones. Many prep school veterans row for a year or two before dropping out of the sport, the usual reasons cited being burnout, boredom, and the pressures of academics and a social life. The oarsmen who go on to make up the varsity boats are the newcomers to the sport, those athletes who were first asked to try out for the team because of their physical attributes.

A look at the roster of crews such as the 1914 Harvard Varsity, shows that every rower came from schools such as Nobles and Greenough, Groton, and Exeter, with no one coming from a public high school. This reflected the make-up of the college itself, with the majority of the student body coming from prep schools and city day schools and the remainder, a small percentage, graduates of public schools.

As admission policies became tougher and attitudes changed, Ivy League colleges, beginning in the 1950s, admitted students wholly on the basis of their individual merits. The crew, long the bastion of athletes who arrived with the basics of rowing already mastered, opened up its doors to the best athletes, when it was evident that stamina and strength were two things that couldn't be taught, whereas style and bladework could.

Although today only a handful of public schools offer rowing as a full sport, many fans and devotées predict that rowing will become as much a part of public high school athletic curriculums as baseball and spring track. Until then, the most extraordinary story in youth rowing in America has been the story of the Holy Spirit High School crew in Absecon, New Jersey. In the late 1960s and throughout the 1970s, Holy Spirit's eight-oared first boat was regarded as one of the strongest and fastest youth crews in the country. When its oarsmen went to college they dominated their boats, dispelling the prep school mystique of rowing and making rowing a much more democratic sport all around.

Of course the high cost of rowing—its omnivorous demands for new shells, new oars, new lauches, and the protective roof of a boathouse—has slowed its spread into public schools, which tend to be wary of using public money to finance a sport open to only a small number of participants. Yet in association with private clubs and schools, more and more high schools have been able to row and row well against well-established teams.

Young rowers in the United States and overseas have an easy opportunity to compete at the international level while still rowing as students. Unlike most adolescent sports, which limit their participants to league and intramural play, rowing is a truly cosmopolitan sport that thrives on competition between countries.

To gain a seat on a crew bound for an overseas championship, a young rower must demonstrate dedication and prowess equal to that of any elite competitor. The selection process is the same as the system used on the adult level. Rowers are invited by the coach of a composite team—akin to an all-star camp—to attend a selection camp held at a host school in the late spring. There they compete on the basis of ergometer scores and seat races, living together and performing odd jobs around the campus to help pay for their costs.

In New England, the New England Composite Crew is an ongoing selection camp held at the Kent School in Connecticut. Young coaches, usually college oarsmen trying to make their name as coaches, scout out the races and the NEIRA regatta, approaching rowers and extending invitations for them to attend the camp and take a shot at making one of the boats.

In late June and through most of July, the young rowers practice twice a day, working hard to make a boat and then concentrating on melding their styles and strength together to make fast, competitive crews. Elsewhere around the country, other young rowers spend their summer the same way, working out and doing their best to row times close to or better than the standard established for their class. Such rowing clubs as the Detroit, Vesper and the Potomac boat clubs sponsor youth crews during the summer months, providing lockers, showers, boats, and launches to elp them train for a chance to represent their country in the summer Junior Worlds.

Just as the best adult elite crews gather at one course to race eliminations to pick the national team, youth crews also set their sights on winning the national championship. Eights, straight fours, pairs, pairs with coxswain, scullers, and doubles are all picked at the all important national trials, raced on the same courses as the elite nationals—Princeton's Lake Carnegie or Cherry Hill in New Jersey and

Schoolgirl rowers sit exhausted after crossing the finish line at the Stotesbury Regatta for high school crews. Philadelphia, 1987.

Lake Waramaug, Connecticut among others.

To qualify for the national team and to receive the stipend that national crews receive from the governing bodies of the sport, a crew not only has to beat every other boat fighting for the right to represent the country, but it also has to meet or beat the time standard set for its class. The reason for applying a minimum time is partly financial. If a crew can't cross the finish line in a time comparable to the average times in international competition, then, so the thinking goes, there is no use in financing and wasting any more time fielding an uncompetitive crew. Happily, most crews make their time standard with ease, and many go on to win medals in the Worlds, at Henley, and other international competitions.

Prep and high school coaches are grateful to the elite youth programs, because any of their charges who are asked to row on a composite or national crew usually return in better shape and with a deeper knowledge of the technical fine points of the sport that can be taught to the less proficient members of the crew. In recent years, youth rowing on the national and international levels has grown in scope and popularity, becoming almost a natural adjunct to the high level of proficiency and competition known at the college and club level.

Take for example one prep school and its rowing. The Brooks School in North Andover, Massachusetts is a small prep school founded in the 1920s by Endicott Peabody, the former rector of Groton, a similar but older prep school in the same area.

Brooks first started rowing in the late 1920s in coxed fours on Lake Cochicnewick, a triangular reservoir at the foot of the campus. Because enrollment was very small, fewer than one hundred students in the early years of the school, every student was required to try out for the crew in the spring and for football in the fall.

A two-story boathouse was built on the shores of the lake thanks to a donation made by a benefactor. Shells built in Seattle by George Pocock were ordered and eventually delivered across the country in Pocock's special railroad car. Every new shell was a cause for celebration. The entire school would turn out on the lakefront to watch the christening and blessing of the shell, a bottle of champagne poured (never broken; shells aren't steel battleships) over the bow, and the wife of the shell's namesake standing by with a few encouraging words.

The crews of Brooks School are called together late in the winter, when the weather is atrocious and the spring break imminent. In the basement, below the auditorium, the veteran rowers shake off their cobwebs in the tank, an oval cement pool with two slides and riggers set along one side. When they finish and their coach has herded them over to the gym for calisthenics and some weight work, the new boys climb onto the slides and are patiently taught the fundamentals of bladework and style.

During spring break, when the rest of the Brooks students go home, the first through fourth boats stay behind for two or three weeks of cold, hard, miserable practices on the lake. If the spring is on time, then the ice usually disappears in time for some rowing. But the water remains cold, and as the crew flogs along the shores, ice forms on oars, riggers, and the rowers' hands.

When the rowers aren't on the lake, then they are running the cross country course, or doing laps around the campus, laden down in their heavy wet green sweatsuits, the charge always led by their indefatigable coach. A man who never seems to tire, a taskmaster with the personality of a deaf ogre, he drives the flaccid rowers panting up steep hills, sometimes up to their ankles in melting snow.

Blisters appear, rip open and fester. A few of the less hardy souls trek into the village to buy a pair of golf gloves, only to throw them away when their stoic teammates catch sight of them. By the end of the session, nearly every oarsman greets the return to school with glee, for then and only then do the double practices end.

In April, when classes recommence, the crews row every afternoon, settling into a routine of hard rowing and constant drills to perfect their timing and style. The coaches begin selecting the boats, trying every possible combination of oarsmen until the fastest boats are selected.

The racing season arrives the second week of April and the coaches use the practices to race their boats down the 3/4-mile course against the clock, giving them an idea of how fast they are and what kind of effort they would need to put out during the Saturday race.

The day before the race, on Friday afternoon, the crews row in their racing shirts, taking it easy and working on the swing of the boat more than the speed. After a short hour on the water, the shells are pulled and placed in slings set up on the lawn outside of the boathouse. Each oarsman painstakingly takes apart his seat and cleans the wheels, then the slide, taking care to remove every bit of dirt and grease from the shell. When the seats, slides, and stretchers are immaculate, the shell is flipped over, and the hull is waxed down with furniture polish and shined to a bright golden patina.

After the shells are placed back into their racks, the crews gather in the trophy room atop the boathouse; there they go over the race with their coach and coxswain, rowing through the race on paper, with every power ten, and change in cadence noted and memorized. Then the crews run together to the locker room at the center of campus, where they shower and don their racing shirts for the evening. Tradition demands that for luck's sake they keep them on until they either win or lose them.

Dinner is served and the crews travel to their coach's homes for dessert and a chance to get the race off their tense minds. Bedtime is called early, with the dormatory prefects taking pains to keep the entire floor quiet so the rowers can get their sleep.

On race day, if the crew has had a rough week of sloppy practices or if the race is particularly impor-

tant (as it would be against the school's arch-rival: Groton) then the crew goes down to the boathouse early in the morning, without the coach or launch, and go out together for a quiet morning row to compose themselves.

"We went down to the lake in our racing shirts and launched the shell into the glassy dawn. Swift (then Brooks coach, David Swift), stayed ashore and so we rowed in utter silence, the only words coming now and then from the coxswain," said Burgess Smith, a Brooks oarsman, who has gone on to become a top U.S. oarsman. "We were a sharp four, very sharp technically, and there was a pleasure in the rowing that morning that has stayed with me today. A sense of knowing we were good, rowing without the pressure of a coach calling pieces, simply basking in the potential speed and knowledge of how much power was waiting in that boat, waiting to explode that afternoon."

Brooks, like many prep schools, conducts classes on Saturday morning before breaking for lunch and the afternoon games. The crews go down early, pull their shells out of the boathouse, and place them back in slings. The visiting crew arrives in a bus, their shells following them on a trailer pulled by a pickup truck driven by the coach. After a while—with both crews studiously ignoring each other—the fourth boats launch and make their way up the lake to the starting line.

After warming up with some starts and power tens on the way up course, the crews wait at the line for the starter to line them up and aim them down the course. The lake is notoriously rough, especially in the early spring when a stiff winds blows over it; so the crews have to do their best to get ready for the start before the starter feels all is equal and sends them charging down the course toward the finish line at the boathouse. There, before a cheering crowd of waiting students, parents, and faculty, the crews cross the finish line, one boat cheering, another quiet in defeat.

Ashore, the losing crew hands over their shirts, if that was the agreed bet, and the boats are put back into the boathouse and back on the trailer. A tea is served in the reception room on campus, and by dinner time the visitors have left to return home.

And so rowing has gone for decades, with some boats going undefeated and winning the NEIRA regatta before being invited over to Henley. Other years it seems that nothing goes rights, every race is lost, the lake is rougher than usual, ice covered longer...but it is a cycle that waxes and wanes every year, a continous blending of oarsmen moving up the ladder from the novice boats to the prestigious first crew.

WOMEN IN ROWING

Its home was on the docks of the ports of England and America; it was a sport born on the Mediterrean aboard warships; and it was a sport that demanded the willingness to withstand considerable agony and punishment. In the nineteenth century, rowing would not have been one that would have seemed to appeal to women.

Nevertheless, women were drawn to rowing early on in its amateur and professional history. In the early and mid-nineteenth century, the closest a woman could come to an oar was as a passenger in a barge rowed by a male. Women who rowed themselves were regarded as novelties. They were discouraged from racing, or rowing hard, being urged instead to perfect their form while paddling languidly along without breaking a sweat.

Those were the days that produced the stereotype of the woman reclining in the stern of a skiff or canoe, one hand twirling a parasol, the other dipping lightly over the side while a man rowed or paddled. The very suggestion that a woman could,

let alone want to, participate in a strenuous activity was risible.

A long tradition of male exclusivity was part of the baggage rowing retained from its origins as a club pastime. Sporting clubs, by their very nature and especially as organized in England and urban America, typically closed their doors (and playing fields) to the female sex. Rowing was in particular a strange sport for the time when one considers the vast gulf that lay between the workingman rower, plying the Thames as a taxi or freighter, and the genteel clubman, rowing in silk togs aboard a flawlessly painted frail barge. The notion of a woman entering the sport from either side was unthinkable. No respectable woman could be expected to fit into, let alone enjoy herself in a sport associated so closely with unsavory sailors, bettors, and sharp professionals.

Remarkably, against these odds and attitudes, women went ahead and founded rowing clubs of their own to learn how to enjoy and eventually

compete as oarswomen. The first races—often organized by men simply for the novelty and supposed humor of seeing women row—weren't races in the true sense of the word but displays of seamanship and grace. Having entered rowing first as passengers, then as novelties, women then rowed as exhibitions to hold the attention of an anxious mob waiting for the race between the two male professionals to begin. The first exhibitions were nothing more than a barge rowed by young women demonstrating proper naval protocol and seamanship. They would slowly row down the race course, turn their barge in a circle, flourish their oars in the air at the finish, and make a graceful docking. The winners of those exhibition races were not the crews who crossed the finish line first (there wasn't one, just as there wasn't a starting line), the winners were the women or crews with the best form and style.

The first actual women's rowing team was founded at Wellesley College in 1877. A year later, Molly Kind, a rower from Kentucky, issued a challenge to any woman from Newport, Covington, and Cinncinati to a 2-mile race for money. Again, the race wasn't to be decided on who crossed the finish line first, but on who displayed the best form.

Paintings of the sport dating back to the midnineteenth century give the first evidence that women rowed. There were women professional scullers in America during the golden age of the sport, just as there were women scullers in England in the 1880s and 1890s. A lithograph from the Philadelphia *Inquirer*, published on Sunday, September 12, 1897,

shows an eight coxed by a woman wearing a highnecked, full dress—the typical rowing uniform for a genteel woman who dared set foot in a shell.

The first American women's rowing club, the ZLAC Rowing Club, was founded in San Diego, California, in 1891. The strange name was drawn from the first initials of the four founders. The women rowed barges, attired in proper feminine style: full dresses. Six years later, in 1897, the Bicycle, Barge and Canoe Club was founded in Philadelphia, then immediately changed its name to the Sedgeley Club. Founded by Midge Corlies and several other interested women, Sedgeley raised the funds to build its own boathouse on the Schuylkill River. Designed by Arthur H. Brockie, the building incorporated an old lighthouse that had stood on the site for nearly a century.

Rowing was taught to the members by volunteer oarsmen, usually husbands who belonged to one of the male-only clubs on Boathouse Row. The female crews would race among themselves and take weekend excursions with their male counterparts. The club ceased rowing by World War I, but it did establish Philadelphia as an early hub of women's rowing, a lead that the city's rowing society hasn't relinquished.

In 1938 the Philadelphia Girls' Rowing Club (PGRC) was founded for the river's "rowing widows." Led by Ernestine Bayer, who is perhaps the most influential figure in women's rowing, the club rented space in the Philadelphia Skating Club and Humane Society, eventually buying the structure in 1965.

Bayer's husband, Ernest Bayer, was an Olympic oarsman who was very involved in Philadelphian

To the left, the Oxford undergraduate women's crew in 1927, preparing on the Isis for their race against Cambridge.

rowing; yet it was she who is best remembered as the leading force behind women's crew in this country. Still rowing in her seventies, Bayer now lives in Rye, New Hampshire, where she helped organize in 1972, and has nurtured since, the Alden Ocean Shell Association (AOSA). It represents the largest class of recreational shells in the world—for men and women—and is the single largest organization within the United States Rowing Association.

The first president of the PGRC, Bayer has an impressive list of barrier-breaking achievements to her credit. In the same year as the founding of the PGRC (1938), she and her partner, Jeannette Hoover, won the first women's race on the Schuylkill River. She also rowed in the first eights race against an outside club in 1956 and later rowed in an eights race with her daughter Ernestine (Tina) at the age of fifty-six. The first American women's eight to compete in the European Championships was organized and managed by Ernestine Bayer in 1967.

The PGRC is only one of more than a dozen women's rowing clubs that were organized in the country after the the turn of the century, the first being the one that existed for a few years at the University of Washington, in Seattle.

In the 1960s colleges and clubs began to set aside funds for women's rowing programs, basically oriented toward instruction. There were a few rare, informal races scheduled against sister crews who happened to share the same river. Wellesley, Radcliffe, and the other all women colleges of Massachusetts, were among the first colleges to adopt rowing for women. They set aside used shells and space in the boathouse, but did not provide the same backing that the men's teams enjoyed through their powerful alumni associations.

In 1964 the National Women's Rowing Association was founded and two years later its first national regatta drew forty-five crews. In those first years, the PGRC was very influential in the sport's success, making an extra effort to raise the visibility of women rowers. In 1965 the PGRC traveled cross-country to Oakland, California, for the first East-West women's race. In 1967, under the direction of Ernestine Bayer, the PGRC sent the first national women's crew to the first World Championships in Vichy, France.

Women's rowing began to truly flourish in the early 1970s as more colleges turned to coeducation and attitudes began to change about the role of the sexes in society and sports. The collegiate oarswomen were truly pioneers, confronting a male-dominated tradition that had flourished and cherished its exclusivity for more than a century. At some schools and clubs, women were insulted, given shoddy equipment, and told to practice at inconvenient times. They showered in mobile homes at Yale University until the entire women's team appeared naked in the office of the director of college athletics to make their point. They filed lawsuits against college administrations unwilling to match the money expended on the men—and they won.

Today every coeducational college in the United States with a crew team provides women with an opportunity to row. The number of women now

Driving to the finish is the University of Washington's 1985 National Champion Women's Varsity Crew.

entering the sport and sticking with it is higher than it has ever been, an influx that accounts for the majority of the sport's recent surge in popularity.

When a woman sits in a shell, grasps an oar and pulls a stroke, she does exactly what a man would do. There are no physical handicaps, no limitations, beside the natural fact that women are generally smaller than men. Hence women row lighter boats, usually the same size and weight as those rowed by a men's lightweight crew.

The oars are often rigged with the buttons, or pivot, set closer to the blade to decrease the angle of the lever. The riggers are pitched lower to compensate for women's shorter heights, and the stretchers have to be able to be adjusted for shorter legs. Yet the stroke is the same, the effort is the same, everything about women pulling an oar is the same as a man.

When the first racing crews began training in the late 1960s at such colleges as Wellesley and Radcliffe, style was emphasized over interval training—intensive work with weights and sprints to build strength for the sprint distance—as it was still believed that women should take it easier than men in training for a race. Gradually, especially as sports physiologists began studying the effects of hard exercise on women, the usual training techniques were adopted with no ill effects. Women were excelling as runners and swimmers, two very hard sports, and thus rowing, which is certainly kinder to an athlete's frame and joints than the constant jarring pounding of running on pavement, soon joined the ranks of the few women's endurance sports.

Women's rowing has progressed from a sport rowed in full-dresses, judged for form and gentility, to a full-fledged Olympic event rowed as competitively as any men's event. Selection camps as rigorous as those used to select the national men's team have been organized, and the youth program in America is just as strong and popular as that for the men.

By the mid-1970s, women's rowing had come into its own. The novelty had disappeared and financial support enabled women to row alongside their male counterparts on prep school, college, and in a few rare cases, clubs. In 1975 the first national selection camp was formed. A year later, in Montreal, women's rowing was included in the Olympic Games and a U.S. woman, Joan Lind, won the silver medal for placing second in the single sculls, the U.S. eight

won a bronze medal at the same games.

At the same time, women's rowing was first offered by many prep schools, the first championships being raced in 1974 at Lake Quinsigamond at Worcester, Massachusettts. Today women's rowing has passed through its childhood and matured into a full-fledged, serious sport that offers competition as tough as any sport in the world. The distances for women's races were first set at the short length of 1,000 meters, but they have been gradually increased to the point where they now match the 2,000-meter standard raced by men's crews.

The times are interesting to compare: the records for eights over 1,500 meters at the New England Interscholastic Rowing Association regatta, the prep school championships, are 4:21 for men and 5:04 for women; a difference of 43 seconds. As in other sports, the margin between men and women is steadily being eroded.

Interval training and its emphasis on improving an athlete's cardiovascular system is the great equalizer in rowing. Brawn and bursts of power are not the ingredients for success. Sustained endurance and an efficient use of strength are attributes that women can train for and attain with the same effectiveness as men.

According to Dr. Frederick Hagerman, the pre-eminent rowing physiologist, men are able to ventilate about 6.1 liters of oxygen during a race, compared to women's capacity of 4.1. Yet, "Rowers...exhibit excellent isokinetic leg strength and power when compared with other elite athletes and oarswomen produced higher relative leg strength values than men when lean body mass is considered. Muscle fiber type distributions in oarsmen resemble those of distance runners while women tend to have a slightly higher proportion of fast-twitch fibers. An average power output of 390 plus or minus 13.6W was produced by oarsmen for six minutes of simulated rowing while women were able to develop 300 plus or minus 18.4 for three minutes of the same activity." Hagerman wrote in *Applied Physiology of Rowing.*

Hagerman wrote in the same paper: "Elite oarswomen average 173cm (5'7") , weigh an average of 70kg (154 lbs.) and range between 12 and 25% body fat. Oarswomen are rather tall athletes with a heavy skeletomuscular structure."

Heavyweight men, on the other hand: "average 192cm (6'3") and 88kg (194 lbs.) body fat averages between 9 and 10%."

In an interview, Hagerman said that any oarsman who is considering competing on the elite international level, should have a minimum VO2 maximum of 6 liters, women a minimum of 4 liters per minute. The highest recorded levels are 7 liters per minute found in two elite oarsmen and 5 in three women.

Science aside, the very recent accomplishments of women in international competition (particularly the meteoric rise in the fortunes of American women during a relative period of stagnancy in the success of the men) has thoroughly debunked the archaic, chauvinistic views of the nineteenth and early twentieth centuries toward women and the potential ill

A women's quad at the 1987 U.S. National Championships.

effects of strenuous activity. Now, more than ten years since women's rowing entered the mainstream of prep school, college, and elite athletics, men have by and large accepted the fact that their position as the "gods of the river" isn't threatened, and that if anything, the addition of women to the scene has done much to humanize the sport and give it a life that it was losing over time.

From the young girls who decide as prep school freshmen to give rowing a try, to the elite oarswomen who strive in total anonymity through dawn practices and poverty to make the Olympic team, there is no questioning the dedication of women to rowing. A good woman rower can be expected to hold her own in a one-on-one race against a man of comparable height and weight. The coaches of the first crews were invariably men, but that is changing as the first trail blazers have graduated and settled into careers as professional rowers, dedicating their lives to teaching the basics and fine points of a difficult sport.

An example of one woman's dedication to rowing despite some formidable odds is Virginia (Ginny) Gilder, an elite-caliber oarswoman who first started rowing at Yale University, home to the best women's rowing in the 1970s and still a dominant force in intercollegiate competition. When Gilder arrived at Yale, the women's team was led by Anne Warner and Chris Ernst, both members of the first U.S. women's Olympic team in 1976. Ernst is still rowing on the elite level, and won a gold medal in doubles at the 1986 World Championships in Nottingham, England. Ernst and Warner were the role models for novice oarswomen like Gilder, providing an example of how far they could go with dedication and willpower.

Gilder tried out for and made the 1980 Olympic team, only to be denied a chance to row by President Carter's decision to boycott the Moscow event because of the Soviet invasion of Afghanistan. As was the case with most athletes, Gilder was frustrated by working so hard for so long, only to be denied an opportunity to compete because of politics; and like many of the nation's best rowers, she decided to hang up her oars and get down to the business of life.

Armed with a Yale degree, she moved to Boston and started work at a computer software company, rising before the dawn to scull on the Charles River and then visit a physical therapist afterward before commencing work at nine. Gilder's solitary workouts paid off in early 1984, when the selection for the Olympic team started again and she found herself at the forefront of the Eastern women scullers, beating everyone, including Carlie Geer, a tough opponent who was a student at Tufts University and who also worked out on the Charles.

Gilder was a long time sufferer of back problems —a common complaint among rowers—and as bad luck would have it, her back betrayed her as the Olympic selection trials drew near. With injections to loosen up the muscles, and sheer determination to see her through the pain, Gilder rowed with a broken rib but lost the first heat of the trials and dropped down to the repechage, the second-chance trial heat for the losers to gain a spot in the semifinals. She won the repechage and gained a coveted spot in the semi-finals, where, halfway down the 1,000-meter course, one of her sculls snagged a lane marker and caused her shell to flip.

Yet the judges decided to restart the race and Ginny had yet one more chance to advance to the finals. She placed third, good enough, but by the finals she could give no more than what she had, and it wasn't enough to gain the coveted crown as the American women's single sculler, that title going instead to Geer. But she did make the Olympic quadruple sculls, and at Lake Casitas that summer, she won her medal, a silver.

The story of Carlie Geer is another fascinating one, but one made even more interesting by the team she's formed with her sister Judy. Acknowledged as two of the best women scullers in the United States, both have met with great success. The Geers hold the distinction of sitting in the first all-women's boat to race at the Henley Royal Regatta, ending the 142-year old masculine lock on that bastion of rowing. Judy Geer has also set the course record in the women's single sculls at the head of the Charles Regatta. Carlie represented the United States as the single sculler in the 1984 Olympics, and together the sisters have held the title of being the national champions in the double sculls.

Their rowing careers started at Dartmouth College. Judy was a member of the 1976 Olympic crew, the first ever fielded. In 1980, at the European Champ-

pionships in Lucerne, Switzerland, they finished a close second to the East Germans in the doubles. That same summer, at Amsterdam, they won the doubles two days in a row and set a course record in the process. In June 1981, they dominated the nationals held at Mission Bay in San Diego. Carlie won the singles, together they won doubles, and with two other women, won the quad.

American oarswomen have become a leading force in international competition in recent years. Anne Marden, the 1985 American sculler, astonished the rowing world at Lucerne when she rowed a double with Monica Havelka at the championships, coming from far behind to finish second to the East Germans in the first championships to race over 2,000 instead of 1,000 meters.

Whereas American oarswomen were once laughed at by men for daring to row, the women athletes from behind the Iron Curtain have long been the butt of nervous jokes because of their size and seemingly grim outlook to the essentially fun world of sports.

Little is known about Soviet and East German training methods except that potential athletes are identified at an early age and cultivated in sports that match their physical attributes. Of course the system isn't all that rigid, ten-year old girls don't row ergometer pieces and run stairs, but they can learn basic bladework and the fundamentals of rowing, a foundation that is wonderful preparation for the hard work that will follow through adolescent and into the twenties when elite competition begins.

A woman's single resting at the finish of the 1987 U.S. National Championships.

W O M E N   I N   R O W I N G

* * *

Just as men's rowing has been broken down into heavyweight and lightweight divisions, large and small oarswomen now have two classes to fit their size. In the early days of women's rowing there often weren't enough women to support a full complement of varsity and junior varsity crews, thus many undersized women resigned themselves to working hard but in boats that often didn't have opponents—a heartless way to row considering the amount of practice time spent in preparation for only a few scarce minutes of racing.

Rowing spread among women by word of mouth and the realization that something pioneering was being done on the rivers and lakes outside of the nation's colleges. Veteran oarswomen came home with stories to regale their younger sisters with, and roommates came home flushed with the success of an afternoon of undefeated seat racing. Within a few years, the turnout at the boathouse the first afternoon of practice equalled if not surpassed the crowd of men trying the sport for the first time.

At Harvard, women have their own boathouse, the Weld, located diagonally across the river from the men's Newell Boathouse. At Yale, men and wom-en share the same indoor tanks, the same bus to and from Derby, and the same boathouse. Women once relied on hand-me-down shells from the better-funded men's teams, but now they are rowing in equipment fully competitive and up to date.

In recreational rowing, where competition is tough but good natured, it isn't uncommon to see a man and a woman rowing together in the same double, racing other couples in their own event, or in some cases, rowing in all male events and sometimes even winning.

Every rower will agree, the entire sport is better off with women participating alongside men. The archaic elitism of the past was pointing rowing on a one-way path toward extinction. The sport was in danger of becoming too inbred, hobbled by an anti-egalitarian image that made it inaccessible to the average athlete or man of average means.

While women and men don't compete for the same seat in the same boats, the camaraderie and affinity between the sexes that exists elsewhere in society is strengthened over the common ground of rowing, where pulling an oar and making a shell move quickly and gracefully is the ultimate goal of all involved.

CHAPTER 12
INTERNATIONAL ROWING

Rowing thrives in Europe, practiced by great numbers who use the Continent's web of rivers and lakes for recreation and competition. Each country has a rowing center, a place where the nation's best rowers practice as a team for international races and where coaches and technicians experiment and test every facet of the sport from shell design to biomechanical models generated by computers. Every riverside town has a boat club, often ancient structures that sag on their pilings and are home to dozens of sculls and skiffs. The lycées and Gymnasiums all have their own teams, as well as do the colleges and old clubs.

Straight fours are the boat of choice for European sweep oarsmen, who are generally in their late twenties and early thirties. Nearly every oarsman is an accomplished sculler, starting out in the unstable boats to learn the basics of balance and style. Eights are very rare and are formed only for international competitions, such as the Olympics. Traditionally, it was not uncommon for a European country's national boat to be put together only one month or less

before an actual race. Two clubs would merge, or a designated coach would invite the eight best oarsmen from around the country to try out for the boat.

Scullers are treated more seriously in Europe and England. Some scullers spend an entire rowing career trying to gain their country's title of champion sculler, a ticket and designation that will ensure them the fame of a professional bicyclist or a soccer star. The chance to compete internationally at the Henley Royal Regatta or the Olympics is a prize that in itself can be the realization of a life's dream.

European rowing, especially in the Soviet Union and East Germany, is more subsidized than it is in the United States, where oarsmen are forced to pay a large portion of their expenses out of their own pockets. European coaches were the first to experiment with the concept of selection camps—annual gatherings of a nation's best rowers at one place for a month of grueling rowing and testing to determine who would wear the country colors and who would go home.

Selection camps were an integral part of Karl

Adam, who has revolutionized rowing. Forming the first camp at Ratzeburg, on a lake located on the East and West German border, Adam worked with the country's best oarsmen for an entire year, forcing them to concentrate on fast sprint rowing suited to the new international course distance of 2,000 meters. Rather than use the American practice of rowing long distances at a low cadence and high pressure to train for races of two, three, and four miles, Adam worked on creating boats that would row hard and fast. His success was copied by American and Soviet coaches throughout the 1960s and early 1970s, but until 1980, American national crews suffered abysmal records whenever they faced elite-level oarsmen from Germany and the Soviet Union.

The most significant result of Ratzeburg wasn't the precise physiological testing and emphasis on aerobic workouts, but the concept of inviting the cream of the crop to one location and creating a high-level rowing camp.

The camp concept was first used in America in 1959 and 1960 in Seattle, Washington. There the Lake Washington Rowing Club fielded a team of oarsmen who lived in the area and practiced together every day, working under the direction of George Pocock. Up to 1960, American boats had been selected at the national championships, with the fastest boat and not the fastest oarsmen being selected to compete overseas for the world championships.

The American eights from 1900 to 1960 were rowed by the best college varsity or club boat. A good, but not necessarily the best, crew could earn a trip overseas if it put on a heroic effort in the Nationals. The better boat and an enormous pool of great talent stayed behind, passed over by the results of one race.

The camp concept of selecting national team rowers has changed all that, ensuring that every qualified rower would have a chance to work for a seat on a national boat, his or her selection based on hard data generated by ergometer pieces, seat races, and physiological testing. The process of selecting a National team begins almost as soon as the World Championships are over. Around one hundred rowers who distinguish themselves from the crowd of collegiate and club teams are offered an invitation to start training for next year's boat at any one of the regional training centers around the country.

Training centers establish, through testing, who will be in next year's boat. Most of the testing is done off of the water. Ergometer pieces, aerobic step tests, body fat percentages, and muscle biopsies are all collected and analyzed by a team of sport medicine physiologists.

The numbers and values that result from these tests give coaches an indication of how fit and how much physical potential a candidate has. Since physiological ranking was established, various criteria for elite competition have emerged; they have established de facto minimums an athlete must expect to meet if he or she hopes to beat the competition.

The leading authority in applying physiological analysis to rowing is Dr. Frederick C. Hagerman, head of the Work Physiology Laboratory, Ohio University, Athens, Ohio. He has said that the purpose of applying science to a sport as sublime as rowing is to give an athlete a standard to measure himself and his progress against.

"Oarsmen are born, not made," Hagerman said. "There are several oarsmen out there that aspire to rowing on the international level, but they simply won't be able to do it. Well over 90 percent of their ability to compete is determined by genetics." Yet Hagerman also said there have been oarsmen who have been exceptions to the rule, athletes who are favored by coaches because of their determination and positive effect on the morale of the rest of the crew or their ability to blend in with seven strangers and adapt to new rowing styles easily.

Hagerman first started testing and studying the physiology of elite oarsmen in the mid-1960s when he was testing middle distance runners in New Zealand. When Fred Strong, coach of a local rowing club asked Hagerman to test his oarsmen, Hagerman was hooked on the scientific potential in rowing. Hagerman helped Strong select the New Zealand national team; the result was a crew that won the North American rowing championships and the U.S. Nationals.

"Older oarsmen always seemed to have an edge when it came time to pick the national boats," Hagerman said. "There was discussion that a lot of politics and too much subjectiveness in the selection. What we did was demonstrate that the young oarsmen, in terms of their physiological data, were much better than many older, more experienced rowers."

Hagerman said he looks for several physical attributes in a potential elite level rower, but the tests mostly measure the capacity of the heart, lungs, and blood vessels. The most important standard a rower is measured against is the maximum volume of oxygen he or she can consume in a minute. Hagerman said the minimum for a heavyweight man is about 6 liters per minute; for women is about 4 liters.

The second quality the physiologists look for is muscle strength, especially the quadriceps or the muscle group on top of the thighs. The physiologists take muscle biopsies (tissue samples drawn under local anesthetic) from the rowers after a hard ergometer piece and examine the sample to determine what percentage of slow and fast twitch muscle fiber the subject has. The testing is exhaustive and not every rower appreciates it, especially when informed that they are pulling an oar with the human equivalent of only a one-half horsepower engine.

Although it may seem demeaning to think of one's self in terms of horsepower, a rower can take heart in the knowledge that he or she is rowing at 20 percent efficiency; in other words, 20 percent of their total effort is dedicated to moving the boat. By way of comparison, an internal combustion engine delivers 9 to 13 percent of its potential in the form of work, with other energy being expended as heat.

The typical selection camp convenes after the first round of cuts have been made at the regional training centers. The designated National team coaches move between these camps during the fall and winter, observing the rowers and weeding down their numbers to make the process faster and more economical. The coaches are selected and paid a stipend by the United States Rowing Association—during Olympic years funding is augmented by the U.S. Olympic Committee. Each oarsman is given small travel chits for several months before the games.

In the spring about forty oarsmen are invited to attend the final selection camp. That camp has been held in Hanover, New Hampshire, at Dartmouth College for the last decade. The invited oarsmen arrive in late May to pit themselves and their experience against the best. For three weeks, oarsmen are cut from the team in ever increasing numbers, but at a decreasing pace. The first tests are on the ergometers, where each rower tries his best at a six-minutes piece. The anxiety that each oarsman holds prior to rowing such an important piece is so great that some simply pack their bags and disappear during the night. Others are pulled aside by the coach and told to try again next year.

After the first round of ergometer pieces and long distance runs, the oarsmen are broken down into pairs and fours. Those small boats are used for seat racing because they allow a comparison of more oarsmen in less time, they are easy to launch, and oarsmen can quickly assimilate the coach's particular style while working in them. Seat racing is often regarded as the most punishing part of a selection camp; oarsmen quickly realize who they are being judged against, but rarely when they are being raced.

The first boat selected is the eight, with the best eight oarsmen rowing what is widely regarded as the most prestigious sweep shell a country can field in an international regatta. Twelve more oarsmen are selected to round out the camp's boats: the four best rowers left over from the selection of the eight row a straight four, followed by a coxed four, a pair, and the remaining two accompany the team as spares, ready to replace any rower who falls ill or is injured. The camp then travels to the National championships, where they race for the final designation as the national team with crews entered by clubs, colleges, and rival selection camps. "Renegade" entrants tend to compete as scullers, because so many single scullers practice alone and coach themselves.

Showing up for a National championship wearing the colors of a certain sanctioned selection camp is no guaranteed ticket to Europe. Oarsmen who are dissatisfied with a camp coach's approach to rowing often break away from the camps and train with a new coach, competing hard at the finals for the right to wear the U.S. team shirt. Even if the crew wins its event, it must do so within a certain minimum, called a time standard. If a crew fails to row the 2,000 meters within the time established for its class, then the national committee may withhold funding until the crew can prove itself competitive.

National teams are remarkable because of their members' ability to adapt to rowing in a strange boat, with new teammates, in a setting that offers no second chances or excuses. Yet they always come together with boats that are fast and able to keep their own when racing down a fixed 2,000-meters course with a crew from Italy on one side and the New Zealand boat on the other.

The first European rowing championships were held in Brussels in 1890. Two years later, four national rowing federations from Belgium, France, Italy, and Switzerland banded together and formed the Fédération Internationale des Sociétès d'Aviron, or FISA. It is now the oldest athletic committee in the world.

FISA was strict in its regulation of races and only recognized records set on closed courses with no current. It established almost draconian standards for measuring and timing courses but still allowed each member country to define what an amateur was.

American crews were slow to participate in European rowing events because of the expense and difficulty involved in traveling at the turn of the century. American rowing also suffered from a mild case of xenophobia at the turn of the century, a bias spawned by the infancy of American rowing and its determination to reach perfection before traveling and by a reluctance to compete against teams they considered their superiors. Foreign oarsmen would often travel to America, however, to compete for fat stakes against the best American rowers. Foreign talent attracted large crowds because of Americans' fierce nationalism and desire to see the new world conquer the old at their own game.

The first American oarsmen to go to Europe was an eight from the Penn Athletic Club who traveled to

Liége, Belgium, in 1903 to win the European championships. Crews from the Schuylkill River had a proclivity for traveling overseas to match their strength against the Europeans. Most of those crews came from Vesper Boat Club in Philadelphia, one of the most competitive rowing clubs in the world. The time of the Penn A.C. eight over the 2,000-meter course was 5 minutes, 18 seconds—a record that stood for a number of years. The next American oarsman to succeed in Europe was John B. Kelly, Jr., representing Vesper. Kelly won the gold medal in the singles at Amsterdam in 1949 and six years later placed fourth in the sculls at Ghent.

Vesper continued to represent the United States in the European championships, winning the silver medal in the eights at Posnan, Poland, in 1958. In 1964 a Vesper pair placed fourth, another pair placed seventh, and a Vesper straight four also placed seventh. The boats later combined to form the Vesper eight that won the gold medal at the 1964 Olympics.

Since 1965 American crews have attended the World championships without interruption—using the annual event as an elite level test to prepare for the quadrennial Olympic games. Although the races were conducted on the European continent from 1893 to the 1960s, recent world championships have been conducted in Canada, New Zealand, and Mexico.

The countries that have dominated international competition are difficult to identify because each country has gone through periods of success followed by complete anonymity. In the early days of the championships, France and Belgium fought it out for the title; but by the time of World War I, Italy and Switzerland were also strong rowing countries. They never regained their lock on the championships after the war, however. The Soviet Union and East and West Germany were latecomers to the sport, finding success in the mid-1950s as their system of rigorous training and testing techniques blazed the way for the rest of the world. Other countries began to row well in specific events. Argentina for example, has yet to field a truly competitive sweep boat but since the early 1960s has consistently sent a top-notch sculler to the Worlds and Olympics.

America again started to row competitively in world competition in the late 1960s, regaining some of the edge it lost for a number of years following the disastrous 1960 Rome Olympics. According to most American coaches, the decline of American rowing had not been the fault of the athletes so much as the coaches themselves. The empiricism of European rowing was beguiling to Americans, who for years had rowed by the seat of the pants, emphasizing timing and a graceful stroke over conditioning and strength. In their rush to catch the Soviets and East Germans, American coaches may have gone too far in the other direction, falling into a trap of relying on numbers rather than their instincts—worrying about biomechanics rather than judging for themselves how a rower pulled an oar.

International rowing for women started in Europe in the 1950s with the backing of the Continent's established men's clubs, although there remained residues of the standing belief that women were too delicate for any sport more strenuous than croquet or riding. Sexist attitudes about sports are less pronounced in the Communist countries; hence the best women crews have tended to come from the Soviet Union, East Germany, Czechoslovakia, Rumania, and Bulgaria.

The first European Championships for women was held in Amsterdam in 1954. American women organized the National Women's Rowing Association in 1964, and participated in the Worlds for the first time in 1967 at Vichy. In 1974 at Lucerne, the East German women won the gold in the four, singles, quad, and eight. The Soviets won the gold in the double, and the Rumanian crew won the pair. For the next five years, crews from the Eastern Bloc and the Soviet Union won nearly every event, and walked off with nearly all the gold, silver, and bronze medals.

American rowing for women, as discussed in the preceding chapter, has been slow to succeed because of the formidable obstacles and attitudes women have been forced to overcome simply to get a shell to row in. Now that women's rowing is firmly and permanently ensconced as a fixture of all rowing, their times are falling, race distances increasing, and better equipment and new shells being rowed instead of hand-me-downs from men's teams.

Women were finally admitted to Henley in the 1980s. When the barrier at Henley fell, women's rowing moved into a modern state long enjoyed by women swimmers and runners. Nearly every college has shells, coaches, and facilities for a women's team, and funding sources from alumni and national organizations has gone far to establish the sport.

Rowing is an expensive sport; one look around a well-stocked boathouse will confirm it. National team rowing is more expensive than at the collegiate level due to the rents that must be paid, the salaries of the staff and coaches, not to mention the rental of shells and the food bills over the oarsmen.

In Olympic years, American rowers are partially backed by the U.S. Olympic Committee. Such rowing organizations as the USRA today conduct ambitious fund raising efforts, but never enough to establish a permanent rowing center capable of hosting year in and year out a world championship or gigantic event on the scale of Henley. Finding a suitable site has proved difficult. Lake Casitas, outside of Los Angeles and site of the 1984 Olympic Games, has two drawbacks: inaccessibility and poor layout. Princeton's Lake Carnegie—a manmade course donated by the financier Andrew Carnegie—has been used as a site for the American national championships, but it doesn't provide the accommodations and facilities for hundreds of oarsmen from around the world. The requirements of a world-class course is that it be sheltered from the wind, be stagnant or devoid of tide and currents, and provide ample seating for spectators.

Some foreign crews solicit gifts from commercial enterprises such as banks and breweries. The British, despite their rigorous standards of amateurism, were

Opening ceremony at the Temple of Luxor for the Nile International Regatta, sponsored by the government of Egypt. Left to right: Great Britain, United States, France, Belgium, Egypt, and the University of Washington.

THE BOOK OF ROWING

among the first oarsmen to accept gifts from businesses. New Zealand crews have cut their expenses with gifts from Rothman's Tobacco Company and other sponsors. The Leander Boat Club, the oldest and most prestigious home of amateurism in all sport, now accepts commercial sponsors. The Oxford-Cambridge Boat Race, the oldest collegiate rowing race in the world, is sponsored by Ladbrokes, the London bookmakers. The Nottingham International Regatta has been backed by Guinness Brewery and several banks; the Tideway Scullers in London are financed by a grant from the Imperial Tobacco Company.

No such sponsorship is allowed in the United States, where oarsmen still rely on informal fundraising and the dedication of its coaches and oarsmen to defray some of the costs of international rowing from their own pockets. Few amateur sports are well subsidized in America, a condition constantly bemoaned when American athletes are compared to the state-backed Russian and East German competitors.

Sponsorship has made some inroads into American rowing, but it comes indirectly in the cases of rowers who are kept on the payroll by their employers or by corporations who help with expenses in return for a chance to point at the sculler or crew with pride and tax deductions in mind. In Europe, some shells are bedecked with the emblems and logos of their sponsors. However, at Lake Casitas in 1984, the Olympic committee ruled that only the builder's marker could decorate a shell.

One of the most unlikely places rowing is found is on the Nile River in Egypt. Since the 1960s the government and the Egyptian Rowing Association and government have invited crews to race on the Nile against the best Egyptian crews, which are clubs composed of policemen, diplomats, and college students. Because it would be too expensive to fly a racing shell to Cairo, foreign crews borrow shells from the Egyptian rowing clubs for their races. In Geneva, the longest rowing race of the year is held every year; a four-day endurance event where coxed fours are raced around the perimeter of Lake Geneva.

Although most countries seem to have at least one rowing center, in England, the entire River Thames is the center of the sport, with most of the boathouses and boat builders occupying either bank between Marlowe and Oxford. In West Germany it is the Ruderakademie in Ratzeburg. In France, Vichy; Italy, it is the town of Donaratico, where some of the world's best shells are built. In Argentina rowing is focused on the Rio Plato at Buenos Aires, and in Australia at Melbourne. In the U.S., rowing thrives in the cities of the Northeast and the major cities of the West Coast.

Modern attitudes about sport have improved the overall organization and intercollegiate cooperation when it comes to composing national teams. Clubs and colleges exchange shells, especially rare classes like the pair with cox, in order to provide the best crews with the best available equipment. Clubs go to great lengths to find lodging for visiting rowers, and colleges provide them with locker space in the boathouse. A network of job contacts moves into gear to help the rower earn his or her keep while training.

The events themselves are a test of the best rowing in the world, and the competitors train with that in mind at all times. Training for the elite level is a year-round process, with the rowing dominating the athlete's life — often taking precedence over jobs and loved ones.

Few rowers, of course, actively aspire to win a medal in the Olympics or World championships. Some spend their entire young lives fighting for the right to try, only to fall short on some critical test or seat race. Truly serious rowers work at menial jobs that don't demand overtime simply to open up their schedules for an extra hour on the water or with a set of weights. They spend their spring and summers on the road, traveling like nomads from one regatta and championship to another—finishing the route at the elimination trials that will decide whether their work has been worthwhile.

C H A P T E R   13
R O W I N G   C L U B S

By the middle of the nineteenth century upper-crust America and Europe were obsessed with athletics. Men divided their sportsmanship between stable and shore, participating in genteel sports that allowed them to socialize, wager, and increase their stature through riding or rowing during their leisure time.

As early as 1762, sportsmen's clubs in Philadelphia were informally racing in four and six-oared barges but it wasn't until fifty years later that clubs dedicated exclusively to rowing began to appear. The rash of rowing clubs, or navies, founded in the 1840s and 1850s were due in part to the new fitness fad but more importantly to the sport and social camaraderie that clubs afforded their members. As competitive rowing left the purveau of workingmen on the Thames and entered the domain of the English public schools and universities, clubs followed. While America was still in its infancy, the upper echelons of society still looked across the Atlantic for direction and fashion. One inevitable import was rowing.

Beginning at Yale in the 1830s, American rowing quickly came into its own. As exercise and sweat became acceptable following a century of dandyism, men began to search for a form of exercise that would set them apart from the masses. Land sports such as football, baseball, and soccer were all but unknown or existed only in crude forms invented by school boys. Yachting was a professional sport with professional crews racing working boats, and there was little opportunity for an outsider to participate. Rowing was very accessible, considered an appropriate masculine undertaking, and also a sport full of grace and style.

With either militaristic aspirations—or their tongues planted firmly in their cheeks—the founders of the first barge clubs dubbed them navies. While no shots were fired, the navies operated under a military command structure that included admirals, commodores, and commanders. Ornate uniforms that would do a ship-of-the-line admiral proud were the rule and not the exception in the first American navies. Barges—so called not because of their ponderous weight but because of connotation of Cleopatra and the ornate craft she traveled upon the Nile aboard—

were usually six-oared craft similiar in design to New Bedford whale boats. Used in the Royal Navy to ferry officers and crews from ship to shore, the traditional naval barge was fourteen-oared and highly decorated. Ceremonial barges were also used to carry royalty during regattas and reviews of the fleet.

Boats were scarce in the beginning, so many clubs made due with heavy gigs and launches bought or borrowed from a merchant shipping company. While most races were rowed among six-oared barges, examples with four, eight, ten, and occasionally even a twelve-oar could be found in an early barge boathouse. Rowing a barge must have been a difficult task when compared to modern carbon-fiber shells with their composite oars. Rolling seats did not exist, riggers didn't arrive for many years, and oarlocks consisted of two wooden pins set close to each other in the gunwale or side of the boat. The stroke was pure back and arms, a hearty swinging motion that must have wrenched arms out of their sockets and left its practitioners hunched over by the end of a row.

Adhering tightly to the naval theme, the uniforms favored by the first boat clubs were ornate by today's standards. Long-sleeved shirts trimmed with satin, broad silk sashes and jaunty, beribboned sailor caps in a broad array of colors guaranteed that a barge would be noticed by Sunday picnickers and dour watermen.

But life wasn't all pomp and strut in America's new navies. Competition among clubs was fierce.

Boats were continuously exchanged for faster, more innovative designs and the crews practiced daily, rowing hard whenever in the vicinity of a rival's clubhouse or barge or just socializing on the weekends by rowing their sweethearts upriver for a picnic.

Oarsmen who would not obey the sometimes strict, but always lighthearted protocol of the club were punished for any evidence of misbehavior or rebellion.

The secretary of the Union Boat Club wrote in 1852:

A midship oar during practice, becoming somewhat careless in his work was requested by the coxswain to feather properly "to turn his oar." The novice to some two hours exercise, in which he had strained every sinew in his body in endeavoring to get command of his sweep, and forgetting for the moment his duty as a "man-of-war's man" suddenly stopped rowing, and with much amazement; accompanied by the display of a terribly lacerated thumb, crustily ordered the coxswain to come and turn the oar himself.

This infraction of discipline was too much, on the return of the crew to the boathouse, a courtmartial was at once held. With mock seriousness it was decided that maritime law applied to the Union Boat Club, for the Charles River Basin was an arm of the sea, and therefore, since the midships oar's reply

Crews from the Vesper Boat Club in Philadelphia row during a training session for the upcoming summer 1987 international competitions.

to the coxswain had been made on saltwater, he was judged "guilty of mutiny on the high seas".

Despite the humor intended in this, the mutinous oar took it seriously. So far as is known he never rowed in a club boat again.

Unlike the modern health club or Y.M.C.A. which anyone can join for a fee, members of a nineteenth century rowing club were judged on how they fit in socially with the rest of the club's membership. Some clubs were exclusively composed of alumni of a specific university, others of a certain profession. The attraction of these clubs to young men of means was magnetic. Membership was not easy to procure partly because there weren't enough boats to sit in. Rowing was an expensive sport: annual dues were steep, chiefly because of the high cost of maintaining and buying barges. And there was the not inconsiderable expense of outfitting oneself with a satin sash, cap, and tights. Because so few applications were accepted, rival clubs were founded as alternatives to the more established clubs. Most major cities supported at least half a dozen boathouses, in addition to those that housed the universities.

Today there are still a few rowing clubs that won't even consider admitting anyone but a WASP with a distinguished family name and the right connections and schools on his résumé.

In most clubs, however, proficiency at the oar is the deciding factor. Some early college and prep school crews, before they were absorbed by the college administration, were open only by invitation, with the founding members asking their friends to join and leaving no doors open.

Because single sculls were very rare, nearly all rowing took place in four- and six-oared barges. Team effort was taken seriously, and a member of a crew was expected to fit in both socially and physically with the other oarsmen of his boat. The gentlemanly flavor of the time followed oarsmen aboard their boat. Much was made of on-the-water etiquette. When one crew approached a boat from another club on the river, they "tossed oars," lifting them out of their locks and into the air as a salute—not an easy matter considering the weight and length of those early oars.

By the 1870s, the Schuylkill River in Philadelphia, the Charles in Boston, New York's Hudson, Washington's Potomac, San Francisco Bay, and Lake Washington in Seattle all had several active competing navies or boat clubs. Rowing had started its golden age.

Philadelphia's reputation as a rowing city was earned largely by the number of boat clubs that lined the banks of the Schuylkill River. Many Philadelphia clubs are still active—stately anachronisms along what is known as Boathouse Row, a stretch of the eastern bank of the river above a short, but respected, set of falls near the Philadelphia Museum of Art. Thomas Eakins, the American painter, did much to immortalize Philadelphia as the center of early American rowing. An oarsman himself, Eakins's depictions of early rowing have done as much to familiarize the general public with the sport as any single object or event. The Schuylkill Navy, founded in 1858, is generally recognized as the organization that provided the structure for subsequent clubs across the country.

Among the Philadelphia boat clubs have been the Undine, University, Pennsylvania, and Bachelors barge clubs; the Vesper, Malta, College, and Crescent boat clubs; the Fairmount Rowing Association; the Schuylkill Navy; the Pennsylvania Athletic Club Rowing Association; and the Blue Devil Club. For women, such clubs as the Philadelphia Girls' Rowing Club and the Sedgeley Club stand out. In the late 1960s, the clubs' crews won the first three women's national championships; they sent the first U.S. women's eight to three European championships in 1967.

Boston is the home of the: Union, University, Boston, and Cambridge boat clubs. As the quintessential college town, the Charles River's banks are home to more college crews than clubs, with the present rowing membership of the city's clubs stocked with recent graduates.

Today, nearly every city on the western and eastern coasts of the United States has at least one active rowing club. Detroit, Seattle, San Francisco, Los Angeles, San Diego, Washington, D.C., Chicago, Philadelphia, New York, and Boston are all home to clubs that not only offer their members an opportunity to row and exercise, but also produce and support some of the most elite and competitive athletes in international competition.

The first known rowing club was the Castle Gar-

ROBERT STEWART © 1988

A view of Boathouse Row, home to some of U.S. rowing's most established private boat clubs, situated along the Schuylkill River in Philadelphia.

den Amateur Boat Association, formed in 1843, which encompassed nine member clubs who rowed on New York Harbor and the Hudson River. The oldest surviving club is the Detroit Boat Club which was founded in 1839.

In 1873, the Aquatics Editor of *Turf, Field and Farm* published the first *Boating Almanac*. In it he listed 289 boat clubs in twenty-five states. Although New York led the list with seventy-four clubs, states as far-flung as Georgia, Iowa, and California all had more than one organization dedicated to rowing.

The early history of this country's barge clubs is a colorful and sometimes comic one. Their uniforms were regularly ridiculed by working sailors and

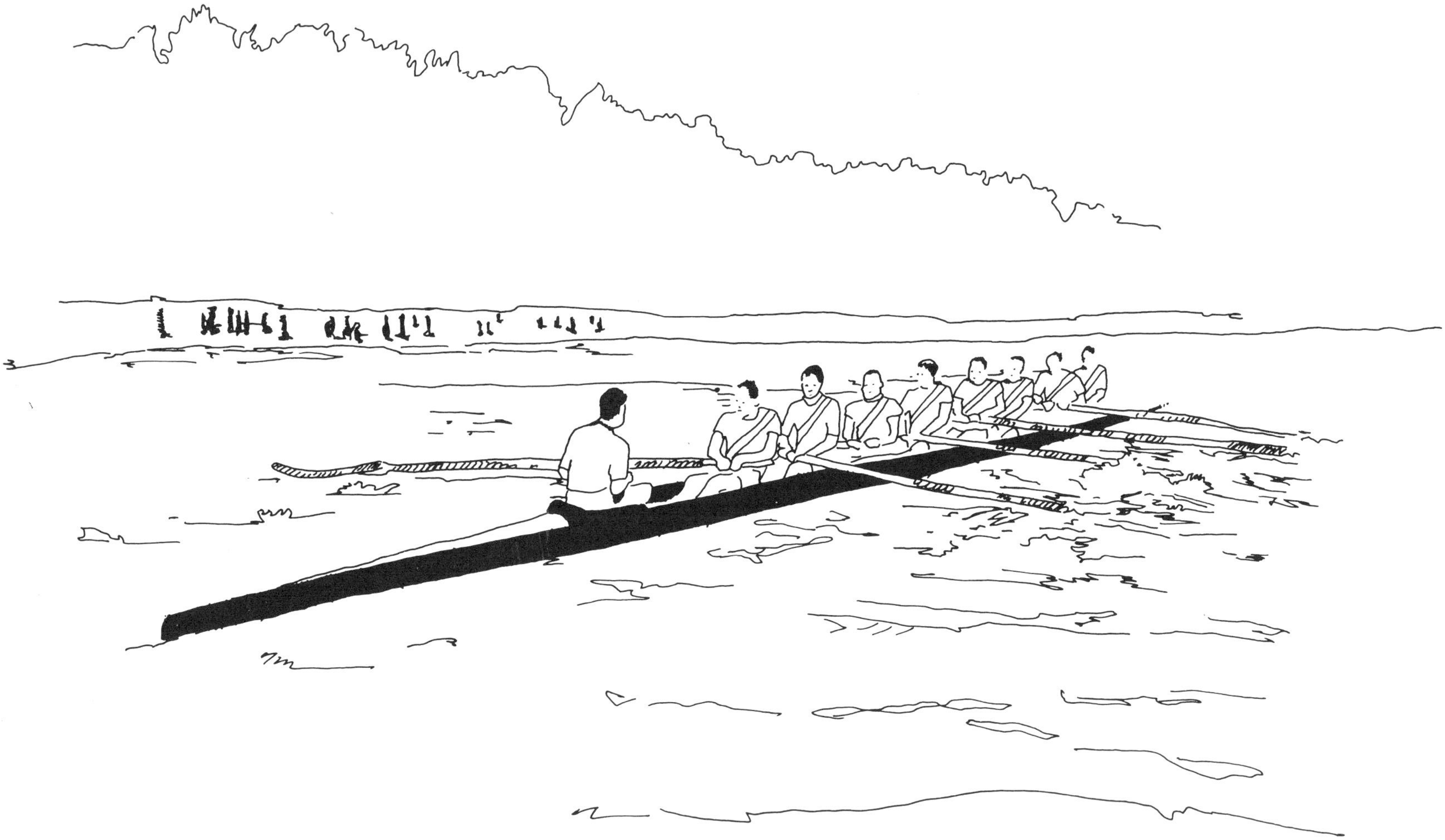

spectators. Yet the entire sport owes a deep debt to the experimentation and dedication of its first participants. Because of their strong financial backing, the clubs could afford to import English shells, boatbuilders, and coaches, introducing the best equipment available to oarsmen who previously had made do with working boats and antique barges. One such group, Boston's Union Boat Club, made do with a heavily built ship's gig once used to transport sailors and cargo to merchantmen moored in the harbor. According to the official history of the club:

> **She pulled four oars and sat quite deep in the water; so deep in fact that unless going with the tide, slow progress was made. Excursions were consequently planned with due regard for the current. To row against it was an offence of a grave nature; an experiment not calculated to preserve a proper respect for the coxswain. From the boathouse to where is now located the Longfellow bridge, was looked upon as a respectable pull, and to cover the distance without halt was a marvelous matter—something to be proud of in pain of endurance, provided, as before mentioned, the tide was made to serve.**

60 Years of the Union Boat Club, (compiled by the secretary of the club, private printing. 2nd edition 1976)

In 1856, the Union Boat Club purchased from a London boatbuilder what has been called "the first true shell to float in American waters." Club members made a point of examining shells and stroke styles whenever they were on the Continent, sometimes purchasing a boat and shipping it home with them.

The first boats used by club crews were often derivations of working boats that had been refitted with extra thwarts, thole pins, and longer oars. Those early, heavy craft served their crews well. Races usually consisted of chance meetings on the river with another club's crew or annual regattas that were often held on the Fourth of July. For the most part, club rowers used their boats for excursions and relaxing paddles with exploration and scenery more important that stroke counts and high speed. But those brush rows against rival clubs and the constant presence of college crews, compelled most clubs to search for the latest and fastest boat designs available to them.

It wasn't until two Canadian crews, from St. John's and Halifax, came to Boston in 1857 to race each other on neutral water, that the Boston clubs had an idea of what a light boat and polished style could do for speed and enjoyment. Both the Canadian crews, being so sure of victory, bet all their money and even their clothing on the outcome of the race. The Halifax crew lost, so they sold their boat to a Boston club. The St. John's crew, not needing their boat anymore, did the same. Those boats were freely

To the left, an eight-oared shell practicing starts.

copied by local builders, who constantly added their own improvements and new design features. Clubs freely sold and traded their equipment among themselves and to new navies, eager to increase the amount of competition in their local waters.

The Union Boat Club of Boston and its six-oared barge, the *Ripple*, also left an impression on the sailors of New Bedford, Massachusetts that same year. A race for whaleboats attracted a fleet that stretched from Fairhaven on one side of the harbor, to the oily docks of New Bedford on the other. So many boats were entered on the narrow starting line that the fleet was forced to split in half, with one starting five minutes before the other.

Although the *Ripple* started in the second fleet, she overcame her handicap and finished first in the first fleet, thereby earning the men of the Union Boat Club the respect of the entire waterfront. So great was the excitement over the victory that New Bedford's Ripple Boat Club was founded that day, with its first boat, the *Adriane*, bought from the UBC.

Some English builders, sensing the burgeoning demand from the number of American orders they were filling, moved across the Atlantic and opened shops in New England, New York, and the Philadelphia region. In St. John's, long a favored source for light, sturdy shells, the foremost builder was Christopher Coyle. In New York, James Mckay, an Englishman, gained a popular reputation as an innovative builder of small racing sculls and singles. Philadelphia's most famous builder was Ellis Ward, the youngest of four racing and coaching brothers who dominated

the professional rowing circuit in the latter half of the nineteenth century.

Competition between clubs and colleges was first organized in the early 1850s, with some cities such as Boston and Philadelphia sponsoring city regattas that drew large crowds. The first organized regatta on the Schuykill occurred in 1835. The first Boston city regatta was held in the summer of 1854 on the Fourth of July.

The historian of the Union Boat Club, in *60 Years of the Union Boat Club* wrote:

> **It had not been advertised long, before the number of entries made evident that there was plenty of interest in it. When the Fourth came, the number of spectators who flocked to all the places on shore that would offer a good view, and the number of boats lying along the course, showed still more plainly that the city had made no mistake.**

Although the regattas were for college and club oarsmen, the amount of interest they raised among the public and on the sports pages of the popular press, served to do much to introduce the sport to the so-called masses. Races of any kind, particularly those that start and finish in front of a crowd, are bound to attract wagers. Crews themselves, such as the Halifax and St. John's boats that raced in Boston, also placed wagers on the outcome of the race. Before long, some clubs were not adverse to placing a few professional watermen aboard their entries.

Thus was born, from the amateur purity of the club systems, the first sprouts of a professional sport that eventually became one of the most lucrative and popular in the country. Professional oarsmen were recruited from the ranks of fishermen and clammers, sailors, and water taximen. To a young, brawny man, rowing offered immediate riches and fame. And in reaction to the amount of money and questionable races rowed and the drop in many people's esteem of the sport's honor, boat clubs banded together to create amateur rowing associations.

In June 1872, the Schuylkill Navy sponsored an amateur- only regatta, which proved so popular that heats had to be run for the first time in the four-oared shell class. Two months later, in August, a group of influential amateur oarsmen convened in New York City. Thus was born the National Association of Amateur Oarsmen, which was formed to organize national regattas and Olympic trials and guarantee the purity of the sport from the taint of the open or covert involvement of professionals.

By the end of the century, professional sculling was all but dead. Clubs continued to compete against each other as avidly as they had in the early, preprofessional days of the sport, with the only change being a renewed emphasis on members pulling oars and not a crew of "ringers" imported to win races and bring the club added fame.

The involvement of professional scullers in club rowing shouldn't be interpreted to mean an attack on the integrity of the typical club. Because the rowing community has always been a small one where every participant is aware of the most prominent figures, it was inevitable that most boat clubs would both come into contact and welcome the expertise of rowing's professional racers. For the simple reason that professional scullers, especially those from a working class background, depended on the quality of their scull and the fitness of their bodies to earn a living; their knowledge of rowing's ins and outs was broader and deeper than the average clubman. It is interesting to note that a parallel relationship was taking place during the same late decades of the nineteenth century among yachtsmen. Hired hands were routinely enlisted to handle the dangerous and arcane work of sailing a powerful racing sloop. This continued until the 1920s when the spirit of amateurism decreed that the sport should belong to everyman and not just those who could afford it.

Because the earliest college crews (Yale and Harvard) were founded as student-run clubs unaffiliated with the school, professional oarsmen found a home in the early years of the collegiate rowing as collegiate coaches. Some of the most successful collegiate coaches of the early part of this century were former professional scullers—a relationship that some college administrations frowned upon as demeaning and corrupting and which a growing trend toward pure amatuerism abolished by 1870.

Because rowing clubs continued to hire professional oarsmen to coach their crews, maintain the shells, and manage the boathouse, a schism developed between them and college clubs. The ex-

Teammates from Vesper Boat Club's four-oared shell with coxswain at the U.S. National Team trials. Princeton, 1985.

ample set by Yale with Bob Cook was followed by several other colleges that prided themselves on their amateurism and dependence on alumni and parents for support. This rift, while not acrimonious, saw clubs and colleges drift apart save where the club's membership was largely composed of a particular college's former oarsmen. Unlike England, where club and college facilities and activities are often indistiguishable, American rowing separated in the 1880s, lagging for three decades as the sport fell out of favor among the public.

Clubs, which were immune to the effects of public criticism, steadfastly continued to employ professionals. Colleges, in part because of administration pressures and also due to the public's huge interest in maintaining the amateur status of collegiate athletics, bowed to the pressure and shed their professional affiliations.

College rowing clubs grew in stature and power as alumni graduated, started careers, and donated money and equipment to their alma maters. As alumni began to take a nostalgic interest in their college rowing clubs, superior boats began to fill boathouse bays. Nearly every collegiate or club shell is named after the person who donated it or in whose name it was bequeathed to the team. The prestige of seeing one's name written in gold leaf on the bow of a victorious racing shell was enough to inspire donations to the point where the average crew is able to row in a new shell every year.

Club rowing also did much to establish the sport in preparatory schools. St. Paul's School in Concord, New Hampshire, was one of the first prep schools to field a rowing team. Other prep schools followed, with rowing arriving in force in the early 1900s. The earliest teams rowed in fours, with the larger schools following the example of their collegiate elders and moving up to eight-oared shells by the beginning of World War I.

Although rowing was the ostensible reason boat and barge clubs were founded, they also offered indoor diversions such as squash racquets, handball, weights, and stationary rowing machines. Winters were spent in the clubhouse, strategizing over the season to come, over boats to replace and oars to order. Collegiate clubs trained through the winter months, while the private organizations socialized and gathered for company and refuge from the pressures of business and responsibility.

Rowing clubs continue to thrive, although not in the glorious numbers of the late nineteenth and early twentieth centuries. Some disbanded for a variety of reasons, including the interruptions of war, escalating waterfront rents, and the competing attractions of country clubs. Manhattan's rowing clubs were forced by the growth of that city to move away from the Harlem River to Old Orchard Beach in the Bronx. Boston rowing actually improved, thanks to the creation of the Charles River Basin, which widened the reach of the river and provided a body of rowing the size of an average lake.

Rowing is essentially a young person's sport; the fiercest competition is among college and prep school students. Veteran oarsmen, entrenched in their careers and burdened with the concerns of family and fortune, found it increasingly difficult to coordinate schedules to the point where an eight- or even four-oared shell could be manned and rowed. The consummate team sport, every member of the boat must be in that boat for the others to get any benefit at all of the exercise. The expense of keeping up a membership in an average urban boat club (about $1000 per year) is prohibitive for most recent college graduates, so many of the more prosperous clubs extend free or guest memberships to college oarsmen for the summer, in many cases supporting the training efforts of oarsmen preparing for Olympic and international competition. Some of them, especially the Vesper in Philadelphia, the New York Athletic Club, and the Union in Boston, field crews that compete against the best the world has to offer and often win Olympic medals or national and world championships. Today, the most prestigious events club crews enter include the annual Henley Regatta, the Head of the Charles, and the Worlds.

Because their numbers have dwindled and because interest in the sport has grown greatly in the past twenty years, it is nearly impossible to join an established rowing club without a solid rowing résumé. Clubs in cities such as Boston have extensive waiting lists, lists that only grow and rarely dwindle. College alumni are sometimes allowed to return to their alma maters to use the facilities. But as more and more of them are opening their facilities to competitive women's crews, the boathouses are barely large enough to store the shells needed for a college and alumni are consequently being squeezed out.

Yet rowing clubs are not the only place someone interested in rowing can practice the sport. Demand creates supply, or so the law goes, so in some areas community rowing programs have filled at least part of the void.

Some such organizations, for a small annual fee, provide access to a dock, a fleet of sailboats, and generally a few fiber glass sculls. Tiff Wood, a noted Olympic sculler from Boston and a graduate of the Harvard Rude and the Smooth varsity heavyweight eight, has organized such a program dedicated entirely to rowing on the Charles River west of the city in Watertown.

Wood has received permission from the Massachusetts District Commission to use an old community skating rink on the southern bank of the Charles as the home of a rowing club open to the public. Advertised in the local newspapers, the initial demand for membership was astonishing.

The program that Wood founded and is guiding to full operation is one of the most ambitious and well received projects in modern American rowing. After depending on the charity of Harvard and the use of the Weld Boathouse (now used by the women's crew), the boating program has grown from a small, word-of-mouth phenomenon, to a major rowing center.

Wood said that after discussing the concept of a program for the first time in the fall of 1984, fliers were posted advertising rowing for the public: "We had about seventy-five people show up and all were current rowers."

But it was a start. Wood and USRA president Daniel Bakinowski decided the long range plan for American rowing was "we ought to do something, not matter how small. We decided to just start something because if we wait for a million members we'll never get anywhere."

The Community Rowing Program has since been formally incorporated and recognized by the Internal Revenue Service as a legitimate, nonprofit organization. Despite some initial problems with the authority that governs the Charles River Basin, the club has finally opened its own docks.

Rowing instruction is done in eights, as Wood said he has found it is the best way to get the maximum number of people on the water at the same time, in a stable craft, with fewer coaches. The program owns a number of recreational singles, one double, and three singles. To give as many people as possible a chance to learn to row, the program is split into three month-long sessions from June to August.

"It's all turning out to be quite popular," Wood said. "Two of the aims of community rowing have been to try to include and actually even attract both junior or youth participants and the disabled. We have a number of blind rowers, for whom rowing is quite a good exercise."

Wood said the program is most aggressively advertising its services to the disabled. "Those are groups that might never otherwise hear about a program like this, segments that could particularly benefit from programs like this. Essentially almost anybody can do it."

Doug Herland, a disabled coxswain and Olympic medalist, has been a leading force in advocating rowing for the disabled. He started his first program in Ann Arbor, Michigan, several years ago and was so successful that he decided to spread the concept, applied for and received a grant from the U.S. Department of Education as a program director.

Wood said of Herland's efforts: "It took a long time to get two or three or four people out on the water, but once he did it was no problem."

Other cities and towns across the country are creating similar facilities, offering dock space and a secure space for the storage of shells. College coaches and oarsmen donate their time to teaching the sport to novices and the membership usually maintains the equipment, with new boats and oars either donated or purchased through gifts. Yet such programs are still painfully few. As more and more budding or experienced oarsmen invest in a scull of their own, public demand may make rowing clubs as commonplace as community swimming pools or tennis courts.

C H A P T E R 14
HEADS, SPRINTS, AND REGATTAS

The Henley-On-Thames Royal Regatta, first rowed in 1839, operated by a set of general rules placed in effect by its board of stewards. The General Rules once stated:

1. No person shall be considered an amateur oarsman, sculler, or coxswain -

   a. Who has ever rowed or steered in any race for stake, money, or entrance fee.

   b. Who has ever knowingly rowed or steered with or against a professional for any prize.

   c. Who has ever taught, pursued, or assisted in the practice of athletic exercises of any kind for profit.

   d. Who has ever been employed in or about boats, or in manual labour, for money or wages.

   e. Who is or has been by trade or employ-ment for wages, a mechanic, artisan, or labourer, or engaged in any menial duty.

The crews that raced the first Henley's were from such clubs and schools as the First Trinity Rowing Club, winners of the first Grand Challenge Cup for eights in 1839, and the Leander Club, oldest rowing club in the world.

The course is among the strangest in rowing. A dogleg bend in the Thames, about sixty-five miles upriver from London and forty-seven down from Oxford. The distance of 1 mile, 550 feet, was picked and retained for 147 years. The reason was simple: it was the longest stretch of good water on the Thames. As the regatta became more popular with the royal family and the throngs of upper classes that accompanied them, pilings were driven into the bottom of the Thames and a long floating boom moored to keep the course clear from errant punters and crews rowing upriver to the starting line.

The atmosphere of a Henley Regatta is as heady

as the races, with oarsmen, coaches, riggers, and stewards performing in their formal summer finery of piped blazers, straw boaters, and silk rosettes. The great boathouses on the river are bedecked with bunting, and gentlemen pole punts inside of the pilings with languid ladies sitting under lacy parasols in the stern.

The entire course and town smells of beer—a light aroma of hops generated by a brewery located near the finish line. On the Berkshire side of the course, down by the Barrier, the beginning of the floating boom, a herd of Guernseys graze on the river bank, coming down to the water's edge to drink, even during the tumult of the races.

Inside of the boom, on the Buckingham or northern bank of the river, once moored four to six extraordinary houseboats rented by the very wealthy. The floating mansions were two-story barges capped with a tented enclosure and outfitted with a large kitchen and several bedrooms. Under great tents in the exclusive Stewards Enclosure, rest the long varnished hulls of the shells. Strawberries and cream are served to guests and the rowers' families inside the striped hospitality tents, where veterans of the regatta recount their races to their wives and friends.

The natural course of the Thames through Henley, according to *Bell's Life* (1851), "is direct from the Henley bridge upon the projecting way of Phyllis Court Grounds, nearly opposite to Poplar Point (not upon the point itself, as so many have supposed); thence it flows obliquely towards the gate below the Point, and then it proceeds still more obliquely and

more quietly to the boughs near Fawley Court."

All racing at Henley is upstream, in the direction of Oxford. The course starts at the Temple, a colonnaded gazebo on the the point of Temple Island, both crews lining up next to each other on the southern side of the temple, two race launches astern, carrying the starter, the timer, and the stewards. By the time the crews settle out of their starts into their racing cadence, the Temple is put behind and the shells enter the Henley Reach for a seven-minute pull straight to the finish.

Fawley Court is considered the midpoint of the course. Since the turn of the century a steward has dropped a flag when the crews pass Fawley, informing the crowd of the crew's positions on a board mounted near the finish.

An anachronism of Henley is instead of splits (times taken as specific intervals in a race, that is 500, 1,000, and 1,500 meters in a 2,000 meter race) a crew's time over the course is divided by a Fawley time. The course has been lengthened, shortened, and readjusted several times, sometimes because of fallen trees or skewed pilings.

As the crews proceed down the course during their race, their positions are announced to the crowd by a large board rigged near the finish line. A steward reads signals from the launches and stations along the course and varies the position of two balls, one white and one black, that hang from a crossarm on ropes. Numbers denoting the speed and position of the boats are hung on the board. In modern times, loudspeakers rigged on poles along the course

provide a discreet commentary on the progress of the contest.

The stewards have kept such precise records over the years that until the 1950s the Henley Course was the standard distance for time trials and collegiate races in America, Canada, and Australia. The records set at Henley have been compared and analyzed to the point where in 1911 it was determined that the average pace of a Henley record holder was 14 feet per second.

By comparison: In 1907 Yale rowed the 4-mile race against Harvard on the American Thames in 20 minutes, 10 seconds (or 17 feet per second), the same speed the record-holding eight set at Henley over a much shorter course.

For the first fifty years, the Henley-on-Thames Royal Regatta was open only to English oarsmen. Gradually, oarsmen from around the Empire were allowed in, with an American opening up the regatta in 1872 as an international arena. A four without cox from Cornell was the first American crew to win at Henley, and since then the regatta has been attended by the very best crews from around the world. American colleges and prep schools routinely send great crews to race at Henley to compete against Britain's best as well as crews from Canada, New Zealand, and the rest of the Western world.

In 1914, after no English crew made the semifinals of the Grand Challenge cup, an unidentified sporting journalist wrote:

In some ways it was a sad Henley. Not a single English crew left in the semi-finals for the Grand Challenge Cup, and the cup ultimately won by Harvard; the Diamond Sculls carried off to Italy by Sinigaglia; a final for the Stewards in which for a good part of the course it seemed as if that cup would go to Germany—all this sounds a melancholy kind of record.

Yet in point of fact the last day of the regatta on Saturday was not melancholy. For one thing, the weather was charming.

The crews are the center of Henley's attention and tradition of pomp. Set apart from the colorful spectators by their white Henley jackets piped with their club colors and emblazoned with an embroidered set of crossed oars, rowers are treated to the hospitality of the local rowing clubs and the occupants of estates in and about the village.

The saga of Harvard's 1914 Varsity Crew at Henley is only the story of one crew to race on the Thames, yet it will serve as a typical example of what happens at Henley.

Led by Robert Herrick, a successful Boston attorney, and captained by Leverett Saltonstall, who went on to become Massachusetts' governor and a United States senator, the crew traveled to Henley aboard the White Star *Olympic*. The eight oarsmen stayed in shape during the tranquil crossing by running around the deck ten times a day. Upon landing in Plymouth, the crew was detained because British

Customs didn't know what to make of the demijohns of Boston drinking water the team had carried across the Atlantic. After convincing the officials that the water was needed to prevent dysentery, the crew boarded the special boat train for London before moving on to Henley, where they were billeted at the Roslyn House.

The day after arriving, the crew tested two English shells, chose one, and rowed the course in 7 minutes, 13 seconds, only a few seconds off of the course record. That night, at the town hall, the drawings for the races were made and Harvard drew the Leander Boat Club, winners of the Grand seventeen times since the first race was rowed, and at the time considered the best crew in England.

Coach Herrick wrote that "Sunday rowing is not considered the thing to do in England, and so everybody went to Oxford in Fords for lunch, and then to the Noble's Estate for tea, taking water with them, which caused great amusement."

An English newspaper cracked, "It is said that the Harvard crew, so careful are they, have even brought their own drinking water over from the States. Is this because they are afraid they won't win on English water?"

On Monday the crew rowed a Fawley piece in 3 minutes, 22 seconds, in the morning and did a course in 7 minutes, 8 seconds, that same afternoon, a time that equaled Leander's best practice time that week.

Tuesday the crew practiced starts but didn't do any hard work, as the first race was rowed on Thursday. That evening "everybody motored over to Sir Frank Crisp's place, which is one of the most remarkable estates in England."

Wednesday was a hot, windless day on the Thames, so the crew saved their strength and rowed two short pieces in the morning and afternoon.

On race day, July 2, Harvard drew the second lane or Bucks, and Leander rowed in the Berks, each lane named for the county (Buckingham and Berkshire) on each side of the river. Harvard and Leander fought down the course, with Harvard opening up a lead after Fawley, which by the finish was opened to a stroke and half.

On Friday, Harvard faced the Winnipeg Rowing Club and won by three-quarters of a boat length, ensuring them a place in the finals against none other that the Union Boat Club, also of Boston and composed of mostly recent Harvard oarsmen.

The British were stunned. They were accustomed to following every account of the regatta avidly, from the results of the informal brushes that inevitably occurred whenever two rival crews practiced on the same stretch of river to detailed analyses in the press of each boat's style. England's rowing public graciously resigned themselves to watching two American crews compete for the top prize.

The London *Times* printed its daily teaser placards that informed the streets of England that Friday, July 3, was a "Black Day for British Sport."

Harvard went on to win the finals against Boston's Union Boat Club.

The Olympic Games have been raced at Henley twice: in 1908 and 1948. A modern, 2,000-meter racing facility has since been built at Nottingham; but it is a forbidding, concrete pool that serves double purpose as a sailing basin. It is a sleek, efficient center for rowing, but it's cold when compared to the lushness of Henley in late June. But little has changed at Henley itself; it is still a regatta where the crowd is as much of a spectacle in its white dresses and ducks. For American crews, it is still the reward that comes after an undefeated spring racing season, an opportunity to cap a year with the best races of them all.

Other British rowing events that should be noted include:

- The Doggett Coat and Badge. First rowed in 1716 and won by either Edward Bishop or E. Gullyford (the record has dimmed with time). It is the oldest race in the world.
- The Oxford-Cambridge Race. Older than the Harvard-Yale series by twenty-three years, it is a microcosm of the history of rowing, with changes in shell design, oars, and seats noted in the ever-improving times over the course from Putney to Mortlake Church.
- The Bumps, or Summer Eight Oars. Rowed at Oxford University since 1836 to determine the college champion, it is an event open only to Oxford students. The races are rowed head style, each crew starting off alone and then followed at a timed interval by another crew, and so on. Each boat tries to bump the crew in front of it, forcing the bumped crew to clear the course and drop out.
- The Wingfield Sculls. It was instituted in 1830 to determine the amateur sculling champion of the Thames. The rules of the event state: "Gentleman scullers of the United Kingdom of Great Britain and Ireland are alone and qualified to row for these Sculls."

American regattas are far less dignified than Britain's, but were no less popular in their time. There would be argument as to which is the American equivalent of the Henley. Some are older, some are richer, and some are bigger and noiser than others.

There have been significant one-time events, such as the Philadelphia Centennial International Exposition of 1876. Held in Fairmount Park, the Exposition featured two sports: sailing and rowing, and attracted three foreign crews and a dozen American colleges and clubs. Races for amateurs were held on the first five days of the Exposition, and professionals raced the last three. The fleets were broken into heats because the course narrowed down and only three shells could be raced at once.

James D. McCabe, author of *The Illustrated History of the Centennial Exhibition*, wrote:

The course was carefully marked off with flags and buoys, and the distance measured with exactness. A grand stand was erected at Rockland, the finishing point, and another on the opposite side of the Schuylkill. The starting point was immediately below the bridge of the Reading Railroad, at the Falls of the Schuylkill, and the finish at Rockland, just above the Columbia Bridge. The stands and the banks of the river were thronged with spectators daily, the crowds frequently numbering as many as one hundred thousand persons, and the utmost good nature and enthusiasm prevailed. The winning crews were greeted with deafening cheers when they came in, and were made to feel that the sympathies of the vast throng were heartily with them. The regatta was in all respects a brilliant success, and the result more than rewarded the generous efforts of its projectors.

The races, especially the coxless fours, were very popular, and other American cities followed Philadelphia's example—though on a less grand scale—hosting festive regattas for amateurs and professionals on the Fourth of July or any occasion worth celebrating. Rowing became so popular in some cities, promoters were hired by sponsors to ensure a large crowd on those busy weekends when a college crew could be racing an archrival, two professionals sprinting for a stake, and a rowing club set-

ting out on its annual summer outing.

As professionalism became the scourge of "good, clean sportsmanship," at the great rowing events, the public's interest waned. Stories were told of welshed bets and about mysteriously broken oars; miraculous cramps that stopped one sculler a hundred feet away from the finish line, but long enough for his rival to cross first. City officials, becoming sensitive to rowing's bad reputation, stopped awarding the silver loving cups to the winners. College presidents handed down strict edicts against their college oarsmen competing in the company of "sculling-sharps."

Although they had coexisted for three decades on the same rivers, professional and amateur rowing was cleanly divorced. The public who retained their interest in rowing switched their loyalty to amateur rowing. The most popular college races—the Harvard-Yale Regatta, the IRA's (first in Poughkeepsie on the Hudson, then Syracuse on Lake Onandaga), Opening Day in Seattle, the Eastern Sprints in Worcester, Massachusetts—remain popular races. None, however, approaches the scale of the regattas of the late nineteenth century or the deep tradition of Henley.

The Sprints are the only time that every large Eastern college crew has the opportunity to race all rivals in one afternoon. Lake Quinsigamond is a long finger of a lake on the eastern end of Worcester. Also home to the New England Interscholastic Rowing Association Regatta, the prep school championship, Lake Quinsigamond is wide enough for six crews to

Henley-on-the-Thames,
home to the prestigious
Henley Royal Regatta,
during race week.

THE BOOK OF ROWING

race abreast down a mile-long course with no turns or obstacles.

At the starting end of the north-south course a highway bridge spans the lake. The crews row under the bridge, turn around, and wait for their race to be called. The starting line has six small aluminum skiffs moored in a line. The crews back their shells up to the skiffs, and a person lying in the skiff holds onto the stern.

The lanes are unmarked by buoys, the coxswains must aim the bow of their shells at six large orange numbers secured to the side of the Route 9 bridge at the southern end of the course.

The lake was first used for racing by Harvard and Yale for their annual regatta in 1859 and continued to provide a good three-mile course until 1870, when the crews moved to their present home on the Thames in Connecticut.

Several rowing clubs popped up on the shore of the lake, as Holy Cross, Clark, and Worcester Polytechnic Institute formed boat clubs and several prep schools in the area decided to start the sport. In 1960 the Eastern Association of Rowing Colleges moved its annual sprints to Worcester, its home today.

The name of the regatta: the Sprints, was a novelty in 1946 when they were first raced. Racing distances in America ranged from 1 to 4 miles, with only prep schools rowing shorter distances. A 2,000 meter race was seen as a "sprint", a test of speed more than endurance. Today, the 2,000-meter distance has been accepted both here and internationally as the standard racing distance. It started in

Europe and soon became the standard Olympic and World Championship distance. The reason is convenience—more boats can be raced in a day over a short course. Some prep schools still row 3/4-mile events, but the long-distance races so popular before World War II are preserved only in traditional events.

In the early 1970s, a phenomenon occurred in Boston that has since brought rowing back to the masses, and opened up the competition to include hundreds of boats, all able to row the same course in one day.

The Head of the Charles Regatta is as well known in this country as the Henley Royal Regatta. Although it is less than twenty years old, the Head, as it has been dubbed, has grown to such proportions that the number of entries now have to be limited to 780 shells and sculls. The racing starts at the western end of the Basin, a long, wide stretch of water that runs along the northern shore of the Back Bay. Every crew is assigned a number (pinned to the back of the boat's bowman) and is called to the line in order by a starter near the Boston University boathouse.

The boats cross the starting line, one after another at regular intervals, settling down into their cadences as they pass underneath the first landmark, a steel railroad bridge painted with Greek symbols and the colors of whatever college crew got there last.

The course curves north into Cambridge at the train yards, opening up into a long stretch of straight water that passes by the Northeastern University and

Riverside Boat Club, and then a series of stone, three-arched bridges, the center span the only one permitted for passage.

After passing the Harvard Boathouses, the crews start an oblique 90° curve into another reach and the last bridge, the infamous Eliot Bridge, bane of many a coxswain who played chicken with another boat and lost the race for the center arch.

Located immediately in front of the Cambridge Boat Club's boathouse and docks, the bridge is the most popular place to watch the race. Crews career around the curve, trying to pass and overtake the boat in front of them. Collisions are inevitable: oarsmen shouting and spectators cheering.

Scullers, their backs to the course, row into river banks, hit buoys, and flip over. Some improvise rearview mirrors by taping dentist's mirrors to their sunglasses; others look over their shoulders, paranoid that they might meet the worst fate of all, running into the bridge. The crowd sitting on the bridge railing scream warnings, but some scullers and some eights for that matter, have rammed the Eliot Bridge head-on, crushing the $1/8$" red cedar bow all the way up to the bowman.

One year, the Harvard and Yale varsity heavyweight eights, a year when Yale had broken Harvard's twenty-year lock on the Harvard-Yale Race and both boats were finishing first or seconds at the Eastern Sprints, neither crew backed down as both approached the bridge at the same time.

With their oars meshing together, the two boats entered the arch together. Yale lost the duel when all the carbon fiber oars on the starboard side hit the wall of the arch and snapped, the noise described by a Harvard oarsman as "four loud gunshots."

Those crews that do make it through, and most do, pick up their cadence and pull the final mile to the finish—two and a half miles from the start. Following the finish, the crews turn around and row back to the start in a slow, narrow file running parallel to the three-mile upstream course.

When the Head was young and only attracted forty crews, some college oarsmen would row two and even three races in one day. Starting off in the morning in a pair, then racing a four after lunch, followed by an eight late in the afternoon. Now, with more shells and more being refused entry every year, rowers are limited to one race each.

Like Henley, the best thing about the Head of the Charles, aside from the rowing, is the scene ashore on the bridges and riverbanks. Crowds of more than two-hundred thousand—college students, tourists, families of the oarsmen, coaches, crews, managers, and riggers—gather along the entire course for the day, picnicking, drinking, watching the boats with one eye, and their friends with the other. Parking is impossible and the best spots are all taken before noon. Yet the regatta continues to grow every year, with crews from the Soviet Union, the Eastern Bloc, Europe, and Canada competing against the best U.S. college, club, and prep school teams.

The crews launch at any one of ten different boathouses along the river. Shells are stored on trailers and in slings on parking lots and open stretches of riverbank; taken through the host boathouse and onto a dock for launching. No launches are allowed on the water; so once the crew has launched, they are on their own. After paddling down to the start, the crews use the wide Basin to practice starts and adjust their stretchers before being called to the starting line.

Since the Head of the Charles has reached the status of being the best fall rowing event in the world, the Head style of racing has spread to other rivers. The Head of the Connecticut, Head of the Merrimack, Head of the Thames, the Lake Washington Head, and the Head of the Chattahoochee have all proved to be popular regional events during the fall rowing season. Until the Head of the Charles was founded, fall racing didn't exist. Colleges used the fall months to teach the freshmen and workout out the summer cobwebs. Fall rowing is nearly nonexistent at prep schools, especially small schools with a limited number of athletes to stock their football and soccer teams.

Now that there are races to be rowed in the fall, American rowing has been given a whole three months of rowing that were once ignored. Head rowing is fun because the pressure is less than the usual sprint or one-on-one match race. Slow boats are overtaken by fast boats. Some oarsmen simply don't want to finish, and row long lazy races to prolong their time on the river. The varsity and national crews race flat out, charging noisy monsters that always win the crowd's approval, as they fight upstream past as many hapless rivals as possible.

Divided into classes, the races are paced so a string of prep school eights will start in sequence, followed by a slower class (such as four with cox) so the two won't blend and cause collisions. The veteran singles are the first off the line, an event open to fifty scullers over the age of fifty. Then the lightweight eights follow, the men averaging 160 pounds, women 130. They are followed by the youth fours, usually small prep school teams, each rower under eighteen, and so on. Every rower, novice or expert, light or heavy, man or woman, oarsman or sculler, has an event at the typical head. Cumulative scores are kept of every club, college, and school with boats rowing in several or all of the events. Points are given on the basis of a crew's place in its event, with penalty points deducted for collisions and straying from the course line.

After the races, the race committee sometimes sponsors a barbeque and beer party open only to the contestants. Oarsmen, in their quest for carbohydrates, can be prodigious beer drinkers, the bane of the Henley pubs and Harvard Square bars.

Opening Day in Seattle is the premier West Coast rowing event. Held on the Montlake Canal that links Lake Union to Lake Washington, the races are rowed in pairs, crew against crew for 2,000 meters before an enormous audience. Home to the legendary Pocock Boatshop and the University of Washington crews, Seattle is a beautiful setting for rowing, with Mount Rainier shining to the southeast and the Olympic Peninsula gleaming to the west.

Like Henley, log booms are anchored along the

course, defining an open course that is filled with one pair of racing crews after another throughout the day. Yachts bedecked with partiers moor alongside the course, while hordes of students and spectators clog the banks of the cut.

The IRA's, or Intercollegiate Rowing Association Championships, were founded in 1895 when several Ivy league schools, blocked from competing against Yale and Harvard, raced a 4-mile straightaway at Poughkeepsie, New York, on the Hudson. Over the years, more colleges asked to race on the wide course, but in time, up to ten eights raced abreast, creating unfair advantages because of the difficulties involved in getting ten shells lined up at the start and off the line together and pointed in the same direction.

In 1929, the varsity 4-mile race resulted in four crews: MIT, then Syracuse, California, and Cornell swamping; and it was decided in 1950 to move the regatta elsewhere. For two years an experiment was tried on the Ohio River at Marietta, Ohio, but flood conditions made the rowing treacherous, and courses had to be shortened because of bad conditions.

Its present home is on Lake Onandaga in Syracuse where the Erie Canal enters the lake near the Syracuse boathouse. The lake is wide enough to accommodate a full fleet of twelve shells in one race; however, there is a problem with wakes tossed up by speeding powerboats that also use the lake. For many years, the IRA's were considered the collegiate rowing championship, and crews from the West Coast began to attend every year—the only two missing colleges being Harvard and Yale. Today there is a true national championships, conducted by the United States Rowing Association in Indianapolis, Indiana. All colleges have been attending this early summer championship, the winners usually gaining an invitation to Henley.

The Dad Vail Regatta is the small college championship of the East. Crews from schools like the U.S. Coast Guard Academy, Marietta College, Boston University, Iona College, Ithaca College, the Florida Institute of Technology (and many more), race for a trophy named in honor of Harry Emerson (Dad) Vail, a former professional sculler who coached at Wisconsin. The prize was offered by Rusty Callow, coach of the Naval Academy, to foster competition among the newer and smaller rowing colleges. It has been raced at Red Bank, New Jersey; Springfield, Massachusetts; Marietta, Ohio; Boston; Poughkeepsie; and finally Philadelphia, on the Schuylkill River.

The San Diego Crew Classic has become an early spring testing ground for the best college crews in the country. With such colleges as Harvard and Yale coming West for the first time, the Long Beach course is the site of some very competitive rowing— the prize being bragging rights for the rest of the season.

Regattas are growing in both the number of rowers who participate in them and the number of new events added to the already long list. Recreational rowing has done much to spawn larger events, and most head races have several events for recreational sculls.

The most important effect of regattas is they bring rowing to the public. It is easy to ignore two shells racing on a Saturday morning while driving along a river, but seven hundred shells is eyecatching. From Henley to New London, from Worcester to Philadelphia, rowing has long been a popular spectacle strong enough to endure the competition of other sports. Now it is appearing on rivers of cities that have never seen a rowing race before, a splendid addition to the scenery and sporting activity of any town.

C H A P T E R   15

THE HARVARD-
YALE
REGATTA

The oldest continuous American collegiate athletic event is the Harvard-Yale Regatta, an enduring blend of sport and society that is raced every June before an appreciative crowd on the banks of the Thames River in New London, Connecticut.

For the 16 oarsmen and 2 coxswains, the race from the I-95 highway bridge to Gales Ferry is probably the most difficult thing they'll ever do in their lives. It is twenty minutes of rowing with something far more important than a rowing shirt or the brief exhilaration of a well-rowed win. As one Harvard oarsman said before the 1986 race, "The results of this race are cast in granite. It isn't a race you want to lose."

What is at stake is a tradition that reaches back to 1852 when the two colleges met on Lake Winnipesaukee in New Hampshire "to test the superiority of the oarsmen of the two colleges."

Yale holds the honor of being the first American college to adopt rowing, an event which occurred in 1843; but Harvard quickly followed, purchasing their first shell only a year or two after Yale, and using it for club rowing and the recreation of some students.

The first Yale boathouse was located on the northern side of New Haven harbor, close to where the present I-95 bridge crosses from East Haven into the city. The first oarsmen were students looking for some exercise and an opportunity to escape the confines of the campus. Rowing was done at a leisurely pace save for times when other barges were passed and the honor of the oarsmen was challenged.

Harvard's first races were on the Charles River and Boston Harbor against crews from the Union Boat Club in a shell named the *Oneida*. The *Oneida* was the envy of the Charles in the early 1850s, with every barge club and professional oarsman trying to beat her in brushes, or informal races, whenever she appeared on the water.

The first boat raced interscholastically by Harvard

was named the *Iris*, an eight-oared lapstraked shell with coxswain. It won the first Yale-Harvard race on August 3, 1852, by two boat lengths over a two-mile course around a turning stake. That race took 22 minutes to win, with Yale coming in about two minutes later in the *Nereid*, a six-oared barge with coxswain.

Another early Harvard boat, a four-oared, rudderless shell named the *Y-Y* (short for *Yang-Yang*) was entered in the second Harvard-Yale race held on July 21, 1855 in Springfield, Massachusetts, three years after the first contest. Determined not to lose the second race because of too few oars, Yale entered the *Nautilus*, a six-oared barge with coxswain against the *Y-Y*.

The Connecticut River course, picked for its convenient location for both crews, was a mile longer than the Winnipesaukee course and was lined by a sizable crowd of Boston and New York rowing enthusiasts. For the second time, Harvard won, much to the chagrin of the Yale crew, who paddled across the finish line in 25 minutes, which was 2 minutes, 13 seconds, after Harvard. Yale's oarsmen blamed their loss on a bad boat. But some members of the Union Boat Club climbed aboard both the *Y-Y* and *Nautilus*, and raced again. This second race ended with the *Nautilus* crossing the line first—a fact dismissed by Yale because the Boston club was considered biased toward their hometown college.

During that era black lead was often rubbed on the bottoms of the barges to make them slip through the water faster. When none was available at the second Harvard-Yale race, the Harvard crew used soap. According to *Sixty Years of the Union Boat Club*:

"In consequence, as they forged ahead, they threw off streak after streak of thick suds which remained visible as far as the eye could reach, much to the surprise of the spectators, who naturally wondered what had happened to the water."

It wasn't until after the Civil War that the two colleges met again, this time in Worcester on Lake Quinsigamond. Worcester remained the site of the regatta until 1870, the race rowed in six-oared coxless shells steered by the bow oar over a three-mile course around a turn. There, Harvard continued an impressive string of victories with the exception of the first two races won by Yale. The last Worcester race ended with another Harvard victory, earned when Yale collided with the leading Harvard barge at the turn, fouling out.

The colleges didn't race head to head from 1872 to 1875, since both participated in the Intercollegiate Regattas in Springfield and Saratoga, New York. A Yale misfortune in the crowded 1874 race at Saratoga, led Yale to resign from the association. Yale invited Harvard to rejoin the tradition of match races, and in 1878, both colleges settled on the Thames River in New London as a good course in a relatively neutral town, convenient to each crew and its supporters midway between New Haven and Cambridge. Yale purchased a piece of property in Gales Ferry on the eastern bank of the Thames, establishing an encampment that is still home of the

Yale oarsmen. Harvard moved into more spacious quarters about a mile down the river on the same bank in Ledyard.

The Thames reach from Gales Ferry to Long Island Sound is straight and wide, a combination of attributes that offered a very rowable, if choppy course and deep lengths of water alongside the lanes where spectators can moor their yachts and root on the oarsmen from start to finish. Old photographs of the course tell the story of the race's popularity through the years and the state of the spectator's taste in yachts as well as their social status. By the early 1900s, New London in late June was an established stop on the circuit of summertime soirées and happenings assiduously followed by the Ameri-

can smart set. For many, the race was just an excuse to gather and see and be seen. Before World War II forced a stop to the races, oarsmen would be invited aboard some of the most opulent yachts, such as J. P. Morgan's palatial craft, for dinner and copious desserts of strawberries and cream. The camps were divided between supporters and alumni of each school, with the excitement fueled by the throngs of undergraduates exuberant from the end of classes and determined to see their boat win.

New London embraced the regatta as train after train pulled into the depot and emptied crowds into the city's hotels and boarding houses, saloons, oyster bars, and grills. On the eve of one regatta, legend has it that the mayor of New London created a new

A close finish to 1962's four-mile Harvard-Yale regatta on the Thames River in New London, Connecticut. Yale won by 1 second in one of the closest races in history.

cliché when he urged Harvard's followers to "paint the town red" should the Crimson crews sweep the afternoon races.

The tumultuous scene on shore was mirrored on the river as the alumni rafted their boats together, hoisted the college colors, and spent the evening walking from deck to deck, racing overloaded dinghys, placing bets, and trading insults until morning.

By 1886, the races were 4-miles long, a downstream run that started at the first bend in the river at Bartlett's Cove, down to the finish at the railroad bridge. Spectators lined the bridge or bought tickets on the race train, riding on flatbed cars fitted with bleachers. Many ventured out in the river in rented skiffs.

The first eight races in New London were all downstream, but the 1886 race went upriver because of a strong south breeze that kicked up a dangerous chop. The races were held in the late afternoon, when the prevailing onshore breeze would usually fade and give the oarsmen a rowable course to race. Both the downstream and upstream course records are owned by Harvard: the 1948 varsity broke the 20 minute barrier at 19 minutes, 21.4 seconds. The 1979 crew nearly duplicated that time rowing *upstream* at 19:22.9.

The cumulative record puts Harvard ahead with 68 to Yale's 47. In 1901, 1911, 1915, 1922, and 1940, the score was tied. Harvard widened the gap beginning in 1963, when Crimson crews started a seventeen-year string of wins under the tutelage of Harry Parker. Yale broke their run of bad luck in 1981 and the two

schools have traded the trophy back and forth ever since, Harvard's freshmen, junior varsity, and varsity swept the 1986 race. Harvard won the contest again in 1987.

The race was not rowed in 1898, at the beginning of the Spanish-American war nor in 1917 because of World War I. World War II caused the 1942 regatta to be rowed at Derby, Yale's home course on the Housatonic River, owing to the gasoline rationing and the closing of the Thames River to the public because of the nearby shipyard and submarine base. The 1943, 1944, and 1945 races were canceled completely.

The regatta was resumed after the war, but it has lost much of its public attention to the lure of professional sports. Where the regatta was once avidly covered by the sporting press, it is barely noticed by the popular press today, save for an occasional feature in the Sunday supplement. Nevertheless, the crowds still arrive at Espinosa's farm on the eastern bank of Bartlett Cove, directly across from Red Top, where they park and picnic on the sloping fields of Quaker Hill.

Although the race train no longer runs along the course, passenger ferries and small tour boats run excursions on the Thames during race day, offering a bar, live music, and a fairly good view of the race from start to finish. The Regatta Association sponsors a luncheon at Red Top for alumni and their families of both colleges, and each college's rowing association sponsors an after-race event at Red Top and Gales Ferry.

Although the two encampments are less than a mile apart, there is absolutely no formal contact between the schools until after the race has been rowed. The boathouses and dormitories are only used during those three weeks at the end of May, locked up the morning after the race, empty and seeming to never change, with the relics of the past staying on the shelves and in the closets until the next regatta.

The walls of the dining rooms and lounges are lined with pictures of past crews, all posed in their shells, their blades set at the catch, their names written on the border. Stacks of magazines and urgent telegrams of support clutter the tables. The living quarters are spartan, the walls unpainted and carved with initials and dates.

Both crews maintain a tradition that stems from 1900 of playing out a croquet tournament during their stay on the Thames. Yale's crew designates one oarsman as the "Ball and Mallet," the organizer of the tournament and the automatic champion given to the rule that only he may cheat. Harvard also takes its croquet seriously, but in their rules, only the coach may cheat.

At the first night's dinner, the members of Yale's freshmen boat stand one at a time, stating their name and the name of the school where they prepped before they are made to sing that school's song. If they don't remember it, then they may sing the song of their choice, until booed back into silence. The rituals of the camps vary slightly from year to year, each year's camp chronicled by the cap-

tain in a perpetual log. At Yale, the captain reads the account of the last race that Yale won at the first dinner of the training camp. For years, the reading of the 1962 race was both a goad and inspiration to the Yale crews, as every intervening year was ignored and omitted from the official record until a win took them out of limbo.

The training methods used are unique, as most crews are accustomed to practicing for the standard 2,000-meter race. Making the transition from short, sprint rowing to the grueling 4-mile distance requires so much time that both colleges forego entering the IRA's and use the time to concentrate on building the pacing and endurance necessary for the New London course.

Only the varsity boats race the full 4 miles. The junior varsity crews row 3 miles, the freshmen 2. Yet varsity and junior varsity row together in practice, racing each other for miles, sometimes from the boathouse 10 miles upstream to Norwich. At least once a week, the crews race the distance they will row during the regatta. The varsity starts under the I-95 bridge and rows upstream past the Coast Guard academy, where the junior varsity joins in and paces the varsity boat up through the second mile mark, where the freshmen boat joins in and helps push the varsity all the way to the finish. Such time trials give the oarsmen a benchmark to measure their condition and speed against and is the only way to familiarize themselves with the rigors of rowing evenly and hard over a long distance.

Practices are held twice a day, once early in the

morning starting at six a.m., when low temperatures and light winds make rowing conditions perfect for a hard practice. The coaches wake the oarsmen and have them take their basal pulse rates before rising; an overall high rate indicates that the oarsmen are still depleted, a low rate clearing the way for a hard workout.

The crews stay on the water for three hours, usually rowing pieces and seat racing in the first week of practice, and then drawing out the length of the pieces from six minutes to ten and twelve. When the boats come off of the water, the oarsmen shower and then eat breakfast before taking off the rest of the morning and early afternoon to sleep, play croquet, read, or play cards.

The afternoon practice doesn't vary much from the morning workout except that an effort is made to row on the race course and work at imitating the conditions and pressures of the final race. Both colleges row past each other's boathouse in full view of each other. Whenever the teams brush together on the water, they usually look away from each other, or stop rowing altogether, to the let the other shell pass. For several years an attempt was made to bring the two teams together for a dinner or evening of conversation. The effort failed dismally, not because of bad manners and ungentlemanly attitudes, but because of the pressure that mounts as the days go by and because there really wasn't much to talk about.

The food served at Red Top and Gales Ferry is cooked by a staff from the Yale dining halls. The quality and quantity is generally greater and better than the fare the oarsmen receive on campus and coxswains and freshmen are pressed into duty as waiters and busboys.

After-dinner entertainment sometimes consists of a movie, or in the case of Yale, a session of filthy limericks composed by the Bard, a freshman in charge of composing and reciting them. The pace of life when the crews are off the water is slow—in part because the oarsmen need the time to recover between practices and also because there aren't many diversions to kill the time. Such experiments in model rocketry and slot car racing have served over the years; but both camps are usually quiet, the oarsmen resting, reading, or writing letters between practices and games of croquet.

A large rock promontory stands on the shore of the western bank of Bartlett's Cove, midway between Red Top and Gales Ferry, and the most hard-fought war before the race is the nightly excursion to paint it blue or red. A race between the team managers and coxswains in fours is another highpoint of the training period. And stealing the other crew's banner from their flagpole and pressing it into service as a tablecloth is a tradition as old as the race itself.

On the day of the race, the crews wake late to find the course lined with yachts and a crowd beginning to gather on the western shore. A huge red banner with a white H flaps from the flagpole at Red Top, a blue and white Y at Gales Ferry. The crews eat a hearty breakfast and then retire to a chair for the

The dock at Red Top, the Harvard crew's quarters for the annual Harvard-Yale race. So called because of its red roof shingles, Red Top is only occupied for several weeks every May and June.

rest of the afternoon, staying off their feet and trying to push any thought of the race out of their minds. The previous afternoon, after a light practice while wearing racing shirts, the crews cleaned their shells and inspected every inch of the slides, footstretchers, oars, and riggers for flaws and dirt.

In the morning, before the spectator traffic is too heavy on the river, the varsity crews row their shells down to the starting line, pulling them out at the U.S. Coast Guard Academy's docks and leaving them there until race time. The reason for getting the shells downriver is to save the oarsmen the extra effort of rowing four miles down to the start before having to race back. The crew rides downstream to the start in a launch, passing down the center of the course to applause and cheers of the spectators.

Both Harvard and Yale share the same dock, fitting their oars to the riggers and lacing into the footstretchers only a few feet away from each other.

The freshmen race first, rowing down to the start because the distance is only 2 miles and used to warm-up and practice starts. When the judges and times return from the finish of the first race, the junior varsities back up to the starting boats and start off on their three-mile course. By six p.m., the varsity crews are by themselves under the highway bridge, two eights waiting for the command that will begin their race into the record books.

From an oarsman's point of view, the race is about twenty minutes of the hardest physical exertion he'll ever know. Although the stroke rate is a few notches lower than the usual 2,000-meter pace, each stroke is pulled as hard as possible. The start of an upstream race usually occurs in fairly rough water, and both crews are filled with the nervous energy and adrenalin that builds up over three weeks of steady practice. Hence, the first half-mile is nearly identical to the beginning of a 2,000-meter race, with both crews fighting early to get ahead and gain the psychological edge that can mean everything in the hard, tough slog through the middle 2 miles.

The coxswain is never more important than in a race as long as the Harvard-Yale regatta, where a missed stroke or bad wave can throw off a boat's timing to the point where nothing can bring back the oarsmen's spirits. Oarsmen have to be closely watched and kept in check, otherwise the tension of the race can cause them to rush their slides and fight against each other, rather than calming down into a perfectly balanced and timed unit that will be more efficient over the long run. Sets of power-tens are taken whenever the shell passes a landmark, half-mile buoy or if it begins to slip behind the other. Coxswains spend half their time monitoring their shell, and the other half yelling with their megaphones pointed at the other crew, demoralizing them by describing their poor progress and weak effort.

With a mile to go, if the race is close, the crews will begin their sprints, working the stroke up slightly and making the final herculean effort to pull ahead and put the race away once and for all. As the shells draw into the range of the spectators, a din of boat horns, whistles, and cheers is final inspiration to the crews, who are finally rowing a race under the critical eye of several thousand fans.

While 2,000-meter races are won by a matter of inches, the Harvard-Yale regatta has finished with times as close as the 1962 race, when Yale nipped Harvard at the finish line to win by one second. The majority of times are separated by a matter of 10 to 20 seconds—a testament to the determination of both crews never to throw in the towel.

Throughout the race, the crews are trailed by launches carrying the coaches, a judges' boat that carries the starters and timers, and crash boats that run alongside and keep the course clear of any wandering spectators who might float out into the path of the charging shells. The course is cleared by the Coast Guard before the start. And the starters wait a few minutes for any motorboat wakes to subside before sending the crews on their way.

At the finish, the shells are pulled together and

Gales Ferry as it used to be. Home to the Yale men's crew, the compound, like its rival neighbor just a few hundred yards downriver, Harvard's Red Top, is only used a few weeks each year as a training center for the all-important Harvard-Yale race.

the losers shuck their shirts off their backs and hand them over to the man who rowed in the opposing seat.

After the shirts, congratulations, and condolences are exchanged, the crews head back to the boathouses, never to meet after the race and discuss it. They simply head back to camp to celebrate or mourn the results of the afternoon's endeavor.

The scene at the winning crew's camp is a joyous one, more so if all the boats have won their races and the crew can hoist a broom up their flagpole to signify the sweep. After the brackish water of the Thames is hosed off of the shell, it is loaded back onto the trailer for the return to Cambridge or Derby. The winners catch their coxswain and, on a count of three, swing him high up into the air, and out into the river.

Before dinner is served, and after the oarsmen have showered and accepted the congratulations of their boatmates and friends, they retire to the coaches' quarters to elect the next year's captain. After every oarsman is publicly polled, a hand vote is taken. Unless it is unanimous, the oarsmen return to their discussions until a man is selected to lead the next year's crew. When the captain is selected, a bottle of champagne is opened and the crews toast the departing seniors, hurling their glasses into the fireplace after they've imbibed.

By invitation to the oarsmen, the dinners are open to their families and friends. The coach is presented with a present, some maudlin speeches are delivered, and without much fanfare, the oarsmen pack their bags and silently depart, the halls of Red Top and Gales Ferry to remain vacant for another fifty weeks.

CHAPTER 16
THE OLYMPICS

Few things in life deserve superlatives in their description as an Olympiad. More records are set there, more underdogs pull off come-from-behind victories, and more athletic careers are capped or launched at the Olympic Games than at any other single athletic festival or championship.

Rowing, while not included at the ancient or even the first modern Olympic Games, eventually became one of the games' most prestigious events. The best at it, for many years, were the Americans.

Few crews arrive at the Olympics at anything less than peak form. Rowers are in the best condition of their lives, their technique and harmony honed to a edge as sharp as it will ever be. The coaches are the best their countries have; most of their crews are backed by extensive budgets; others arrive having to borrow equipment from local schools or clubs.

The Olympics is generally the pinnacle of every rower's career with an oar. Some countries keep their national teams more or less together from an early age with the aim of one day having them mature into a crew capable of capturing an Olympic medal. Other rowers, particularly those from the United States, row together for only a few months as a crew before backing their shells into the Olympic starting blocks.

Many prominent figures in American rowing have bemoaned the lack of coherence in its rowing programs. American crews held the Olympics in a tight and seemingly unshakable grasp for nearly fifty years, and at the center of that dominance was the college system of selecting Olympic boats. Beginning in 1969, American crews, particularly eights, were selected through camps held in one location, usually on the East Coast near the traditional rowing centers of Boston, New York, or Philadelphia. What emerged were crews composed of the best individual oarsmen in the country attempting to merge their dissimilar styles together in one boat, in a very short time.

At the same time however, there were no coherent training goals set for aspiring Olympians during non-Olympic games, just the work set out for them at their colleges by their coaches, each of whom coached according to different philosophies and

The U.S. 1936 Olympic Gold Medal crew from the University of Washington: (left to right) Hume (stroke), Rantz, Hunt, McMillan, White, Adam, Day, Morris; Moch (coxswain).

methods. There was no one national coach, no national training center, no national rowing organization devoted expressly to the success of American Olympic rowing. The results were nearly two decades of defeat.

The modern Olympic Games were resurrected in 1896 by Baron Pierre de Coubertin, a French nobleman who, in reaction against the increasingly professional tinge of athletics, organized a revival of the original celebration of amateur athletics, the Greek Olympiad. The ancient Olympiads were displays of sheer physical and military prowess; held originally as an annual harvest celebration, they developed as a way for the Greek city-states to test themselves against each other. The events were generally limited to track and field events, with wrestling and javelin throwing examples of the more belligerent events. Later, the Olympics were held every four years in the summer in honor of Zeus. Traditionally; the first was held in 776 B.C., and thereafter the Greeks reckoned their calenders by Olympiads, or four-year units.

It wasn't nostalgia or scholarly curiosity that led the formation of the modern games, but the inspiring spectacle of the 1889 Paris Universal exposition and its symbol, the Eiffel Tower. Baron de Coubertin, was most impressed by the international flavor of the Exposition's opening ceremonies. For the next seven years, de Coubertin labored to convince enough like-minded sportsmen and athletes that the preservation of the amateur principle of the Olympic spectacle was an event worth resurrecting. In the end, it was the nationalistic pride of the Greeks that ensured the revival of the Olympic Games. Backed in large part by the donations of a Greek businessman, Georgios Averoff, the games emerged in modern times in 1896 in the reconstructed Panathenean Stadium in Athens. Thirteen countries attended and the first modern Olympics gave birth to an athletic spectacle that has grown in magnitude ever since.

The games gained full attention in 1900, when de Coubertin brought them to Paris. Twenty-two countries entered athletes, a credit to de Coubertin's lobbying and cajoling. The 1900 Olympiad also marked the beginning of Olympic rowing, which was dominated by the host country, France, who won the unofficial team championship.

Four years later, the United States hosted the third Olympiad in St. Louis on the occasion of the Lousiana Purchase Exposition, in effect, a world's fair. There, the first American games saw a decline in the number of participating countries, reduced to a dozen due to a series of factors, foremost being the lack of organization and preparation given to the St. Louis games.

The most recent summer Olympiad, hosted by America and based in Los Angeles, drew athletes from 142 countries.

Based on the number of medals won in rowing, the unofficial team championships in Olympic rowing are as follows:

1900:	France	1948:	United States
1904:	Great Britain	1952:	Great Britain
1908:	United States	1956:	United States
1912:	United States	1960:	United States
1920:	Germany	1964:	Italy
1924:	United States	1968:	United States
1928:	Germany	1972:	United States
1932:	East Germany	1976:	East Germany
1936:	East Germany	1980:	East Germany
	1984:	United States	

Since 1968 the East Germans have won seventeen out of the possible thirty gold medals in men's competitions. In 1980, in Moscow, the men nearly swept all eight rowing events but missed in the single sculls. Why East German rowers have dominated men and women's international and Olympic rowing is a hard question to answer. The convenient reply is the same used by nearly all Western fans and athletes in other sports: deep government support, almost unnatural dedication to one sport at an early age, and the ability to train as if the sport was one's job.

East German rowers enjoy the luxury of big budgets, state-of-the-art equipment, and advanced sports medicine. However, their main advantage probably stems from the fact that the average East German elite oarsman or oarswoman start rowing at a far earlier age than his or her Western competitors, staying with the sport through a structured, well-ordered program that emphasizes such basics as bladework and general physical training.

It is unfortunate that most discussions of Olympic competition, rowing, and any other sport in which the East Germans and Soviets participate and are successful in, come to the misconclusion that totalitarian governments engender totalitarian athletics. Some would argue that there is nothing amateur about Communist athletics and that if democratic athletes were given the same breaks competition would be far more even.

The truth, according to any elite athlete, is that many Western sports programs have grown complacent and unwilling to take the risk of embracing new technology and philosophies to get ahead in the international arena. Many Western rowers visiting the Soviet Union have been struck by how used and repaired the Russian's boats and oars are. While the best Soviet crews may launch the best shells and use the best oars in Olympic competition, they practice in shells that many American prep schools would have long since junked.

The beauty of the Olympics is the level of competition. Nowhere else in the world of sports does the world watch each event with the intensity of an Olympiad. Even rowing, once a sport that fans had to stay awake until the wee hours of the morning to watch, has gained better and more frequent play in television's coverage of the games. In fact rowing gained so much airplay in the 1984 games that one newspaper television critic complained there was too much rowing!

It has been said by some rowing insiders that there is nothing like an Olympiad to raise the image of rowing in the public's mind. After the American successes in 1984, rowing has been rapidly growing into a sport that both Madison Avenue advertisers and the consuming public have come to recognize as a distinctive spectacle full of excitement, beauty, and hard competition.

That year, 1984, was a banner one for American rowing. It was also the first time in more than fifty years that America hosted the summer games, and it marked the first time American rowers had tried out and trained for the Olympics in an organized, highly efficient manner.

In 1984 the United States Olympic Committee with cooperation from the United States Rowing Association, established regional rowing centers in Boston, Seattle, and Newport Beach, California. A full-time coach, Kris Korzeniowski, was hired to do nothing but move among the three centers and oversee the selection and training of the country's best oarsmen.

Korzeniowski was a Polish rower who defected in 1972 at the end of the Munich Olympic Games, where he had been an assistant coach for the Polish eight that took sixth place in the finals. He worked as a coach in Italy and Canada, successfully coaching both women's and men's crews in those countries to medals before coming to the United States to coach the Princeton University women's crew.

In 1979 his women's eight won a bronze medal in the World Championships; two years later his crew won a silver at the Worlds.

When Korzeniowski was hired as coach by the USRA, a lot of college coaches felt slighted. He was Polish, he spoke with an accent, he represented Eastern Bloc techniques rather than home-grown American "values" and he was virtually unknown by most rowers and fans of the sport.

"A lot of noses were knocked out of joint," said Dick Erickson, men's coach of the University of Washington heavyweight crew. After all, the Olympic goal is not one only aspired to by rowers; for many coaches, particularly those who never participated as rowers, an Olympic assignment represents the peak experience of their career.

When Koreniowski started working with American rowers four years earlier in preparation for the 1980 Olympics, he met some opposition from the veterans of elite rowing who were returning for another try at an Olympic medal or even a seat in a boat. Where the rowers were once accustomed to winning their seats through seat racing and ergometer pieces, they found the Pole more concerned with technical matters, such as bladework and integration of each rower's style into a coherent whole.

Korzeniowski's greatest contribution to elite rowing in America, according to many of the rowers who

The 1964 national trials to select the American entry in the Tokyo Olympics was won by Philadelphia's Vesper Boat Club.

BRIAN HILL © 1988

The American four after being awarded their gold medals in the 1984 Olympics.

rowed under him in 1984, is his emphasis on stylistic coherency. All the strength and impeccable conditioning in the world won't make eight dissimilar rowing styles equal speed and victory. A key element of European crews' success is the time the individual rowers spend in the same boat with each other. Familiarity breeds speed. In 1984 Korzeniowski proved this point with the American crews.

The selection of the 1984 Olympic team started in Boston, Newport Beach, and Seattle as the best rowers in the country settled into a month of training and competition to determine who would travel to

Princeton, New Jersey, to race in the eliminations. While Korzeniowski was absent from one of the three locations, he depended on local coaching assistants to work the crews until he could arrive on site and make a first-hand evaluation.

In May the surviving rowers congregated in Princeton for the final selections. Those who survived that competition were then issued their official American uniforms and racing shirts and told to make an appearance at Harvard University where the final preparation for the Olympics would begin.

Organized as the Charles River Rowing Association, a quaint term used by many crews that have trained on the Charles without the benefit of a collegiate or club sponsor, the Olympic team spent several weeks rowing on the legendary Charles. Harry Parker, coach of the Harvard heavyweight men's crew, coached the male scullers, while Korzeniowski handled the sweep shells.

Before heading to the games, the rowers first had a European tour to complete. The European circuit would be the proving ground for nearly all of the crews bound for Los Angeles in August. It would also be the one opportunity for the best crews of the West to row against the best of the East, for there were no boycotts in Europe. (The Soviets and most of the Eastern Bloc countries had already announced that they were planning to boycott the Olympics.)

The American eight headed to Europe as the Charles River Rowing Association, racing first at Vichy, France. The boat won at Vichy, and headed on to Grunau, East Germany, site of the 1936 Berlin Olym-

BRIAN HILL © 1988

pic rowing where the University of Washington Huskies won a gold medal. Nearly fifty years later, the American crew, with two Washington oarsmen aboard, beat the Russians and East Germans on their home course, an upset regarded as one of the most important wins in modern American elite rowing.

In the 2,000-meter trials at Grunau, the American crew beat the Russian boat 5:56.3 to 6:04.2, an eight-second margin that may appear slim on paper but which is, in the parlance of Harvard's Rude and Smooth crew, a "horizon."

The Russians were so shocked by their defeat that they swapped out half of their boat for the finals. But all the seat changing and replacement of oarsmen in the world couldn't help the Soviet crew, as the Americans beat them again by four seconds in the finals.

It quickly became apparent in Europe that the Americans would face their real competition from the Canadian crew, a country renowned for serious rowing, yet a country that has never been a consistent power due to the disadvantage of its brief rowing season. The Canadians beat the American team in pre-Olympic competition and the Americans returned the favor in a later race. Unfortunately the Americans dismissed their loss to the Canadians as a bad day at the races; the crew focused on the Soviet and East German eights more than the British, New Zealand, and Canadian boats.

The women, the fours, pairs, and scullers also met with success on the European summer circuit against crews that had rowed together longer. For

American Anne Marden, silver medalist in the 1984 Olympics.

BRIAN HILL © 1988

Americans, the prestige event was clearly the eight-oared shell; however, in Europe the sculling events were the most hotly contested.

The American male scullers were coached in 1984 by Harry Parker, the renowned coach of the Harvard heavyweight crew. Bob Ernst, coach of the University of Washington women's crew, coached the Olympic women sweep rowers, and John Van Blom, coach of the University of California, coached the women scullers.

The saga of the scullers was well chronicled by David Halberstam, the journalist and former Harvard oarsman who, in *The Amateurs*, described the intense competition among the top four American scullers for the right to represent the country as the single sculler. As Halberstam noted, the simple fact that there is only one single sculler gives that event the cachet of being the one event in crew for the best rowers in the world. An Olympic eight-oared crew may consist of eight of the best rowers in the country, but the sculler is clearly set apart as the number one rower in the country, the person who is most qualified to sit alone in a shell and face off against the rest of the best.

In 1984 the best sculler going into the Olympics was Pertti Karppinen, a 6 foot, 7 inch, fireman known to his countrymen as the Floating Finn. Karppinen had dominated his event since 1976 in Montreal, when he won his first gold medal. He repeated that performance four years later in Moscow, establishing himself in the informal scullers' hall of fame. His time over the 2,000-meter course became the benchmark, or goal, for scullers everywhere.

Karppinen's closest rival has been Peter-Michael Kolbe of West Germany, a former world champion, and every bit as dedicated a sculler as the Finn. At 6 feet, 6 inches, he was almost as tall. Kolbe is known for his technical innovation, rowing for a few years in a new single with sliding riggers—a design that is banned from Olympic competition where the scullers must race in the traditional fixed-rigger sculls.

The American men's sculler in the 1984 Games was John Biglow, a Seattle, Washington, native who helped lead the renaissance of rowing at Yale in the late 1970s. Biglow was a small rower compared to Karppinen and Kolbe, yet he made his name as a rower through his tenacity and nearly super-human ability to find a phenomenal drive and stamina in the closing quarter of a race, rowing through the finish and ending the last stroke totally depleted.

In the women's single, the American entry was Carlie Geer. Her greatest challenge would be her race against the Rumanian sculler, Valeria Racila, who lost a medal in the 1983 world championships when she flipped 150 meters from the finish, losing an open-water lead in an instant.

The Rumanian women dominated elite rowing in 1984. Once the domain of the East German women, the Eastern boycott left the field open to the Rumanians, who were cheered at the opening ceremonies in Los Angeles for their courage in attending despite the Soviet boycott.

There are no records kept for comparison purposes in Olympic rowing. To be certain, the course times are kept, published, and filed away. But there are too many extraneous variables that keep rowing from being a precise sport of time trials, splits, and hypersensistive quartz timers. The English may analyze every detail of the Henley Royal Regatta, dwelling on one crew's time to the Temple and Barrier, comparing the merits of the Berkshire or Buckingham lanes—but in Olympic rowing there are no records, only medals. A crew rowing in the latest and lightest shell, using the best oars technology can offer, may suspect they row the same distance faster than a crew fifty years before, but they will never be officially deemed as doing so. Some races are rowed into hard headwinds, others are helped along by tailwinds. Some races were rowed under the lax direction of officials who didn't restart races despite the fact that one or more crews may have jumped the gun. Rowing coaches agree that there is no question that modern rowers are in better condition and have better abilities than their average predecessors, yet there is no absolute way to be sure that the crew of 1987 is better than the crew of 1887.

The most important condition to Olympic rowing is the course. Some host countries undertake the expense of a custom course, others make do with the nearest available body of water. The historic Henley reach of the Thames has been used for the games, as have lowly barge canals and deserted lakes. The most important consideration, in the end, is ensuring that all the crew have the same water and handicaps that the others do. There can be no curves, nor any lanes that are particularly exposed or sheltered from the wind or current.

The search for an appropriate course for the Los Angeles Olympics took the planners to nearly every body of water, including the Pacific Ocean, between Mission Bay in San Diego to Puget Sound in Washington state. Lake Casitas, located outside of Santa Barbara, was eighty miles away from the rest of the games in Los Angeles. The reservoir was finally selected because it was big enough (2,700 acres) and because its shores were sufficiently undeveloped to accommodate special docks to launch the shells from, boat tents to store them in, and changing areas for the athletes.

The negotiations for use of the lake took some time, as the local municipal water district wanted to placate the local fishermen who were slightly vexed that the rowers were taking up most of the lake with their racing and practicing. The solution? The Olympic Committee donated $12,000 to be used to stock the lake with fish.

The lake lies in a beautiful setting, so photogenic that it undoubtedly contributed to the decision of the ABC television network to give rowing more coverage than normally would have been expected. The network invested heavily in equipment and cameras to cover the sport. A special floating platform was constructed, a double-hulled, catamaran-type craft that made no wake or waves as it followed alongside the racing shells. Every day of the games, ABC opened its coverage with a shot of Lake Casitas.

Because most of the racing took place early in the morning when the lake was smooth before the afternoon winds kicked up a chop, rowing was the mainstay of ABC's morning coverage and the only event of all the games that was broadcast live in Europe.

According to *Rowing Magazine* (then the name of the official publication of the United States Rowing Association), at least two-thirds of the racing where American crew participated was broadcast. Most

rowers, who saw the coverage, agreed it was the best rowing footage ever produced. Some did feel left out of all the Olympic excitement, being eighty miles away from the heart of the activity in Los Angeles. Most agreed, however, that being removed from the frenetic atmosphere of Los Angeles was conducive to good hard rowing.

The first round of racing ended with the American men qualified in seven out of eight events. The

American women were even more impressive: all six entries qualified for a shot at a medal in the finals. The American crews led the list of finalists at thirteen, followed by the Canadians with twelve, and the West Germans with eleven.

There was talk, as there was in 1980 when the U.S. boycott was in effect, that the 1984 games wouldn't be a true test of who were the best rowers in the world. The level of competition in the women's events were expected to be hurt as the Russians and particularly the East Germans—the two traditional powers of women's rowing, were staying away. Despite the criticisms and feeling that Lake Casitas would be a somewhat handicapped test of excellence, it was the largest rowing event in the world, one that attracted crews from the People's Republic of China and North Korea, one that pitted the best against the best of the world.

Although rowing was called the purest amateur sport by the father of the modern Olympics, de Coubertin, 1980 marked the first time trademarks and brand names made an appearance on the race course. In 1984, seven countries' crews placed the name or corporate logo of sponsors on their shells. All fourteen American shells carried the name of Hunt-Wesson Foods, who gave some financial support in return for a bit of recognition. It wasn't the International Olympic Committee, the enforcers of the principles of amatuerism and pure athletics, that cracked down on the new trend; it was the media, led by ABC, that made a strong protest against the ads.

With commercial advertising commanding a steep price during the games, the network felt Hunt-Wesson Foods and the other sponsors were getting away with a free ride, so to speak, and so demanded that the offending stickers be removed.

The issue was resolved when the stickers were peeled off. Some rowers preferred them off, others lamented the loss of the only commercial backing rowing could hope to receive, and probably the last.

There was one other controversial incident that marred the competition at Lake Casitas. Nearly half-way into the repechage, or consolation heat, of the men's eights, the gate on the rigger of the French crew's seven man opened, causing him to lose his oar and forcing the shell to limp over the finish line with seven rowers. Accidental oarlock openings are rare but not unheard of in rowing. Most equipment failures can be traced to sloppy maintenance or inattention to detail on the part of the rower or his crew's rigger. But in the case of the French breakdown, the gate, the piece that is hinged at one end and swings over and down to lock the oar into the oar lock, opened at the hinge end, a rare occurrence. Most gates open at the free end because the rower had neglected to tighten it shut. An examination of the French boat's hinge pin showed it had been filed through on a angle sometime before the French crew arrived at Lake Casitas. Oddly enough, a similar misfortune befell the U.S. junior women's four at the FISA Junior Championships in Jonkoping, Sweden, a month before. After FISA officials investigated the Swedish incident, they came to the conclusion that sabotage was to blame. In the case of the French crew at the Games, FISA once again found the mishap was clearly the result of sabotage. Rather than row the race over, the French were allowed into the finals, making it the seventh entry in what was planned to be a six-boat race.

The finals of the 1984 Olympic Games were played out before a full house of spectators, and tickets to the races were among the most difficult to come by in all the Olympic events, despite the lake's distance from Los Angeles. Nearly all of the races ended with close finishes. Few crews walked away from their competition by wide margins, nearly all the medalists finished within fractions of a second of each other—so close that several photo finishes were recorded that caused a delay in declaring the winners until the judges could view the films.

American rowers finished the 1984 Olympics with eight medals—the most collected by any single country. The men left Lake Casitas with one gold, three silvers, and a bronze, the most medals the American team has won since the 1956 Games in Melbourne, Australia. The women won one gold and two silvers. That single gold medal, won in the eights, was not only the first an American women's crew had ever won in Olympic rowing, but also the first gold ever won by a non-communist women's crew in any World or Olympic competition. The men's eight, predicted to win the first gold medal in that event since 1964, lost to the Canadian crew by 32/100ths of a second, a heartbreaking loss for a crew that many viewed as the best and most internationally competitive the country had fielded in twenty years.

The success story of the games, however, wasn't the American men, nor the Canadians, but the Rumanian women's team, who won five golds and a silver medal in six events.

The Olympics are the end of the road for most rowers. There is simply no other event in the world worth training so long and hard for, except of course, the next Olympiad. Many rowers keep coming back, reliving their youths in sculls and shells, always pursuing an elusive medal that seems to just barely escape them. But most leave the sport, graduating on to careers as coaches, or to a single scull stored in the bays of a rowing club, to be pulled out once or twice a week for a lonely morning row, a row that usually relives those final back-breaking strokes, with the best of the world in the lanes to each side, pulling their hearts out for a chance to stand on the staggered steps and feel the weight of a medal fall around their necks.

C H A P T E R   17
OCEAN
ROWING

The very notion of crossing an ocean in a small boat is staggering to the average person. Attempting to do it with oars alone is justifiably considered lunacy. Yet more than a dozen men and women have crossed the Atlantic and Pacific oceans in rowboats. Many more have tried and failed.

Ocean rowing has always been a necessity for those who make their living on the sea. From the earliest galleys and dromonds rowing from island to island in the Aegean and Mediterranean to the dorymen of the Grand Banks, sailors have plied the open oceans with oars, taking awesome risks in boats that seem ridicuously small and frail.

The Vikings, the first adventurers from the Old World to land on the New, rowed longboats that had oars but mostly depended on a single large sail for long voyages. The age of sail ushered in the age of discovery, but rowing remained the method favored for charting unknown waters and exploring forbidding shores for untold riches.

The first European settlers in America relied on heavy ships' boats left behind after their ships returned to England for another cargo of people. Those boats meant the difference between life and death for the earliest settlers, allowing them to explore the coast and rivers adjacent to their settlements. Typically, one of the first industries to appear in a colonial settlement was a shipbuilder, who started off by building small fishing boats intended to be rowed or sailed only to a point in sight of the shore.

The fishing industry has traditionally used rowing rather than sails, which are difficult for one man to control while engrossed in the task of setting nets, baiting hooks, and landing fish. Hence oars in very seaworthy small boats were the safest and most efficient way to fish.

One of the most enduring North American boat designs is the dory: a high sided, flat-bottomed, two-man boat with a pointed stern. Dories were used on the fishing schooners that sailed out of Newfoundland, Nova Scotia, and Gloucester. They were

At right, an ocean-going dory equipped with a sliding seat and sculls. Built by the Lowell's Boat Shop in Amesbury, Massachusetts.

stored in nests on deck, one stacked on top of and inside another, and launched when the banks were reached and fish were found.

The dory proved itself to be a very stable design for the dangerous seas of the northern Atlantic. They could be loaded with a huge amount of fish and still maintain their balance in choppy, windblown waters. Dorymen were a tough breed of sailor, their hands calloused like leather from handling hundreds of fathoms of hooked lines and the heavy, coarse-handled oars.

Dories are still built today, but many are built with a special well that can accommodate an outboard motor. Lowell's Boat Shop in Amesbury, Massachusetts, on the banks of the Merrimack River, still builds traditional dories based on designs used when the shop was founded in 1793. Lowell's, under the direction of Yale and Harvard business school graduate Edward Hand, now builds beautiful pulling boats outfitted with sliding seats and racing sculls.

One famous doryman who rowed his way into a place in history was Howard Blackburn, a Nova Scotian fisherman who made his living aboard the *Grace L. Fears*, one of the many fishing schooners that fished the Grand Banks off the coasts of Canada and New England. Blackburn earned his place in maritime history by enduring a terrible accident and ordeal that would have and has killed many a less determined and less lucky doryman.

Blackburn and his dory mate, a man named Welch, were fishing several miles away from their schooner when a sudden snowstorm covered them,

dropping an impenetrable shroud over the fishing grounds and cutting off their only connection with the ship. The foghorn was sounded over and over to guide the dories back home to safety, but Blackburn and his mate had a lot of lines still in the water and pulling in fathom after fathom of twine took a long time.

By the time they were ready to ship their oars and start pulling for the schooner, they could only see a few feet in front of them. They anchored, waiting for the visibility to improve so they could row for the ship. The snow lifted and the lights of the *Grace L. Fears* glimmered in the darkness. Blackburn and Welch took to the oars and made for the ship, but the seas were too high, so they anchored again.

By either an oversight or in haste, the schooner made no attempt to find or assist Blackburn and his mate, leaving them alone on the vast ocean in a small boat laden with fish. While bailing, Blackburn lost his mitts, but kept scooping the water out of the bilge and knocking off any ice that threatened to make the small dory top-heavy and subject to capsizing. Still at anchor, they sat waiting for the schooner to come to them, but when the weather cleared enough to start rowing again, the schooner was gone. By that time, Welch was dead, covered in a shroud of ice.

The loss of his mitts was a terrible stroke of bad luck for Blackburn as his fingers soon began to freeze and lose their feeling. Blackburn realized that without his mittens his hands would soon be rendered useless by the cold water and frozen sleet. He ran his oars back out into the oarlocks and bent his fingers around the oar handles, letting them freeze around them so he would still be able to row.

Blackburn kept rowing, resolutely forcing himself to do the only thing that offered hope. He had no idea where he was, no idea if he was rowing toward land or farther out to sea. Eventually his persistence and will to live paid off. During the night, as he was close to death but still putting his back into every dip and stroke of the oars, Blackburn heard the sound of surf running against a rocky shore. He held himself out to sea until morning, when he could see where he was and find a safe and protected inlet in an island to bring the dory and his dead mate's body ashore.

Blackburn found a deserted house and despite having spent three terrible days and night at sea, forced himself to stay awake rather than die comfortably in his sleep. The next day he found help and was nursed back to heath. Most of his fingers, thumbs, and toes were lost from frostbite.

The saga of Howard Blackburn didn't end with his heroic voyage across the open winter ocean in an ordinary fishing dory, but in fact was the start of a life that is remarkable for its accomplishments. Of course his usefulness as a fisherman ended when his frostbitten fingers were cut away, leaving him only blocks for hands, but he remained a hearty strong man who loved the sea and refused to turn his back on it for an invalid's life on the shore.

He returned to his home in Gloucester, Massachusetts, and built a small, seaworthy sloop he named

the *Great Western*, after the largest and most renowned ship of the day. Crippled by any sailor's standards, Blackburn sailed alone on June 1899 from Gloucester, Massachusetts, to Gloucester, England. On the eighteenth of August he arrived at his destination, where he was met by an enormous crowd. Later, he returned to America and built a smaller boat, the twenty-five-foot *Great Republic*, and sailed her to Portugal in thirty-nine days.

Never content to live out the life of a crusty old salt on the Gloucester waterfront, Blackburn pushed his luck and had built an even smaller yacht, the seventeen-foot dory *America*, which he sailed in 1903 for a third solo trip across the Atlantic. This time he failed, capsizing 165 miles east of Cape Sable. But his experience in the same waters in that other dory, stuck with him; Blackburn righted his small craft, bailed her out and, deciding enough was enough, set sail for home.

In 1896 George Harpo and Frank Samuelson, two Norwegian fishermen who had recently emigrated to New Jersey, decided to row home one summer to visit their family and friends. In an ordinary dory fitted with two spare sets of oars, they departed from Sandy Hook one late spring morning with only a few spectators to wish them bon voyage.

They made the crossing in sixty-two days—a record among the handful of men who have attempted a transatlantic row. When they came ashore in Le Havre, near death from starvation and thirst, they joked that they were game to row home after a hearty meal and a rest. Although their feat was first scoffed at as a hoax, their story was verified by several vessels that veered off course to offer assistance and rescue what seemed like two obviously shipwrecked sailors. But the two men rejected the offers of help, to the amazement of the ships' captains and their crews.

An oarsman who takes a wherry, dory, or ocean shell for a coastwise cruise, rowing in the ocean during the day, the shore comfortably in view at all times, is certainly rowing in the ocean. Yet he is doing nothing remarkably different from what an oarsman does on a river or lake except roll over the waves and taste the salt in the spray. Ocean rowing, for the purpose of this chapter, is the stuff of adventures, voyages far from the sanctuary of a harbor or sheltered cove, prolonged rows that test an oarsman's fortitude, seamanship, and navigational skills.

Many men and women have crossed oceans alone in sailboats, some have even circumnavigated the world alone in small sailboats. Very few have dared to attempt a long voyage across an open ocean with nothing but a pair of oars to pull them along. Sailing is something of a passive endeavor. There are moments of intense tension and effort, but for the most part the sails and rig do most of the work, the sailor maintaining the integrity of the hull, the strength of the rigging, and keeping on course.

But an ocean rower, a person pulling himself from home to destination with nothing more than his arms, is painfully aware of every wave, every mile of ocean put under the keel.

No rower has ever crossed an ocean by himself. At present, several are trying. Some, like Blackburn, have rowed great distances by themselves, but it would be nearly impossible to cross an immense expanse of water as wide as the Atlantic or Pacific Ocean without another person for the following reasons:

First, there is the matter of sleep. When a solo sailor wants to get some rest, he can entrust the helm of his yacht to a self-steering device or an autopilot. But an oarsman, if he stops rowing, ships his oars, and lies down in the bilge for forty winks, may wake in the morning to find that the wind and current have carried him back to where he was before bedtime. Hence two oarsman are necessary, one to keep rowing while the other sleeps. Generally, the two take shifts at the oars throughout the night and row together during the day or in particularly strong headwinds to keep up their progress.

Several attempts to cross the Atlantic and Pacific have ended mysteriously and most likely tragically. The voyage of the *Puffin*, a boat touted by its designer, Colin Mudie of London, as the most seaworthy pulling boat afloat, is an example of how dangerous long open water rows can be. David Johnstone, a British journalist from Farnham, Surrey, prepared for a transatlantic row during the summer of 1965. After running an advertisement in the London *Times* for volunteers, Johnstone selected David Hoare, a reporter from Leicester, to help pull the *Puffin* from America back to England.

On May 21, 1966, the *Puffin* set sail from Norfolk, Virginia. For a week Johnstone and Hoare tried to pull the small boat away from the American coast to the helping push of the Gulf Stream. The winds slowed them to a virtual standstill, wasting provisions and undoubtedly trying the patience of the two men. At one point they were blown back to within a mile of the Virginia coast, more than a week after leaving. Using a small cabin stuffed with stores for their shelter, Johnstone and Hoare probably took turns at the oars while the other caught what sleep he could. During the day, when the opportunity presented itself, both could row, using only their arms and backs as the boat wasn't fitted with sliding seats. On June 13, a very early storm, Hurricane Alma, swept up the Eastern Coast about a hundred miles offshore. It missed land, but it may have been

the death of Johnstone and Hoare. Months later, near the end of the year, the *Puffin* was found by a ship in the mid-Atlantic, floating bottom up, with no sign of either David Johnstone or John Hoare.

Remarkably, at the same time Johnstone and Hoare rowed to their deaths in the Atlantic, two fellow Englishmen, two paratroopers in the British army, John Ridgeway and Chay Blyth, made modern rowing and seafaring history.

Ridgeway was inspired to attempt the voyage when he heard Johnstone describing his plans on a BBC radio show. Ridgeway phoned Johnstone, and met with him personally to volunteer for the row, but Hoare had already been picked and Ridgeway was left to plan a row of his own. His first task was to find a stout, seaworthy boat capable of surviving the often wild ocean. The *Puffin's* price tag of 2,000 pounds was far beyond Ridgeway's reach, and he almost scrapped the idea until a friend suggested he take a look at a design known as a Yorkshire Dory, a craft whose design was based on the same Nova Scotian dories that men like Blackburn fished and survived in for centuries.

Built by Bradford Boat Services in Yorkshire, the dory cost a mere 185 pounds and was already built and in stock. Ridgeway's next task was to find a partner to help him pull the dory. His first choice dropped out because of seasickness and Ridgeway looked frantically for someone capable of withstanding the mental and physical stress the voyage would bring to bear.

Chay Blyth, Ridgeway's platoon sergeant, volun-

A man and a woman racing Alden Ocean Shells in the annual Isles of Shoals race, an open ocean event from New Hampshire's Isle of Shoals to Portsmouth Harbor.

teered for the job. Blyth and Ridgeway had won a 70-mile canoe race from Reading to London, but Ridgeway had not considered Blyth for the ocean-going adventure because Blyth was a married man. Blyth persisted in going, and it wasn't until his wife, Maureen, consented, that Ridgeway found his partner.

They dubbed the dory the *English Rose III* and set about modifying her for the trip. Ridgeway would be in charge of seamanship, navigation, safety, and the radio; Chay handled the rations, medical supplies, and clothing. On May 17, 1966, the two soldiers boarded an R.A.F. plane for Canada, where they boarded a Greyhound bus to Boston, the *English Rose III* having been sent ahead by freighter. They planned to depart from Cape Cod on the same day as the *Puffin*, but Ridgeway developed a septic infection in his foot upon arriving in Boston and was forced to spend a week in the Chelsea Naval Hospital. On May 21, when Ridgeway was still lying in a hospital bed, a nurse told him that the *Puffin* had sailed from Norfolk.

After his discharge, Ridgeway joined Blyth at Orleans, a small village on the ocean side of Cape Cod's upturned arm. There they were taught the fine points of rowing by the local sailors, old men who believed from the beginning that the two Englishmen had a chance to succeed if only they followed the rules of the sea.

At 5:30 p.m. on June 4, Blyth and Ridgeway stepped from the shore into the *English Rose III* and started rowing toward the eastern horizon. A small flotilla of well wishers followed them until darkness, when they were left alone, in the Atlantic, with nothing pulling them toward their goal save their strength and determination.

For more than two weeks, they labored to pull the dory away from the New England coast, across the Grand Banks where generations of dorymen rowed from fishing schooners, and into the Gulf Stream. Along the way, they were also hit with Hurricane Alma, a terrifying experience recounted in their account of the voyage, *A Fighting Chance*. After surviving the storm, both knew they could depend on their craft to keep them afloat in nearly any conditions, it was up to them to pull it the rest of the way.

Misfortune struck when they opened their provisions and discovered that Alma had spoiled more than half of the provisions with saltwater. So they went on half rations and refused offers of food from several ships until they grew so delirious that they finally accepted some provisions when they were more than half-way across.

Their voyage is a tale of abject misery: saltwater raising horrendous boils on their skin, their clothing rotting away, sharks bumping the bottom of the *English Rose III*, and whales making dangerously playful runs at them in the middle of the night. Ships passed within a few hundred yards of them in the fog. Sleep was nearly impossible as they had no cabin, only a canvas awning, which leaked and offered little more than the psychological comfort of shelter.

On September 3, 1966, ninety-one days and thirty-five hundred miles after setting off from Cape Cod, Ridgeway saw land. It was the island of Aran, off the western coast of Ireland.

They rowed ashore in a driving storm, dodging the reefs and cliffs through the surf until they could rest in the lee of a lonely lighthouse. The keepers, seeing two men in a rowboat, thought they had been shipwrecked and waved them off from attempting a landing on the wave swept isle. Within two hours a lifeboat sailed out of Aran and towed them ashore.

Since then, oarsmen have crossed the Pacific Ocean, and plans are afoot to row the six-hundred mile distance from South America to Antarctica, the roughest, most inhospitable water in the world.

Ocean rowing is not a sport, but a challenge that few are capable of attempting, let alone completing successfully. But as with singlehanded sailing, where nearly every challenge left has been sailed from east to west, west to east, north to south and so on, someone, someday, will surely attempt to row around the world.

Ocean rowing is gaining the kind of popularity that off-road bicycles has enjoyed in recent years, and for the same reasons. While sculling a racing shell forces an oarsman to only venture forth onto very calm, protected bodies of water, a seaworthy ocean shell can be taken out into the open sea, where it can ride the waves and be pulled into a fairly stiff breeze, a challenge posed by the elements that is very challenging and incredibly satisfying to master. Shells can surf down waves, balanced perfectly and held in complete control by subtle changes and checks of the oars.

Arthur Martin only recommends coastal and inter-island rowing through open ocean for experienced oarsmen who are able sailors and understand the principles of seamanship. Those who fit the bill can be rewarded with some of the most exciting fun the sea has to offer.

Martin wrote: "Experienced oarsmen can move very fast in a following sea without broaching (spinning sideways onto the face, or front, of the wave), and it is an exhilarating feeling to be able to harness the power of the sea and achieve such a thrilling speed. This is known as surfing."

The longest ocean event in the United States is a 36-mile pull from Catalina Island to Marina Del Rey on the California mainland. Oarsmen in a wide range of different ocean-going shells, including experimental designs entered by manufacturers, endure the rigors of racing in the open sea, where progress is often determined by the direction of the wind and the break of the seas rather than the shortest distance between two points.

Any trip across an exposed open stretch of water should be undertaken cautiously and only under the best conditions. An oarsman should try to row in open water only in the company of another scull should something go wrong and quick assistance is necessary. The dangers of hypothermia is great in most American and European waters, especially in the fall and winter when water temperatures are low and potential rescuers scarce. While some builders claim their boats are ocean shells, upon close examination they turn out to be fiber glass racing shells, fit only for rowing in sheltered circumstances.

Every ocean race should be staffed with power boats in case a shell overturns or a piece of equipment is broken. Oarsmen who find themselves overwhelmed by the wind and waves need only keep the bow of the shell pointed into the wind, and use the oars to keep the shell from sliding sternfirst down the face of the waves. With the right hands, an oarsman can row a boat in hurricane force winds. Martin did, during a tropical storm that swept across Portsmouth Harbor in the late 1970s. He said that when he was back ashore, he called the local airport and learned that there were gusts to 80 knots. A photograph of a Martin rowing into the teeth of the gale as blithely as he would on a bright summer day was used as an advertisement in many sailing magazines for several years.

Most ocean rowers content themselves with such "short" ocean races as the annual race to Catalina Island from Marina Del Rey, and the Isles of Shoals Race off the coast of New Hampshire. In Australia, the lifeguards race enormous surfboats through thundering waves. In San Francisco, New York, Baltimore, and Boston, crews race lifeboats. Even Outward Bound, the famous survival school, places its students in heavy pulling boats, rowing them around their camp on Hurricane Island in Maine.

Lifeboat racing is becoming very popular in cities such as Boston and San Francisco as civic events.

Vocational schools, Boy Scout troops, and clubs build and race their own boats, taking traditional coast guard cutter designs and transforming them into beautiful works of varnished mahogany.

Until a few years ago, college crews and crews from maritime academies regularly raced against crews from ocean liners and freighters in lifeboats around Manhattan Island. Such races are still held, occasionaly, the most recent being in the summer of 1986 at the hundredth anniversary celebration of the Statue of Liberty.

R. D. Culler, a Cape Cod builder and designer of many rowing boats, wrote in the preface to his famous *Boats, Oars, and Rowing*: "In a rowing craft you find that you are closer to the water than you ever were before, no matter how much boating you have done in other craft. You are much more aware of sea and weather conditions, and see more of your surroundings than you ever did before. You get into places, holes and creeks you never really knew existed."

Adventures such as those of Ridgeway and Blyth are more difficult to attempt due to new U. S. Coast Guard regulations that allow the authorities to inspect a boat for its seaworthiness before it sets sail. Although it is only a formality, it has prevented several fools from setting out to a certain death.

As John Ridgeway wrote in *A Fighting Chance*: "I kept at it for I knew that this was not the moment to give up. One piece of relaxation and we might be lost, for I kept thinking over and over that the cruel sea would only strike if you gave it a chance."

CHAPTER 18

RECREATIONAL ROWING

Arthur Martin wanted to design a kayak that would carry his mother-in-law in comfortable safety. She would have a place of her own, low in the boat, to sit and store her bag. Arthur planned to do the paddling, his mother-in-law relaxing while enjoying the scenic inlets and rivers that branch north from Portsmouth harbor into Oyster Bay.

Unfortunately, she died before she could enjoy Arthur's creation, a wide kayak with a flat bottom and a nearly plumb or vertical bow. Martin liked that bow ("I thought it was very good") but the stern dragged underwater whenever he paddled hard. The bow was perfect for driving into the chop of Portsmouth harbor and gliding up and over the sea swell rolling in from the Atlantic, so Martin put up with the plunging stern for two years before giving up and taking a saw to it.

A diligent experimenter and accomplished naval architect, Martin only had to look inside of his garage to find a stern that would complement the best bow he ever designed. He took a saw to that boat, glued and fiber glassed the good halves together and found himself with the best small boat he ever designed.

Martin began to miss the rowing he learned as a small boy on the Isles of Shoals, eight miles off the coast of New Hampshire, and perfected at the Kent School. So he found a pair of riggers, ordered a set of sculls and built a sliding seat and footstretchers.

"You could row the thing," Martin said, taciturn and surprised it ever amounted to much. "That's how it started in 1968. I had no idea of ever selling one."

What he started has since become the best thing to ever happen to rowing. Two years after making his prototype, Martin went to work for Boston's John Alden & Co., a renowned brokerage, designer, and builder of yachts. There he met Neal Tillotson, who offered to build several copies if Martin would pay for the molds and guarantee twenty sales. Martin said goodbye to his life's savings and turned the designs over Tillotson-Pearson, an experienced builder of sailing yachts. He named the result the Alden Ocean Shell after John Alden, partly out of honor to the great naval architect and partly because "the name was better known than mine."

It wasn't long until all twenty were sold and being rowed.

"A lot of people tried one and said, 'I've been designing that boat in my mind for years,'" Martin said. The yachting press began to write about the new boats, and checks began to arrive with the order to send a shell as soon as the next batch was finished. By the end of 1971, the first year the boat was on the market, 165 had been sold.

"It was quite a pleasant surprise," Martin said, 3,500 Aldens later.

Recreational rowing is a broad term that could be construed to include any voyage without a purpose or load of cargo such as fish or paying passengers. The first barge clubs on the Thames started rowing because it was an exciting way to escape the shore and explore the river's upper reaches and winding tributaries. Only when other barge clubs were founded and set more barges out exploring the same rivers did racing begin on an informal basis.

Early amateur oarsmen were recreational rowers, meeting at regular times to launch and take their oar in six, eight, ten and even twelve-oared barges known as centipedes. Because a shell's performance requires an oarsman for each position, casual rowing requires a lot of coordinating and committments. If an oarsman wished to strike out on his own, when he

wanted, rowing wherever he pleased, then he could row a wherry; a lapstrake skiff that it is much heavier and beamier than a racing scull, but also large enough to carry a passenger in a safer, less delicate hull. Racing singles were rare in the early days of club rowing and have always been expensive, prone to capsizes, and hard to keep tuned to racing standards. Professional boatmen and scullers didn't have to afford the costs of a racing scull, getting their craft free from the many builders vying for orders from the private clubs and university crews.

Wherries are still used to teach novices the basics of sculling. Many boathouses still have several tucked away in a dark corner, brought out in moments of boredom or amusement when the coxswains want to race or a sweep oarsman wants to try two-oar rowing.

In Europe, most oarsmen start rowing at the age of ten or twelve, and nearly all learn sculling first. In America one starts off in a four or eight, learning how to scull only at the end of one's competitive career. There is a belief that sweep rowing is harmful to a young oarsman because of the wrenching, repeated twist of the torso in one direction that the one-oared sweep stroke forces.

To master the nuances of setting up a boat and learning the fundamentals of precisely controlling a delicate shell, novice Europeans are started off in racing sculls and race them until they reach the elite level where sweep-oared boats are formed to compete in international competition.

In the past, when an American oarsman gradu-

ated from college, he usually had to say goodbye to rowing in a racing shell with a sliding seat. If they were yachtsmen, then they could get some fleeting pleasure from rowing a dinghy from the dock to mooring; but except for an invitation to row at a school reunion, the average oarsman had to settle for fond memories. True, rowing clubs have existed for a long time, but more clubs closed than opened in America from 1900 until 1970, when community boating programs, health clubs, and groups of professionals such as doctors or financiers opened a new opportunity for veterans and novices to enjoy the sensation and physical benefits of sliding seat rowing.

The inevitable pressures of purchasing new boats, maintaining the clubhouse, and still limiting membership to a level that was both exclusive and self-sustaining caused many urban clubs to disband, their waters dammed up and polluted by the industries that profited from easy access to piers. At least one boat club, the New York Athletic Club, has moved its boathouse and docks out of the city to the shores of Orchard Beach in Long Island Sound. The Union Boat Club in Boston considered disbanding when the city decided to dam the Charles and create a lush park along the southern shore along the Back Bay and Beacon Hill. But the city allowed the Union to build a new boathouse on the shore of the promenade, its docks floating in a sheltered lagoon near the community sailing program.

Even though fiber glass sculls are much cheaper than wooden or composite racing singles, their big-

gest drawback is their size; storage remains a perpetual headache for urban oarsmen who consider themselves luckier to find a rack in a boathouse for their boat than finding a parking space close to their apartment. But advocacy on the part of concerned oarsmen and new rowing clubs is opening up pieces of urban waterfront and unused buildings, renting out space and boats to recreational scullers and businessmen who want to exercise close to their office.

A group of stockbrokers on Wall Street have recently opened the West Side Boat Club for morning rows on the Hudson. In Boston, a similar club has opened near the financial district. All across the country, in nearly every major city that is close to a harbor, river, or lake, new clubs are forming—but not enough to keep up with the demand for dock space and rack room from shell owners.

Many oarsmen say recreational rowing could boom if there was enough room to store the boats, or simply parking lots convenient to a dock. Many urban oarsmen simply find a parking space near their water, feed the parking meter and launch right from the bank or beach, getting their feet wet as they walk the boat out to enough water to row away. Many oarsmen are discouraged from rowing in the city during the summer because of the number of other boats, especially power boats criss-crossing channels and lurching blindly into docks to discharge passengers. Large wakes can swamp an unwary sculler, who must always keep looking over his shoulder to make sure he isn't paddling blissfully into an oncoming water skiier or racing sailboat.

Most recreational rowers take to the water early in the morning, when the only people on the water are fishermen, and the wind hasn't started kicking up waves. Because a half hour of hard rowing is the equivalent of running five miles, it is much faster and far more enjoyable than a timed run over a set distance.

Martin wrote in his pamphlet, *How to Row An Alden Ocean Shell*:

> **Unless you are an exception, you will find that you will be forcing yourself to jog a predetermined time or distance, and looking forward to the moment when you can stop. When you are rowing, on the other hand, you will probably find it difficult to force yourself to come ashore. There are so many places to go, and things to see, and the pleasure of moving swiftly and quietly through the water is so great that you will also be unaware of the passage of time.**

The physiological benefits of recreational rowing over jogging and other aerobic sports are obvious. For one, jogging exerts pressure on a runner's joints, with an large, continuous amount of shock hitting the feet, ankles, and knees. Although cycling on a ten-speed is much smoother, like running it completely ignores the athlete's upper body. The effort experienced by an oarsman during a stroke is evenly distributed over every muscle, throughout the drive,

when the oar blades are in the water and the oarsman is driving back on his slide with his legs, finishing the stroke with back, shoulders, arms, and wrists.

Martin said he sells more Aldens to physicians than members of any other profession. Dr. Benjamin Riggs, seventy, a Charleston, South Carolina, psychoanalyst and naval architect, has constructed his own recreational scull for rowing on the Wando River.

Riggs rowed at Groton and Harvard, and like most oarsman had to substitute other sports for rowing once he graduated and moved to Charleston, where sculling has never been a very popular sport. "In college, the main things I loved were snow skiing, rowing and tennis," Riggs says. "The thing that stayed with me longest was rowing. It's beautiful recreation and even better exercise than swimming."

Although retired oarsmen are the most avid recreational rowers, many competitive elite oarsmen have purchased fiber glass shells for training and relaxation. The number of races for recreational oarsmen is always being expanded, including events at regattas as prestigious as the Head of the Charles. The Alden Ocean Shell Association sponsors a race every summer between Martin's childhood home, the Isles of Shoals, and Portsmouth. To keep the race an even contest, novice oarsmen start first, followed by progressively more experienced boats until the last oarsmen over the starting line are among some of the best scullers in the country.

The Alden association encourages oarsmen across the country to band together and establish clubs

Arthur E. Martin (right), the father of recreational rowing, with Fred S. (Ted) Perry of Alden Ocean Shells. Behind them are the boats of the Martin Marine line.

wherever two or more shells are rowed. One such club in Toledo, Ohio, donated space and equipment to the University of Toledo, which has joined with the Alden oarsmen to lobby the city into opening a public rowing center. The university now owns several racing boats, including an eight they row competitively against other Midwestern crews.

The average person who buys a recreational shell shouldn't be too concerned about how well the hull will fare in a tropical storm, but more about its weight and strength. Launching a recreational scull should be an easy task for one person. The ability to lift a shell over one's head and down onto a car's roof rack is the first thing a person shopping for a shell should consider. Although racing sculls often weigh less than thirty pounds, recreational sculls average fifty pounds and are often a little longer, making it much harder to walk from car to water's edge without knocking the bow or stern into a tree or building.

Most recreational oarsmen aren't lucky enough to own waterfront property, their own dock, or the rights to a rack in a boathouse. Lack of access to the water is the biggest headache of rowing, with legal parking, safe launching and docking facilities at a premium everywhere. City oarsmen are especially pinched as development closes off more and more open access to the waterfront. To stem the flow, oarsmen are banding together to purchase waterfront land and build docks—a resurrection of the forces that spawned the original barge clubs in the early nineteenth century.

Owners of recreational shells are banding together and organizing races, regattas, and expeditions together across the country. Collegiate oarsmen, trying to stay in shape during the summer months and finding themselves a good distance away from a rowing club's facilities, buy, rent, or borrow a recreational scull. Some of the best elite oarsmen rowing today in Olympic and international competition, including oarsmen such as Andy Sudduth, the American sculling sensation, learned how to row in a recreational scull.

Oarsmen who don't feel the urge to use their shells for hard workouts and training for races have found that recreational rowing can also include a passenger, or, in a pair, another oarsman. Most recreational pairs can be set and rowed by one oarsman, the extra seat and stretchers removed to make room for a passenger, dog, or small cargo.

Pair rowing is an excellent way to introduce a novice to the sport. An experienced oarsman can balance the shell and coach a novice through each stroke, pointing out problems as they occur until the novice reaches the point where he or she can row alone.

There is a wide selection of recreational sculls now on the market. They range from very stable ocean boats, such as the Alden, to very sturdy fiber glass or composite racing sculls. Some are close adapations of traditional sculls, their riggers, slides, and stretchers installed exactly the same way as they would be in a racing shell. Others have more innovative arrangements; the slide, riggers, and stretchers come all packaged in a single modular unit that can be installed or removed from a shell by merely tightening a few wingnuts.

Alden shells use a self-contained rowing unit called the Oarmaster while the rigging of shells such as the Laser are more like the rigging of a racer. Because recreational shells aren't subject to the same standards that are applied to racing boats, designers have been able to experiment and try out innovative ideas such as sliding riggers, where the seat is fixed, but the riggers and footstretchers are united and move together on slides.

Recreation doesn't necessarily mean an idle diversion or amusement; it connotes a leisure activity without the burden of competition. Yet recreational rowing has developed into a competitive sport, with races abounding and its devotées as serious about their style, speed, and equipment as any collegiate or elite oarsman. Regional and national championships are held for many classes, and distance races, such as the Isles of Shoals and Catalina-Marina Del Rey marathons are becoming more and more popular with oarsmen of all ages and abilities.

America seems to have a fascination with endurance sporting events, such as triathlons and marathons that push participants across long distances, dangerous terrain, and physical absolutes. That fascination has given rowing a new prominence and distinction: where rowing's image was once one of elitism, Ivy League, and the East Coast establishment, its new-found reputation as an ultimate test of

an athlete's physical and mental skills has placed it on a par with running and bicycling.

What keeps rowing and other endurance sports from turning their athletes into robotic automatons is the wonderful part the mind plays in a winning oarsman. Oarsmen who score poorly when connected to a heart monitor, respirator, and treadmill, can still shine as oarsmen for reasons known only to themselves. No seat is earned in a shell on the basis of the numbers alone.

Seat races are the final judge of an oarsman's inherent ability as a rower. It is the only time—save for a sculler—when an oarsman is tested one-on-one against a teammate.

Recreational rowing has been the beneficiary of the new rowing. The health benefits of the sport are well recognized, and its reputation as a life-prolonging and graceful form of exercise is rapidly finding people who have never before been exposed to it. The newer boats are forgiving craft that do away once and for all with rowing's reputation as a very difficult sport. They can blithely ram rocks, be driven into beaches, and fill up with water without showing any ill effect. They can be stored in the garage, transported on a car roof, and launched nearly anywhere.

On any body of water where two shells are rowed, their owners will inevitably seek each other out and race to test the fruits of many solitary morning workouts when the only competition was a watch and destination. Dedicated rowers are eager to share the sport with others, making available their own boat for lessons and practice rows. Before long there are enough shells converging on the river, lake, or harbor every morning to warrant friendly races or excursions to a secluded beach. When fall comes and the summer house has been closed for the winter, the shells are driven to the big regattas—the Head of the Charles, the Head of the Connecticut, the Merrimack, the Schuylkill—to participate in the spectacle of rowing as a link in a chain of eights, fours, pairs, doubles, and singles, their rowers deriving immense pride from passing lighter racing sculls and receiving the cheers of the crowds sitting on the bridges and riverbanks.

The effects of rowing and the impression it leaves on novices and veterans is difficult to describe in technical terms. Stoic oarsmen usually turn poetic when they describe their love for the sport and what it is about it that is worth sacrificing so much for.

Arthur Martin wrote:

> If you are a philosopher, and not in too much of a hurry to stop and dream a little, picture yourself as an oarsman in the calm of early evening, when the glaring sun has receded in the west—and with it the wind, gliding along through the clear water, arms, legs, and back moving in near-perfect rhythm, the silence complete but for the regular click of the oars in the oarlocks, and the waters rippling and swirling away from the shell and the blades. Above your own aerobic breathing, you can hear a fish in the distance, slapping the water with his tail after a leap for a hapless prey. You will see your wake in the dim light, bubbling away in a straight line under the stern, rising to a crescendo at the end of each stroke, and fading away at the start of the next one, and in the darkening sky above you will see a lone seagull returning to shore. You will not be in a hurry, for you already are where you want to be. You will not be bored, for the challenge of the sea is eternal. You will not be worried, for there is no room in the boat for the heavy burden of life ashore. You will not disturb the marine ecology, for your silent passage discharges no poisons on the water, nor harms a living thing.

> You will feel humble in the grandeur of your surroundings, but you will be envious of no man. You will be completely alone, but not lonely. You will have an inner glow and peace that neither power nor alcohol nor drugs can duplicate.

> You will be living.

CHAPTER 19

THE SPRINT

There are few sports that bring out the lyrical and romantic side of its devotées as rowing. While many sports are celebrations of grace and fluid motion, few have the quiet addiction of rowing.

What is it that compels a man or woman, boy or girl, to go down to the water in a small boat and row? Is it the lure of competition, that desire to beat another and take his shirt, to stand on a dock and with bowed head receive a medal? Is it the need for control, to push an otherwise chaotic life into the tight regimen of a rower, training for hours every day, rising early to row on calm waters, forcing one's self to excel with every stroke, oblivious to the surroundings, consumed by the sensation of moving silently over a fluid surface?

Rowers are a laconic lot. They row by a code of honor that is unwritten and certainly unspoken. The first rule is not to let down the boat, to pull every stroke as if it were your last. The second rule is there is no pain. Grimacing and shouting in agony are strongly discouraged. Every rower knows the agony, therefore there is no need for one to vocalize it.

This is a sport that is an addiction. There are those who know of nothing else from the age of fourteen to thirty. They postpone their lives to excel at a pastime that few outside of the sport's tight circle know anything about.

But that is all changing. No longer is rowing a pastime for the superdedicated, for those athletic misfits who fit in to rowing's fraternity by dint of their size, their conditioning and that special mental something that allows then to row through more pain than marathoners endure.

Today rowing is a sport for all people, a pastime one can enjoy at the same pace as a Sunday stroll through a park in springtime. Rowing is a way to escape the hustle of the mobs and pull away to a quiet place, an undiscovered place, a place where motor and sailboats can't fit, or pass by at speeds too high to comtemplate the pleasures of being afloat.

Arthur Martin and George Pocock are only two of the many men and women who have written of the lyrical grace of rowing well. Anonymous athletes who would be dumbfounded if asked to describe why they have dedicated their time to the sport, will suddenly burst into a poetic mood and conjure up a metaphor for rowing that no one has ever heard before. It might be difficult for the nonrower to imagine what rowers find to talk about. That great crab Ed caught in the race against Princeton? The time the kids shot BB guns at the scullers on the Potomac last summer before the nationals? When Joan and Linda had an ice cream eating contest on the bus back from the Dad Vail Regatta?

Rowers talk shop as much as any set of athletes. They compare shells, they weigh the benefits—real and imagined—of composite or synthetic oars versus spruce oars. They compare ergometer scores and diets.

Recreational rowers may happen upon each other while working out in the early morning mists of a summer day. Like two ships captained by skippers who imagined themselves to be the sole navigators on a forgotten sea, they may react with surprise to see another shell on the same waters, an informal race may spring up without a word being spoken—two slightly out-of-shape rowers burning with the desire to pull ahead and open a margin of open water between their stern and the other sculler's bow.

Yes, rowing is a sport of solitude. Even in an eight, powering down a 2,000-meter course in the world championships, the rowers don't speak to one another. Only the coxswains scream, trying to out-psyche the crews in the adjoining lanes while keeping their eight heaving engines in control, ready to unleash them with a decisive power ten at the precisely correct moment. For a word in such a race is a word that uses energy that should be going into the oar. From start to finish, the only sounds in a shell are those made by the cox, the eight slides, the eight oarlocks, and the eight oar blades splashing in and out of the water.

Most rowers don't listen to music as some joggers do. A few may, but most are content to listen to the sounds of the water; much about how one is rowing can be discerned from the sound of his oar entering and exiting the water.

This sport has been called the most amateur of all sports; it is a sport where fame and fortune will never occur, no matter how many advertisers feature the graceful spectacle in their commercials to sell deodorant and financial services. It has also been called the most grueling sport, one that can make a healthy participant vomit or faint from exhaustion. It has been called the most snobbish of sports, the most mechanical, the most fascistic by its detractors. It is a sport that lends itself to cartoons in the *New Yorker* and brief shots in movies for romantic background.

Above all, rowing is a sport for its participants. Spectators will derive little pleasure from watching two shells race side by side down a river, unless those spectators happen to be the families of the rowers or former rowers themselves equipped with stroke timers and binoculars, commenting on every aspect of the race as if it were a science.

For the uninitiated, a walk through the boathouse

or inside the tents where the shells are stored is usually enough to elicit some interest. For the length and narrow beam of a wooden shell, golden in the darkness, bespeaks nothing but speed and graceful strength. No other sport has equipment so delicate, except perhaps cycling or sailing. Take a spectator out onto the water in a coach's launch and let him see, closeup, the way a crew works, and what was once so mechanical and boring from the shore is a startlingly precise activity of perfect timing and herculean effort.

To start rowing takes about $2,000 if one wants a shell of one's own. That money will get you a fiber glass shell, a pair of sculls, and a roof rack to carry it around with. To find out what rowing feels like, and to learn how to do it moderately well in the company of others, takes a $50 membership in a community rowing program.

Rowing is more expensive than running and far less accessible. A business executive on a trip can lace on a pair of running shoes and find a good workout on the sidewalks surrounding his hotel. A swimmer can find a pool, pond, or river without too much trouble, and simply dive in, without worrying about the availability of a dock to launch from. A bicyclist can ride anywhere save a major highway. But a rower has to take into consideration the length of the body of water and how rowable the water is; a small puddle of a pond will give three or four strokes of good rowing before the rower has to dig in with the oar blades to stop the boat. Too rough and

the rower will put himself in danger, or at the least have a difficult time balancing the scull over the waves. Too congested with commercial traffic or speeding pleasure boats and a recreational scull stands the risk of being run down or swamped by a power boat's wake.

No, rowing is not the perfect sport by any stretch of the imagination. It is not a sport that one can easily enjoy. It is a not a sport for every pocketbook, which, unfortunately, may explain much of its current popularity. As is the case in polo, the expense of rowing can make it a status symbol of the moment, a fleeting luxury that one day will take its place in the garage with a set of nearly new cross-country skis and a barely used Italian racing bike.

Rowing is a sport for the dedicated. That is why those who take the pinch of buying a shell of their own, or sacrifice the brightest years of their lives to row four hours a day, are those who reap the rewards of the sport. There are moments of nearly religious grace awaiting in a shell for the faithful— moments that even transcend that high of rowing highs: swing.

For me rowing will always mean a memory of rowing in an April snowstorm in a four-man shell, no one talking, the coxswain silent for once, all of us shrouded in silence and paddling along so slowly that I could hear the snowflakes dropping on the water. Yes, there were the moments, a stroke or two before a hard-reached finish line, when I knew that I had won another shirt to wear in off-season. Moments of victory so sweet that the work of 2,000 meters didn't effect me at all, whereas had I lost I would have slumped over my oar and shrieked air back into my burning lungs.

There were moments when a coach would take me aside and praise me. And no praise ever sounded so sweet.

There were moments when my hands, blue with the cold, were pinched between the gunwale and oar handle because someone in the boat caught a bad stroke. There were times when I was so bored with the monotony of rowing through the cycle of catch, drive, finish, and recovery, times when I counted through that cycle . . . one, two, three, four . . . one, two, three, four . . . that I thought I was becoming retarded with the boredom.

Rowing is not the be all, end all of the world. The history is remarkable because it is a history of the upper and lower classes both here in America and elsewhere. For rowing is the first truly organized sport, a statement that historians of other sports will surely challenge, but take heed of the firsts:

The first organized sport in English public schools . . . not cricket, not rugby: Rowing.

The oldest intercollegiate sporting event in the world: The Oxford-Cambridge boat race.

The oldest intercollegiate sporting event in the United States: The Harvard-Yale Regatta.

The oldest professional sport: Rowing.

In the early 1970s rowing was high and dry. Aside from Harvard, where its crews were making headlines, collegiate rowing was moribund. Yale, the place where collegiate rowing began in this country, had troubles fielding a full complement of three boats: twenty-four oarsmen and three coxswains. It had been years since an American crew had won an medal in international or Olympic competition.

It seemed as if no one but former rowers, gray haired and prone to reminiscing, cared one whit about rowing. The activism of the time, the long-haired protests and liberal reaction against the Establishment, was like a knee to rowing's groin. No self-respecting college student in those days would row lest he be branded an elitist. Those who did row did so because they learned how in prep school and fell in love with it there. Walk-on participants, the life's blood of the sport today, were very rare.

Rowing was written off as an anachronism by several college and prep school athletic departments, who could no longer justify the considerable expense of equipping and transporting a crew team over the needs of other sports that were certainly more popular than crew.

Yet through it all the devotées of the sport kept to their boathouses and oars, keeping alive a tradition for the pleasure of the sport and for the sake of the tradition.

The turning point came in 1975, the year that women's rowing suddenly became something more than a novelty designed to amuse the husbands of rowing widows on regatta day. With the 1976 Montreal Olympics just around the corner, women's rowing came into the mainstream, and suddenly rowing became the rage among women on college and prep school campuses, a rage that helped the sport deflate its balloon of pomposity and open its doors to people other than well-to-do male WASPs.

Consider the numbers: membership of the United States Rowing Association doubled from 6,000 members in 1979 to close to 12,000 in 1984. Estimates of the number of people who row range, according to the USRA, from 25,000 to 40,000.

This is a sport that has recently been discovered by the media. Starting in 1984, on the eve of the summer Olympiad in Los Angeles, rowing regained a place on the sports pages of most major metropolitan daily newspapers. At least five books have been written about the sport in the past five years—one found a place on the best seller lists.

There have been two movies made about rowing. Countless advertisements have been filmed and photographed with rowing as their centerpiece.

But most important are the inroads rowing has made into the mass public. Rowing has finally become a sport that anyone can enjoy. In Seattle, the parks and recreation department runs a summer rowing program and has built a special boathouse to accommodate the demand. Other cities with public rowing facilities include: New York; Baltimore; Cleveland; Waterloo, Iowa; Syracuse; and Boston. Undoubtedly more are on their way. Several programs for the handicapped have been established, with the blind and the physically impaired finding rowing one of the easiest and safest sports to enjoy.

Rowing is finding its oars again.

GLOSSARY

AEROBIC: The physiological condition where energy is supplied by oxygen.

ANEROBIC: The physiological condition that follows the aerobic plateau when the body begins converting sugar and fat to energy.

BARGE: The predecessor to the modern racing shell, a barge was a 35 to 50 foot longboat with a narrow beam or width that seated up to twelve rowers. Barges featured fixed seats, thole pins instead of oarlocks, and a coxswain steering in the stern. A more modern version of the term applies to the twenty-four seat floating behemoths used by some colleges and schools to train large numbers of novices at the same time. Such craft are extremely heavy, have sliding seats, adjustable stretchers and riggers. The center of such teaching barges usually have a path for the coach to walk up and down while watching each rower practice the stroke.

BEAM: The width of a shell, barge, scull, or any craft as measured at the mid-point of the hull.

BICEPS: The muscles of the upper arms.

BLADE: The flat piece of wood or synthetic material fixed to the end of an oar or scull. Blade styles have evolved from thin, long hooks, to broad, "tulip" shapes.

BLADEWORK: The action of feathering, or turning an oar's blade in and out of - the water. A rower said to have "good bladework" is regarded as a precise stylist.

BOAT: In rowing, the craft used for rowing is called a shell or scull. Boat refers to the members of the crew who sit in a shell or scull. For example, a crew team's first boat is its best, or varsity, the second, the junior varsity, and so on.

BOW: The front of a shell or boat.

BOW-BALL: Generally a tennis or rubber ball, painted a bright color, sliced and fixed to the prow, or extreme tip of the bow. Used as a safety measure to prevent injuries should shells collide, and also as an indicator for judges in the event of a close, photo-finish.

BROAD COMP: A wide-beamed scull for a single rower. Generally used as a boat for teaching novice scullers, a heavy weighted boat for a hard workout, or a more stable craft for windy, rough water conditions.

BUTTON: The ring of plastic or laminated leather that encircles the loom, or shaft, of an oar or scull about one-third of the way down from the handle. Used to keep the oar from sliding too far down in the oarlock.

CARBON FIBER: Synthetic, high-technology fiber used to contruct lightweight, strong shells, sculls, oars, and riggers. Typically used on only the most competitive classes of shells.

CATCH: The point in a stroke when the oar first bites into the water.

CHECK: A slight, but sharp pause in a shell that occurs at the catch when one or several rowers hit the water with the back of their oar blade at the catch. "Check all!" or "Way Enough!" is a coxswain's command for the rowers to stop a shell by squaring their blades in the water.

COLLAR: An eight-inch-wide band of leather or nylon that encircles the loom of an oar where the oar pivots in the oarlock. Used to prevent the shaft from wearing away.

COMBING: A strip of wood affixed to the deck of shell to keep rough water out of the boat.

COXSWAIN: The person, male or female, who steers a shell and encourages the crew, pointing out faults and exhorting them to row harder. Coxswains are generally light (80 to 120 pounds). In some private rowing clubs, the coxswain is the equivalent of a yacht club commodore.

CRAB: The biggest mistake a rower can make, so named because the oar slices downward and out of control into the water like a crab catcher's net. Crabs usually occur when a rower drives his oar blade into the water at an angle. The oar goes out of control and can result in the rower losing his grip altogether, or even causing the shell to capsize.

CUTTER: A large, heavy craft used by navies to ferry supplies, cargo, or passengers from ship to shore. Cutters were one of the earliest boats raced in England. Also used to denote a barge.

DECK: The thin silk, canvas, or plastic skin stretched and fixed to the bow and stern sections of a shell.

DINGHY: 8 to 12 foot small craft used by yachtsmen to get from ship to shore and vice-versa.

DOGGETT'S COACH AND BADGE: The oldest event in rowing. Held annually on the Thames River in London for amateur scullers and apprentice watermen.

DORY: A double-ended working boat design renowned for its seaworthiness and durability. Designed for commercial fishing and utilized throughout the North Atlantic fisheries, dories have become popular as recreational ocean-going row boats.

DOUBLE: A shell for two scullers.

DRIVE: The portion of a stroke when the oar is pulled through the water, by extending the legs, leaning back, and hauling on the oar or sculls. The term "leg drive" is used to describe to a rower's leg strength.

EIGHT: An shell with eight rowers and a coxswain. Length averages 60 to 70 feet. The most popular and prestigious class of shell widely used in prep, college, and international competition.

ELITE: Elite-level rowing is generally world-class level rowing, where crews are selected from a pool of national candidates and funded by a parent organization or government.

EMFBO: Every Man For Better Oarsmanship. Motto of the University of Washington men's crew.

ENGINE ROOM: The middle four rowers in an eight are sometimes referred to as the engine room. Because the four heaviest and usually strongest members of a crew are seated in the 3, 4, 5, and 6 seats to balance the shell, they are often called the "engines" of the shell.

ERGOMETER: A rowing machine used for off-water workouts and quantative measurement of a rower's strength. The machines consist of an oar handle, affixed by lever or cable to a flywheel. A counter ticks off the revolutions of the flywheel, a timer paces the rower, and an adjustable brake may be set to account for body weight and the level of work.

FEATHER: The angle of an oar blade. Feathering is the act of turning an oar in its oarlock.

FINISH: The end of the stroke's drive, when the oar blade exits the water and the hands stop in the lap of the rower.

FISA: Federation Internationale Societe Avion. The international organization of rowing and the oldest governing body of any sport.

GATE: A hinged bar that closes an oar into an oarlock.

GIG: A small craft manned by up to six sailors, used by navies to ferry officers from ship to shore.

GRIPS: Rubber handles that fit over the handles of sculls.

GUNWALE: The topside of a shell's hull.

HANDS: A term used by coaches when critiquing a rower's bladework or recovery speed.

HEAD START: A form of start used in large regattas when it would be impossible to start many boats at the same time on the same starting line. A head start is a running start, where crews cross the starting line while moving at predetermined intervals. The time it takes each crew to traverse the course is calculated, with the shortest time belonging to the winner.

HEAVYWEIGHT: A rower or crew where every individual weighs more than 170 pounds, with an average weight of 190 pounds.

HENLEY ROYAL REGATTA: The most venerable rowing event in the world, held every July on the Thames River in Henley-on-the-Thames, England.

KEELSON: A thin, rigid piece of wood that runs the length of a shell, from bow to stern, joining the sides of the hull together and providing stiffness.

LAUNCH: The act of placing a shell in the water from dock or beach. Also, a small craft used to ferry passengers and crew from ship to shore.

LIGHTWEIGHT: A rower or crew with no one individual weighing more than 170 pounds, and the boat's average weight is 160 pounds.

LOOM: The shaft of an oar or scull.

NAAO: The National Association of Amateur Oarsmen. (Defunct; now the United States Rowing Association.)

OAR HANDLE: The extreme end of an oar or scull, formed to fit the hands of a rower.

OCTET: A shell, similiar to an eight, except each member of the eight-person crew sculls, with two oars apiece. A rare sight.

ORTHODOX: The orthodox style of rowing originated on English racing barges before the advent of the sliding seat. It was a style that emphasized the swing of the upper body as the oar dipped in and out of the water. Also referred to as English orthodoxy.

PADDLE: The slowest pace in rowing, where just enough pressure is applied to the oars to slowly propel the shell. Also: a short oar used without oarlocks.

PAIR: A shell rowed by two rowers, each with one oar, or sweep. Coxed pairs feature a coxswain sitting in either the stern or the bow of the shell.

PETIT FINALS: The semifinals of a rowing regatta.

PICK DRILL: A series of rowing exercises designed to teach precise bladework and foster improved timing among a boat.

PITCH: The angle of an oar blade relative to the water. Can be adjusted by tuning the riggers.

PITCH METER: A scale used by riggers or coaches to determine the pitch of an oar.

PORT: Standing at the stern of a shell and looking up the length of the hull, port is the left side.

PUNT: A small, square bow and stern craft propelled by a pole that is driven into the river or lake bottom and drawn forward. A popular craft on the Thames in England, especially at the Henley Royal Regatta.

QUAD: A shell for four scullers.

QUADRICEP: The muscle atop the thigh and one of the most important for strong rowing.

RATE: The pace of rowing. Thirty-six strokes per minutes is considered a racing rate. The low 20s are paddling and anything in the high 30s or low 40s is sprinting.

"READY ALL?": A coxswain's command to a crew to get them prepared to row.

RECOVERY: The cycle of a stroke where the oar is out of the water and moving away from the finish to the catch.

REGATTA: A series of races, involving several different classes of shells, men and women, youth through elite levels.

REPECHAGE: The consolation heat of a regatta, Olympic series, or world championships.

RIGGER: A set of metal or carbon fiber tubes affixed to the gunwale of a shell for the oarlock and gate. Developed in the late nineteenth century to increase the leverage of the oars while reducing the beam of the shell. Also, the person in charge of rigging and maintaining shells, overseeing a boathouse's operations, and coordinating travel to distant races.

RUDDER: A hinged fin mounted on the stern or beneath the hull of a shell. Rudders are controlled by two cables connected to tiller or two wood handles called clackers.

RUN: The distance a shell travels between strokes.

RUSHING: When a rower's timing is out of synch with the rest of the crew, then he or she is said to be "rushing" their slide. Rushing causes the forward run of shell to check.

SCULL: A shell for one rower.

SCULLS: Sculls are nine-foot-long oars with slender grips to accommodate one hand. Used in sets of two.

SEAT RACE: A race when a coach orders three shells to row at full speed for two to three minutes. At the end of the interval, two rowers switch boats and the three shells race for another interval as long as the first; at the finish, one of the first two rowers is switched with a new rower from the third boat. Another interval is rowed, and so on. The purpose of seat racing is to determine what effect an individual rower has on a boat's performance. Only the coach knows who is being compared to whom. One rower always knows he is being seat raced, but none of the other six to twenty-four know until the coach orders the boats to pull together and makes a new swap.

SETTLE: The one stroke following the starting sprint, when the crew or sculler "settles" into a lower cadence for the body of the race.

SET-UP: The balance of a shell. Setting up is one of the most difficult tricks of rowing to master and is accomplished by having every oar the exact same height above and in the water throughout all stages of a stroke.

SHELL: A craft propelled by oars for racing.

SINGLE: A one-man scull.

SKEG: A metal fin fixed to the bottom of shell, on the keelson, to keep the shell on a true course.

SKIFF: A sturdy wooden boat, under 15 feet long, used for rowing from ship to shore, for fishing and general harbor and protected water work.

SKYING: The style flaw by which a rower raises the blade of the oar too high off the water during the recovery.

SLIDE: The seat, wheels, and tracks combine to form the slide. Also used to describe a rower's use of the seat, as in "rushing one's slide."

SPOON BLADE: An early oar blade design that was square at the tip, but curved inward to form a slight hook, the thinking being that the oar would "grip" the water better.

SPRINT: The end of a race when a crew raises the rate and drives hard to the finish line. Also, a race 2,000-meters or shorter.

SQUARE: A blade is square when it is perpendicular to the surface of the water and submerged.

STARBOARD: Standing at the stern of a shell and looking up the length of the hull, starboard is the right side.

STERN: The rear of a shell, the end the rowers face when seated.

STRAIGHT FOUR: A four-man shell with no coxswain.

STRETCHER: An adjustable foot rest that ties a rower's feet down so he or she can pull their slides forward during the recovery. Some stretchers use leather flaps and shoelaces to do the job, others are expensive running shoes, slit in half and held together with Velcro so a rower can rip his or her feet out should the shell capsize.

STRIKING: The rate at which a crew is rowing; for example: "Yale was striking 40 at the start before they settled to a 36."

STRINGER: A thin, rigid piece of wood that runs inside of a shell to provide strength and stiffness.

STROKE: The action of moving an oar into, through, and out of the water. The rower who sets the pace for the rest of the crew.

SWEEPS: Rowing in a multiperson boat, with each rower using one oar. The opposite of sculling.

SWING: A state in rowing where the rowers fall into perfect timing and the - shell seems to accelerate without additional effort.

TANK: A pool of moving water used to teach rowing and train rowers when the elements rule out an outdoor row.

THOLE PINS: A pair of wooden dowels four to six inches apart set upright along the deck or gunwale of a barge, gig, cutter, or launch. Thole pins were the ancestors of the modern swiveling oarlock.

THWART: A piece of wood that runs across a barge, gig, cutter or launch that serves as a seat for one or two rowers.

TILLER: A coxswain's steering bar made of wood or metal, connected to the tiller ropes, which in turn are connected to the rudder.

TRAINER: A stable shell used to teach rowing to novices. Also, the person affiliated with a team who administers to the rower's aches, pains, and blisters.

TULIP BLADE: A style of oar blade which resembles a tulip blossom. Currently the most popular blade type for racing.

TURNING STAKE: In the nineteenth century, most races started and finished in the same place for the sake of the spectators, with the racing shells turning around a single or pair of buoys or stakes at the race course's mid-point.

USRA: The United States Rowing Association, the national body that oversees collegiate and national rowing. It's address is 251 North Illinois St., Suite 980, Indianapolis, IN, 46204.

WAIST: The middle seats in a shell, also called the engine room.

WATERBOX: The combing and planks that surround a crew and keep water from splashing into the shell.

"WAY ENOUGH!": A coxswain's command for a crew to stop rowing.

WHERRY: A small craft with a sliding seat and short riggers, designed for rowing in rough water.

BIBLIOGRAPHY

Adam, Karl. *Ratzeburg Rowing Clinic.* University of Alabama.: The University of Alabama Crew, 1978.

Allen, Jane E., and Allen, Roger E. *Flashing Oars: Rowing on the Schuylkill.* Philadelphia: Philadelphia Maritime Musuem, 1985.

Bourne, Gilbert C. *A Textbook on Oarsmanship.* Oxford, England: Oxford University Press, 1923.

Burnell, Richard. *The Complete Sculler.* Marlow, England: Simpson, 1977.

Burnell, Richard. *150 Years of the Oxford and Cambridge Boat Race.* London: Marlow, 1979.

Burnell, Rickard. *Henley Regatta.* Oxford, England: Oxford University Press, 1957.

Cleaver, Hylton. *A History of Rowing.* London: Herbert Jenkins, 1957.

Cook, Theodore A. *Rowing at Henley.* Oxford, England: Oxford University Press, 1919.

Culler, R.D. *Boats, Oars, and Rowing.* Camden, Maine: International Marine Publishing, 1978.

Edwards, H. R. A. *The Way of a Man with a Blade.* London: Routledge and Kegan Paul, 1963.

Fairbairn, Steve. *On Rowing.* Ian Fairbairn, editor. London: Nicholas Kaye, 1951.

Gardner, John. "The Early Days of Rowing Sport." *The Log of the Mystic Seaport*, Vol. 19, No. 4, pp. 114-123 (reprinted in the Log, Vol. 32, No. 1, pp. 3-9.)

Glendon, Richard A., and Glendon, Richard J. *Rowing.* New York: Lippincott, 1923.

Halberstam, David. *The Amateurs.* New York: Morrow, 1985.

The H Book of Harvard Athletics, Vol. I, 1923 (1852-1922). John A. Blanchard, editor, Vol. II, 1964 (1923-1963). Geoffrey H. Movius, editor. Cambridge, Mass.: Harvard Varsity Club.

Heaton, Peter. *The Singlehanders.* New York: Hastings House, 1976.

Herrick, Robert F. *Red Top.* Cambridge, Mass.: Harvard University Press, 1948.

Howard, Ronnie. *Knowing Rowing.* San Diego, Calif.: A.S. Barnes, 1977.

Kelley, Robert F. *American Rowing.* New York: Putnam, 1932.

Kiesling, Stephen. *The Shell Game*. New York: Morrow, 1981.

Kirch, Barbara; Hoyt, Reed W.; and Fithian, Janet. *Row for Your Life*. New York: Simon & Schuster, 1985.

Lehmann, R. C. *The Complete Oarsman*. London: Methuen, 1908.

Mendenhall, Thomas C., III. *A Short History of American Rowing*. Cambridge, Mass.: Charles River Press, 1981.

Morrison, J. S., and Williams, R. T. *Greek Oared Ships*. Cambridge, Mass.: Cambridge University Press, 1968.

National Association of Amateur Oarsmen. *Official Guide*. (published annually, 1910-1975).

Newell, Gordon. *Ready All! George Yeoman Pocock and Crew Racing*. Seattle: The University of Washington Press, 1987.

Norsen, Irene W. *The Ward Brothers, Champions of the World*. New York: Vantage Press, 1958.

Rowe, R. P. P., and Pitman, C. M. *Rowing*. London: Longmans, 1898.

Sixty Years of the Union Boat Club (1851-1911). By the Club Historian. Boston: The Union Boat Club, 1976.

Warre, Edmund. *On the Grammar of Rowing*. Oxford, England: Claredon Press, 1909.

Wilson, Paul C. *Modern Rowing*. Harrisburg, Pa.: Stackpole, 1969.

Young, Charles Van P. *Courtney and Cornell Rowing*. Ithaca, New York: Cornell Publications, 1923.

ROWING TEAMS, CLUBS, AND ORGANIZATIONS OF AMERICA
(with person to contact when available)

NORTHEAST

Albany Medical College Rowing Club
c/o Alumni Office
Mail Code 5
47 New Scotland Avenue
Albany, NY 12208

Albany Rowing Center
PO Box 857
Albany, NY 12201

Alden Ocean Shell Association
34 Sunset Drive
S. Easton, MA 02375

Alte Achter Boat Club
PO Box 812301
Wellesley, MA 02482-0017

Amoskeag Rowing Club
c/o Manchester YMCA
30 Mechanic Street
Manchester, NH 03101

Aqueduct Rowing Club
P.O. Box 202
Rexford, NY 12148-0202

Arlington High School Crew
North Campus, Route 55
Pleasant Valley, NY 12569

Arlington Rowing Association
c/o ARA
PO Box 1171
Pleasant Valley, NY 12569

Assumption College Crew
500 Salisbury Street
Worcester, MA 01615

Bantam Boat Club
c/o Trinity College
Ferris Athletic Center
300 Summit Street
Hartford, CT 06106

Barnstable Rowing Club
PO Box 1024
Centerville, MA 02632

Bates College Rowing Association
Bates College Alumni Gym
130 Central Avenue
Lewiston, ME 04240

Beach Channel High School Crew
100-00 Beach Channel Drive
Rockaway Park, NY 11694

Belmont Hill School Crew
c/o Belmont Hill School
350 Prospect Street
Belmont, MA 02178

Berkshire School Rowing Association
245 N. Undermountain Road
Sheffield, MA 02157

Berkshire Sculling Association
43 Roselyn Drive
Pittsfield, MA 01201

Brandeis University Crew
Gosman Athletic Center
Mail Stop 007
Waltham, MA 02254-9110

Blood Street Sculls
RFD #3, Blood Street
Old Lyme, CT 06371

The Blue Blades Boat Club
3 Shaler Lane
Cambridge, MA 02138

Boston College Crew
141 McElroy Commons
Chestnut Hill, MA 02167

Boston Masters Women
Four Harrison Avenue
Gloucester, MA 01930

Boston Rowing Center
23 Dunstable Street
Lawrence, MA 01843

Boston "T" Club
25 Kelly Road, #3
Cambridge, MA 02139

Boston University Crew
285 Babcock Street
Boston, MA 02215

Boston University Women's Crew
c/o Athletic Department
285 Babcock Street
Boston, MA 02215

Bowdoin Crew
Athletic Department,
Bowdoin College 9000
College Station
Brunswick, ME 04011

Brewster Academy Crew
80 Academy Drive
Wolfeboro, NH 03894

Brooks School Crew
1160 Great Pond Road
North Andover, MA 01845

Brown Rowing Association
838 Greenwich Street, #5F
New York, NY 10014

Brown University Crew
Box 1932, Athletic Department
Providence, RI 02903

Brunswick School
100 Maher Avenue
Greenwich, CT 06830

Buckingham, Browne & Nichols
Gerry's Landing Road
Cambridge, MA 02138

Bulldog Rowing Club
415 Concord Street
Holliston, MA 01746

Burnt Hills Rowing Association
PO Box 248
Burnt Hills, NY 12027

Cambridge Boat Club
7 Meadow Way
Cambridge, MA 02138

Cascadilla Boat Club
Box 4032
Ithaca, NY 14852

Casco Bay Rowing Center
5 Lupine Court
Yarmouth, ME 04096

Castle Rowing Club
15 Innis Lane
Old Greenwich, CT 06870

Cazenovia College Crew
Cazenovia College Athletic Complex
Cazenovia, NY 13035

Cazenovia Rowing Club, Inc.
PO Box 533
Cazenovia, NY 13035

Champion International Collegiate
  Regatta

PO Box 3
Centerville, MA 02632

Charles River Rowing Association
60 John F. Kennedy Street
Cambridge, MA 02138

Charter Oar Rowing Club
16 Sycamore Road
Hartford, CT 06117

Choate-Rosemary Hall School
  Crew
114 Quonnipaug Lane
Guilford, CT 06437

Clark University Crew
950 Main Street
Worcester, MA 01610

Colby College Rowing Association
Athletic Department
4900 Colby College
Mayflower Hill, ME 04901

Colgate Rowing Club
210 Huntington Gymnasium
Colgate University
Hamilton, NY 13346

College of the Holy Cross Crew
Holy Cross College
Worcester, MA 01610

Columbia/Barnard Rowing
Mail Code 1905
119th & Broadway
New York, NY 10027

Columbia University Crew
Mailcode 1905
119th & Broadway
New York, NY 10027

Community Rowing, Inc.
PO Box 382604
Cambridge, MA 02238-2604

Community Rowing, Inc.
Youth Program
PO Box 382604
Cambridge, MA 02238-2604

Connecticut Rowing & Boating
  Society
12 A Dayton Court
Newington, CT 06111

Connecticut College Rowing
  Association
Connecticut College
Box 1582
New London, CT 06320

Connetquot River Rowing Association
150 Idle Hour Blvd.
Oakdale, NY 11769

Cornell University Crew
Crew Office, Teagle Hall
Campus Road
Ithaca, NY 14853

Cornell University Women's Crew
Crew Office, Teagle Hall
Campus Road
Ithaca, NY 14853

Cotuit Rowing Club
PO Box 393
Cotuit, MA 02635

Craftsbury Sculling Center
PO Box 31
Craftsbury Common, VT 05827

Cygnet Rowing Club
6 Ballord Place
Cambridge, MA 02139

Dartmouth Rowing Club
6083 Alumni Gymnasium
Dartmouth College
Hanover, NH 03755

Deerfield Academy Crew
Deerfield Academy
Main Street
Deerfield, MA 01342

DeWolfe Rowing Club
285 Babcock Street
Boston, MA 02215

Dowling College Crew
Dowling College
Idle Hour Blvd.
Oakdale, NY 11769

Downtown Boat Club
241 W. Broadway
New York, NY 10013

Dresden Rowing Club
PO Box 419
Hanover, NH 03755-0419

Durham Boat Club
220 Newmarket Road
Durham, NH 03824

Eastern Association of Rowing
  Colleges
9 Main Street
New Preston, CT 06777

Eastern Association of Rowing
  Colleges Regatta
PO Box 3
Centerville, MA 02632

East Lyme Rowing Association
PO Box 36
East Lyme, CT 06333

East River Rowing Club
300 East 74th Street
New York, NY 03824

Empire State Rowing Association
PO Box 2916
Church Street Station
New York, NY 10008-2916

Erie Canal Rowing Club, Inc.
5875 State Route 26
Rome, NY 13440

Exeter Boat Club
Phillips Exeter Academy
Exeter, NH 03833

Exeter Rowing Association
11 Hall Place
Exeter, NH 03833

Fairfield University
1073 N. Benson Road
Fairfield, CT 06430

Farmington Valley Rowing
  Association
542 Hopmeadow Street, Suite 101
Simsbury, CT 06070

Fat Cat Rowing Club
579 Midline Road
Freeville, NY 13068

Floating the Apple
400 W. 43rd St., #32R
New York, NY 10036

Florida Rowing Center
1140 Fifth Avenue
New York, NY 10128

Fordham Rowing Association
Lombardi Memorial Center
Fordham University
Bronx, NY 10458

Franklin Pierce College
PO Box 60
Rindge, NH 03461-0060

Friends of Barnstable Crew, Inc.
86 Willow Street
Yarmouthport, MA 02675

Friends of Niskayuna Crew Club
938 Morgan Avenue
Niskayuna, NY 12309

Friends of Shenendehowa Crew,
  Inc.
15 Brookline Drive
Clifton Park, NY 12065

Gentle Giant Rowing
29 Harding Street
Somerville, MA 02143

Grace Harbor Rowing Club
102 Columbia Street
Huntington Manor, NY 11746

Grateful Oars Rowing Club
140 Green Meadows Road
Winthrop, NY 13697

Greater Lowell Rowing, Inc.
Greater Lowell Rowing
PO Box 1493
Lowell, MA 01853-1493

Groton School
Box 991
Groton, MA 01450

Gunnery School Crew
The Gunnery School
99 Greenhill Road
Washington, CT 06793

Hamilton Crew
198 College Hill Road
Clinton, NY 13323

Hanover Rowing Club
6083 Alumni Gymnasium
Dartmouth College
Hanover, NH 03755

Hartford Barge Club
551 Bell Street
Glastonbury, CT 06033

Harvard Business School Boat
  Club
75 Cambridge Parkway, #205
Cambridge, MA 02142

Harvard Law School Crew
14 Line Street, Apt. #3
Somerville, MA 02143

Harvard Sculling Club
60 John F. Kennedy Street
Cambridge, MA 02138

Harvard University Crew
60 John F. Kennedy Street
Cambridge, MA 02138

Head of the Charles Regatta
PO Box 380052
Cambridge, MA 02238-0052

Head of the Connecticut Regatta
PO Box 1
70 College Street
Middletown, CT 06457

Heritage Park Rowing Foundation
4 Kirock Place
Westport, CT 06880

Hiawatha Island Boat Club
47 Frederick Drive
Apalachin, NY 13732

Hobart and William Smith Rowing Club
Winn-Seely Gym
HWS
Geneva, NY 14456

Holy Cross College Crew
Holy Cross Athletics
1 College Street
Worcester, MA 01610

Housatonic Rowing Association
574 Amity Road
Woodbridge, CT 06525

Hudson River Rowing Association
12 Pennock Road
Poughkeepsie, NY 12603

Hull Lifesaving Museum Rowing
Association
PO Box 221
Hull, MA 02045

Huntington Barge and Paddle Club
15 Briarwood Circle
N. Easton, MA 02356

Hyde Park Rowing Association
19 Gilbert Drive
Hyde Park, NY 12538

Intercollege Rowing Association
PO Box 3
Centerville, MA 02632

Independence Rowing Club
PO Box 1412
Nashua, NH 03061

Intercollegiate Rowing Association
Regatta
PO Box 3
Centerville, MA 02632

Interlachen Rowing Club
PO Box 330
Corning, NY 14830

Iona College Crew
Hill Center
Ithaca College
Ithaca, NY 14850

Kent School Boat Club
Kent School – Route 341
Kent, CT 06757

Kings Crown Rowing Association
280 Madison Avenue, Suite 1404
New York, NY 10016

Lasell College Crew
1844 Commonwealth Avenue
Newton, MA 02166

Lesley College
29 Everett Street
Cambridge, MA 02138

Lightweight Development
Camp/Club
60 John F. Kennedy Street
Cambridge, MA 02138

Litchfield Hills Rowing Club
PO Box 42
Litchfield, CT 06759

Little Brave Canoe Rowing Club
Manhattan College
Bronx, NY 10471

Lourdes Rowing Association
Cara Lourdes Crew Club
64 Martin Drive
Poughkeepsie, NY 12603

Maine Rowing Association
PO Box 267
Camden, ME 04843

Mandela Town Hall Health Spot,
Inc.
1855 Washington Street
Lower Roxbury, MA 02118

Manhatten College Crew
Manhatten Crew – Athletic
Department
Manhatten College Parkway
Riverdale, NY 10471

Marist Colleg Crew
McCann Center
Marist College
Poughkeepsie, NY 12601

Massachusetts Maritime Academy
Men's Crew
101 Academy Drive
Buzzards Bay, MA 02532

Massachusetts Maritime Academy
Women's Crew
101 Academy Drive
Buzzards Bay, MA 02532

Masters Womens Rowing Camp
36 Montgomery Street
Cambridge, MA 02140

Merrimack River Rowing Association
PO Box 686
Lowell, MA 01854

Middlebury College Crew
D-28, Middlebury College
Middlebury, VT 05753

Middlesex School Crew
Middlesex School / 1400 Lowell
    Street
Concord, MA 01742

Middletown Boat Club
831-D Long Hill Road
Middletown, CT 06457

Middletown Rowing Association
Middletown High School
Huntin Hill Avenue
Middletown, CT 06457

Mid Hudson Rowing Association
PO Box 683
Poughkeepsie, NY 12602

MIT Boat Club
MIT Box D
Cambridge, MA 02139

MIT Lightweight Crew
MIT Box D
Cambridge, MA 02139

MIT Rowing Association
MIT Branch PO Box D
Cambridge, MA 02139

MIT Sloan Crew
174 Putnam Ave, #2
Cambridge, MA 02139

Mohawk River Boat Club
5010 St Hwy 30
Amsterdam, NY 12010

Monadnock Rowing Club
PO Box 239
Harrisville, NH 03250

Motley Rowing Club
119 McKee Road
Morrisville, CT 05661

Mount Holyoke Womens Regatta
10 Harwich Place
South Hadley, MA 01075

Mount Madison Volunteer Ski Patrol
PO Box 78
McCormack Station
Boston, MA 02101

Mystic Valley Rowing Association
Tufts University
36 Sawyer Avenue
Medford, MA 02155

Narragansett Boat Club
PO Box 2413
Providence, RI 02906

Navy Masters Rowing Club
1021 Mill Road
E. Aurora, NY 14052

NE Sculling & Rowing Center
PO Box 2060
Duxbury, MA 02331

Newburgh Rowing Club
13 Lexington Drive
Newburgh, NY 12550

New Canaan High School Crew
153 Sunset Hill Road
New Canaan, CT 06840

New England Interscholastic
    Rowing Association
PO Box 1024
Centerville, MA 02632

New Haven Rowing Club
105 Mill Rock Road
New Haven, CT 06517

New Rochelle Rowing Club
523 Croton Heights Road
Yorktown Heights, NY 10598

New York Athletic Club
2560 Stedman Place
New Rochelle, NY 10805

New York Maritime College
Director of Athletics
6 Pennyfield Avenue
Bronx, NY 10465

New York University
Coles Center
181 Mercer Street
New York, NY 10021

Niskayuna H.S. Crew Club
33 Hill Avenue
Alplaus, NY 12008

Noble & Greenough School Crew
507 Bridge Street
Dedham, MA 02026

Nonesuch Oar and Paddle Club –
ME
500 Fowler Road
Cape Elizabeth, ME 04107

Northeastern University Men's Crew
219 Cabot Gym
360 Huntington Avenue
Boston, MA 02115

Northeastern University Rowing
Association
219 Cabot Gym
360 Huntington Avenue
Boston, MA 02115

Northeastern University Women's
Crew
36 Montgomery Street
Cambridge, MA 02140

Northfield-Mt. Hermon School
Box 4075
206 Main Street
Northfield, MA 01360

Norwalk River Rowing
Association
56 Walter Avenue
Norwalk, CT 06851

Notre Dame College Rowing
PO Box 416
Henniker, NH 03242

NYSU Maritime College Crew
Fort Schuyler
Bronx, NY 10465

Oars
Rec. Services
3 Keaney Road, Suite 1
Kingston, RI 02881

Old Lyme Rowing Association
4 Jean Drive
Old Lyme, CT 06371

Onata Lake Rowing Club
PO Box 411
Williamstown, MA 01267

Peck's Boat Club
PO Box 47
Rowayton, CT 06853

Pequot Yacht Club
130 Willow Street
Southport, CT 06490

Phillips Academy Crew
Phillips Academy
Andover, MA 01810

Phillips Exeter Academy
20 Main Street
Exeter, NH 03833

Pioneer Valley Rowing
Association
72 Reservation Road
Suderland, MA 01375

Pomfret School Crew
Pomfret School
Pomfret, CT 06258

Porcellian Boat Club
PO Box 306
Exeter, NH 03833

Quinsigamond Rowing Association,
Inc.
PO Box 254
Worcester, MA 01613-0254

Radcliffe Crew
Harvard Athletic Department
60 John F. Kennedy Street
Cambridge, MA 02138

Rensselaer Crew Club
Box 17
Rensselaer Student Union
15th and Sage
Troy, NY 12180

Riverfront Recapture, Inc.
One Hartford Square West
Suite 104
Hartford, CT 06106

Riverside Boat Club
769 Memorial Drive
Cambridge, MA 02139

Rochester Institute of Technology
   Crew
RIT Athletics
51 Lomb Memorial Drive
Rochester, NY 14623

Rochester Rowing Club
7 Orchard Street
North Chili, NY 14514

Roger Williams University Crew
Head Crew Coach
One Old Ferry Road
Bristol, RI 02809

Rome Area Chamber of Commerce
139 W. Dominck St.
Rome, NY 13440

Row as One Institute, Inc.
421 High Street
Westwood, MA 02090

Rude & Smooth Boat Club
46 East 91st Street
New York, NY 10028

Sagamore Rowing Association
PO Box 453
Glenwood Landing, NY 11547

Saint Mark's Boat Club
St. Mark's School
Southborough, MA 01772

Salisbury Boat Club
Emmons Lane
Canaan, CT 06018

Sarah Lawrence College
1 Meade Way
Bronxville, NY 10708

Saratoga Rowing Association
PO Box 750
Saratogo Springs, NY 12866

Saratoga Springs Rowing Club, Inc.
PO Box 1132
Saratoga Springs, NY 12866

Saugatuck Rowing Association
PO Box 3083
Saugatuck Station
Westport, CT 06680

Shimma Rowing Club
One Rockefeller plaza
New York, NY 10020

Shrewsbury High School Rowing
Shrewsbury High School
45 Oak Street
Shrewsbury, MA 01545

Simmons College Crew
300 The Fenway
Boston, MA 02115

Simsbury High School Crew
152 Tariffville Road
Tariffville, CT 06081

Skidmore College Crew
Saratoga Springs, NY 12866

Smith College Crew
Ainsworth Gym
Smith College
Northampton, MA 01063

South Kent Crew
South Kent School
South Kent, CT 06785

Spackenkill Rowing Club
30 Cathy Road
Poughkeepsie, NY 12603

Sparhawk Sculling School
222 Porters Point Road
Colchester, VT 05446

Springfield College Crew
263 Alden Street
Box 425
Woods Hall
Springfield, MA 01109

Squamscott Scullers
371 Washington Road
Rye, NH 03870

St. Anselm College Crew
100 St. Anselm Drive, Box 308
Manchester, NH 03102-1310

St. Anthony's Crew, Inc.
St. Anthony's High School
Library C – Session 275
Wolf Hill Road
South Huntington, NY 11747-1394

St. John's High School
378 Main Street
Shrewsbury, MA 01545

St. John's University Crew
Union Turnpike and Utopia Parkway
Jamaica, NY 11432

St. Lawrence Rowing Club
St. Lawrence University Crew Coach
CMR #2262
Canton, NY 13617

St. Paul's School Crew
St. Paul's School
Concord, NH 03301

Star and Crescent Boat Club
c/o Union College Athletic Department
Schenectady, NY 12308

Stonington High School Rowing
   Club
8 Godfrey Street
Mystic, CT 06355

Style Driven Rowing Club
145 Pickney Street, #134
Boston, MA 02114

Syracuse Alumni Rowing
   Association
PO Box 7202
Syracuse, NY 13261

Syracuse Chargers Rowing Club
409 Bronson Road
Syracuse, NY 13219

Syracuse University
Manley Field House
Syracuse, NY 13210

Syracuse University Men's Crew
Syracuse University Boathouse
Longbranch Road
Liverpool, NY 13090

Syracuse University Varsity
   Rowing
Archbold Gym Crew Room
Syracuse, NY 13244

Tabor Academy
Tabor Academy Athletic Office
Marion, MA 02738

Thames River Sculls
800 Pequot Avenue
New London, MA 06320

To the Water, Ltd.
75 Federal Street, Suite 1405
Boston, MA 02110

Town of Groton Boat Club
45 Fort Hill Road
Fairfield, CT 06430

Trinity College Crew
Ferris Athletic Center
Hartford, CT 06106

Triton Rowing Club
9 Lenape Drive
Montville, NJ 07045

Tufts University Crew
Cousens Gym
36 Sawyer Avenue
Medford, MA 02155

Turkey Pond Rowing Club
PO Box 719
Manchester, NH 03105

The Tuxedo Rowing Club
50 East Orchard Street
Allendale, NY 07401

U.S. Coast Guard Academy Crew
U.S. Coast Guard Academy
New London, CT 06320

U.S. Merchant Marine Academy Crew
U.S. Merchant Marine Academy
Kings Point, NY 11024

U.S. Military Academy Crew
Department of ElecEngr & Compsci
USMA
West Point, NY 10996

Union Boat Club
Rowing Committee
144 Chestnut Street
Boston, MA 02108

Union College Rowing Association
Union College Athletic Department
Schenectady, NY 12308

United Sports Association Rowing Club
395 East Putnam Avenue
Cos Cob, CT 06807

University at Albany
Campus Center 116
1400 Washington Avenue
Albany, NY 12222

University of Connecticut Crew Club
2095 Hillside Road, #U-78
Storrs, CT 06268

University of Connecticut Men's
   Crew
PO Box 762
Storrs, CT 06268

University of Massachusetts Men's
   Crew
416 Student Union Building
University of Massachusetts
Amherst, MA 01003

University of Massachusetts
   Women's Crew
230 Boyden Building
Amherst, MA 01003

University of Massachusetts – Lowell
Department of Athletics
1 University Avenue
Lowell, MA 01854

University of New Hampshire Crew
Whitteman Center
Durham, NH 03824

University of Rhode Island Crew
3 Kearney Road, Suite #1
Kingston, RI 02881

University of Rhode Island Rowing
   Association
Recreation Office Tootell Center, URI
Kingston, RI 02881

University of Rochester
River Campus Sports Complex - 201
Alumni Gym
Rochester, NY 14627

University of Vermont Crew Team
Geology Department
University of Vermont
Burlington, VT 05405

Vassar College
Box 259
124 Raymond Avenue
Poughkeepsie, NY 12604

Warren Rowing Club
245 East 63rd Street
Apt 1516
New York, NY 10021

Water Sports Center
41 Wolfpit Avenue, #3K
Norwalk, CT 06851

Wellesley College Crew
Wellesley College/PERA
Wellesley, MA 02181

Wesleyan Alumni Rowing Club
Freeman Athletic Center
Wesleyan University
Middletown, CT 06459

Wesleyan University
Freeman Athletic Center
161 Cross Street
Middletown, CT 06457

West Side Rowing Club
Foot of Porter Avenue
Buffalo, NY 14202

Whaling City Rowing Club
57 Arnold Street
New Bedford, MA 02740

Wide Load Boat Club
285 Babcock Street
Boston, MA 02215

Williams College Boat Club
PO Box 411
Williams College
Williamstown, MA 01267

Winsor School
Pilgrim Road
Boston, MA 02215

Worcester Polytechnic Rowing
   Association
Worcester Polytechnic Institute
100 Institute Road
Worcester, MA 01609

Worcester Public High Schools
12 Winter Street
Medford, MA 02155

Worcester Rowing Association
20 Old Colony Road
Shrewsbury, MA 01545

Worcester State Crew
Student Center
486 Chandler Street
Worcester, MA 01602

Yale University Boat Club and Crew
PO Box 208216
New Haven, CT 06520

Yankee Rowing Club
PO Box 377
Amherst, MA 01004

87 Gold Rowing Club
72 Little Nahant Road
Nahant, MA 01908

1980 Rowing Club
204 Larch Road
Cambridge, MA 02138

1992 Olympic Rowing Club - Death
  Warmed Over
36 Wareland Road.
Wellesley, MA 02181

MID-ATLANTIC

Alexandria Crew Boosters Club
PO Box 3202
Alexandria, VA 22302

Allegheny River Rowing
548 Penn Street
Verona, PA 15147

American Express Rowing Association
SE Corner 16th & JFK
Philadelphia, PA 19102

American Rowing Association
16 Aldwyn Lane
Villanova, PA 19085

Annapolis Rowing Club
Box 4191
Annapolis, MD 21403

Atlantic City High School
112 25th Street
Brigantine, NJ 08203

Atlantic County Rowing Association
PO Box 802
Northfield, NJ 08225

Atlantic Ten Conference
2 Penn Ctr. Plaza, Ste. 1410
Philadelphia, PA 19102

Bachelors Barge Club
6 Boathouse Road
Philadelphia, PA 19103

Back Bay Viking Rowing Club
2 South Rosborough Avenue
Ventnor, NY 08406

Baltimore Rowing Club
3301 Waterview Ave
Baltimore, MD 21218

B-CC Crew Boosters, Inc.
4525 N. Chelsea Lane
Betheda, MD 20814

Better Motion
829 Taney Street
Philadelphia, PA 19130

BMA Boat Club
27 Western Avenue
Morristown, NJ 07960

Bonner Rowing Association
PO Box 72
Drexel Hill, PA 19026

Brigantine Rowing Club
1402 Sheridan Blvd.
Brigantine, NJ 08203

Brooke High Crew Parents
Brooke High School
Cross Creek Road
Wellsburg, WV 26070

Bryn Mawr College
Schwartz Gym
Bryn Mawr, PA 19010

Bucknell University Rowing Club
Bucknell University
Department of Athletics
Lewisburg, PA 17837

Bucknell University Women's Crew
Bucknell University Crew
Department of Athletics
Lewisburg, PA 17837

Camden Country Rowing Foundation
PO Box 1346
Camden, NJ 08105

Camp Dimension
641 East Shawmont Avenue
Philadelphia, PA 19128

CAMSIS Boat Club, Inc.
721 North Overlook Drive
Alexandria, VA 22305

Capital Rowing Club, Inc.
PO Box 66211
Washington, DC 20035-6211

Carlow College Crew Club
Director of Athletics/Crew Coach
3333 Fifth Avenue
Pittsburgh, PA 15213

Carnegie Lake Rowing Association
PO Box 330
Princeton, NJ 08540

Carnegie Mellon Univ. Rowing Club
607 Greenfield Avenue
2nd Floor, Front Apt.
Pittsburgh, PA 15207

The Catholic University of America
Office of Campus Programs
200 University Ctr W
Washington, DC 20064

Charleston Rowing Club
University of Charleston
Charleston, WV 25304

Chester River Rowing Club
PO Box 616
Chestertown, MD 21620

College Boat Club
University of Pennsylvania
235 S. 33rd Street
Philadelphia, PA 19104

Combined Cathedral Crew
1054 31st Street NW, Suite 300
Washington, DC 20007

Compote Rowing Association
4045 Ridge Avenue
Philadelphia, PA 19130

Conestoga High School Crew Club
Conestoga High School
Irish Road
Berwyn, PA 19312

Crescent Boat Club
#5 Boathouse Row
Kelly Drive
Philadelphia, PA 19130

Dad Vail Rowing Association
1812 Webster Lane
Ambler, PA 19104

D.C. Strokes
PO Box 53019
Washington, DC 20009

Drexel University
3141 Chestnut Street
Philadelphia, PA 19104

East Arm Rowing Club
691 Birchwood Avenue
Wyckoff, NJ 07481-1006

Ellis School
6425 Fifth Avenue
Pittsburgh, PA 15206

Fairmount Rowing Association
#2 Boathouse Row
Kelly Drive
Philadelphia, PA 19130

Fairfax Crew Association – Woodson
   Chapter
PO Box 2881
Fairfax, VA 22031

Father Judge High School
1008 Huntington Pike
Huntington Valley, PA 19006

Fort Hunt High School
PO Box 6211
Alexandria, VA 22306

Fox Chapel Crew Club
501 Guyasuta Road
Pittsburgh, PA 15215

Franklin & Marshall College
171 East Main St.
Mountville, PA 17554

Gar-Field Crew Booster Club
625 Bethlehem Park
Ambler, PA 19002

George Mason University Crew
Room 251, Student Union 1
4400 University Drive
Fairfax, VA 22030

George Washington University Crew
Department of Intercollegiate
  Athletics
Smith Street
Washington, DC 20056

George Washington University
GWU Athletics—Men's Crew
600 22nd Street NW
Washington, DC 20052

George Washington University
GWU Athletics—Women's Crew
600 22nd Street NW
Washington, DC 20052

Georgetown Day School Crew Club
5032 Upton Street, NW
Washington, DC 20016

Georgetown University Rowing
  Association
Department of Athletics
McDonough Arena
Washington, DC, 20057

Georgetown Visitation Prep School
  Crew
764 College Parkway
Rockville, MD 20850

Gonzaga College High School Crew
1301 Vacation Lane
Arlington, VA 22207

Hampton Roads Rowing Club
6011 Westwood Terrace
Norfolk, VA 23508

Haverford School
450 Lancaster Avenue
Haverford, PA 19041

Holy Spirit High School Crew
California & New Road
Absecon, NJ 08201

Hoya Boat Club
10115 Glenmere Road
Fairfax, VA 22032

Hun School of Princeton Crew
176 Edgerstoune Road
Princeton, NJ 08542

Hylton Crew Boosters Club, Inc.
PO Box 2558
Woodbridge, VA 22193

Interscholastic Sculling Association
6508 Rivington Road
Springfield, VA 22152

J. E. B. Stuart High School Crew
  Boosters
5905 Dawes Avenue
Alexandria, VA 22312

Johns Hopkins Crew
White Athletic Center
Homewood
Johns Hopkins University
Baltimore, MD 21218

Johns Hopkins University Crew
3400 North Charles Street
Department of Athletics
Baltimore, MD 21218

La Salle University Crew
20th & Olney Avenue
Philadelphia, PA 19141

La Salle University Men's Crew
1900 West Olney Avenue
Philadelphia, PA 19141

La Salle University Women's Crew
1900 West Olney Avenue
Philadelphia, PA 19141

La Salle College High School Crew
8605 Cheltenham Avenue
Wyndmoor, PA 19038

Lafayette College Crew Club
PO Box 9407
Easton, PA 18042

Lehigh University Crew Club
39 University Drive
Box L12
Bethlehem, PA 18015

Loyola College Crew Club
4501 North Charles Street
Baltimore, MD 21210

Loyola College Rowing Club –
  Maryland
Loyola College Crew Club
8518 Hillspring Drive
Lutherville, MD 21093

Malta Boat Club
463 Lombardy Road
Drexel Hill, PA 19026

Malvern Preparatory School
840 Heatherstone Drive
Berwyn, PA 19312

Mary Washington Crew Club
Box 3774, College Station
Fredericksburg, VA 22401

McClean Crew Club
7322 Ronald Street
Falls Church, VA 22046

Mercyhurst College Crew
501 E. 38th Street
Erie, PA 16546

Mercyhurst Prep School Crew
538 East Grandview Blvd.
Erie, PA 16504

Middle States Rowing Association
712 Monument Road
Malvern, PA 19355

Misery Bay Rowing Club
PO Box 904
Erie, PA 16505

Monongahela Rowing Association
1837 Listravia Avenue
Morgantown, WV 26505

Mt. Lebanon High School Crew Club
153 Main Entrance Drive
Pittsburgh, PA 15228

National Women's Rowing Association
512 West Sedgewick
Philadelphia, PA 19119

National Rowing Foundation
PO Box 6030
Arlington, VA 22206

Navesink River Rowing Club
PO Box 6153
Fair Haven, NJ 07704

Nereid Boat Club
4 Briarwood Court
Ramsey, NJ 07446

North Allegheny Rowing Association
134 Burns Road
New Brighton, PA 15066

North Catholic High School
300 Seminole Avenue
Pittsburgh, PA 15237

Northeast Catholic Crew
#1 Willig
Philadelphia, PA 19125

Northeastern Women's Rowing
  Association
1409 Orchid Court
Virginia Beach, VA 23454

Northern Virginia Rowing
  Association
4220 25th Street
Arlington, VA 22207

Northern Virginia Scholastic Rowing
  Association
c/o NVSRA, PO Box 23042
Alexandria, VA 22304

Oakland Catholic High School Crew
6830 Juniata Place
Pittsburgh, PA 15208

OAR – Organization of Allderdice
  Rowing
901 Hastings Street
Pittsburgh, PA 15217

Occoquan Boat Club
9527 Blackburn Drive
Burke, VA 22015

Ocean City Rowing and Athletic
  Association
520 Bay Avenue
PO Box 880
Ocean City, NJ 08226

Ohio Valley Rowing Club
PO Box 2313
Parkersburg, WV 26102

Old Dominion Boat Club
ODU Rowing Club
HEPE Building, Room 192
Norfolk, VA 23529

Oneida Boat Club Rowing Association
3 York Street
Burlington, NJ 08016

Patriot Crew Booster
PO Box 3536
Parkersburg, WV 26101

Peddie School
South Main Street, PO Box A
Hightstown, NJ 08520

Penn A.C. Rowing Association
1503 Firethorne Road
Wyndmoor, PA 19038

Penn Academy Rowing Association
5838 North 4th Street
Philadelphia, PA 19120

Penn State Crew
302 Rec Hall
University Park, PA 16802

Philadelphia Frostbite Regatta
219 Summit Trace Road
Langhorne, PA 19047

Philadelphia Girls Rowing Club
5035 Pulaski Avenue
Philadelphia, PA 19144

Philadelphia Rowing Program for
   Disabled
#4 Boathouse Road
Kelly Drive
Philadelphia, PA 19130

Pittsburgh Mercy Foundation
The Mercy Foundation
1709 Boulevard of the Allies
Pittsburgh, PA 15219

Port Events, Inc.
355 Crawfird Street, Suite 101
Portsmouth, VA 23704

Potomac Boat Club
3530 Water Street NW
Washington, DC 20007

Potomac Crew Club
PO Box 924
c/o Potomac Crew
Dumfries, VA 22026

Potomac River Development Center
1517 North Taylor Street
Arlington, VA 22207

Potomac Sculling, Inc.
4883 Old Dominion Drive
Arlington, VA 22207-2744

Prince William Crew Association
PO Box 2393
Woodbridge, VA 22193

Prince William Rowing Club
12471 Dillingham Square
Box 150
Woodbridge, VA 22192

Princeton Training Center
177 Nassau
Princeton, NJ 08540

Princeton University Rowing
   Association
Princeton University Crew
Department of Athletics
Box 71
Princeton, NJ 08544

Princeton University Women's Crew
Dillon Gym
Princeton University
Princeton, NJ 08540

Raritan Valley Rowing Association
PO Box 1149
Piscataway, NJ 08845

R. C. Williams High School Crew
3330 King Street
Alexandria, VA 22302

Red and White Rowing
PO Box 4291
Parkersburg, WV 26104-4291

Regatta Sports
16 West River Road
Rumson, NJ 07760

Rivanna Rowing Club, Inc.
PO Box 5797
Charlottesville, VA 22905

Rude and Smooth Boat Club
19 Wertsville Road
Neshanic, NJ 08853

Rutgers University Crew
83 Rockafeller Road
Piscataway, NJ 08854

Rutgers University Women's Crew
L. Brown Athletic Center
83 Rockefeller Road
Piscataway, NJ 08854

Scholastic Rowing Association of
   America
214 Glendalough Road
Erdenheim, PA 19046

Schuylkill River Development
  Council
2314 South Street
Philadelphia, PA 19146

Schuylkill Navy
7001 Wayne Avenue
Upper Darby, PA 19082

Schuylkill Navy of Philadelphia
Boathouse Row
#4 Kelly Drive
Philadelphia, PA 19130

Sidwell Friends School Rowing Club
3902 Rosemary Street
Chevy Chase, MD 20815

Southern Intercollegiate Rowing
  Association
2111 Kanawha Avenue SE
Charleston, WV 25304

Special Olympics Rowing Program
2826 Pickertown
Warrington, PA 18976

St. Andrew's School Crew
Middletown DE 19807

St. John's College Rowing Club
Box 2800
Annapolis, MD 21404

St. Joseph Preparatory School
534 W. Springfield Ave.
Philadelphia, PA 19118

Steel City Rowing
157 James Street
Verona, PA 15147

Stockton State College Crew
Stockton State College
Pomona, NJ 08240

Swan Creek Rowing Club
PO Box 153
Lambertville, NJ 08530

Temple University Crew
418 Cedarwood Lane
Philadelphia, PA 19027

Thomas Jefferson H.S. Crew Booster
Thomas Jefferson High School
  6520Braddock Road
Alexandria, VA 22132

Thompson Boat Center
2900 Virginia Avenue, NW
Washington, DC 20037

Three Rivers Rowing Association
300 Waterfront Drive
Pittsburgh, PA 15222

Tiber Creek Rowing Club
6705 Queens Chapel Road
University Park, MD 20782

Towson University Crew Club
Towson University
Burdick Hall, Rm. 150
Towson, MD 21252

Trinity College Crew
Trinity College
125 Michigan Avenue
Washington, DC 20017

Triton Boat Club
24 Elmwood Avenue
Belleville, NJ 07109

Undine Barge Club
6470 Drexel Road
Philadelphia, PA 19151-2401

University Barge Club of
  Philadelphia
108 Fisher Road
Jenkintown, PA 19046

University of Delaware
Delaware Field House
Newark, DE 19716

University of Maryland/UMBC Crew
Baltimore, MD 21228

University of Pennsylvania Crew
235 South 33rd Street
Philadelphia, PA 19104

University of Virginia Rowing Assoc.
PO Box 3785
University Hall
Charlottesville, VA 22903

University of Virginia Women's Crew
PO Box 3785
University Hall
Charlottesville, VA 22903

University of Baltimore Rowing
   Association
Office of Student Activities
Charles Street & Mount Royal
   Avenue
Baltimore, MD 21211

University of Delaware
Delaware Fieldhouse
Newark, DE 19716

Upper Marion Boat Club
Competitive & Rec. Rowing
738 Hidden Valley Road
King of Prussia, PA 19406

Upper St. Clair H.S. Crew Club
1825 McLaughlin Run Road
Upper St. Clair, PA 15241

U.S. Dragon Boat Association
456 Militia Hill Road
Southampton, PA 18966

U.S. Naval Academy Crew
U.S. Naval Academy
Annapolis, MD 21402

U.S. Naval Academy Men's Crew
566 Brownson Road
USNA, NAAA
Annapolis, MD 21402

U.S. Naval Academy Women's
   Crew
566 Brownson Road
USNA, NAAA
Annapolis, MD 21402

Vesper Boat Club
10 Kelly Drive
Philadelphia, PA 19130

Viking Rowing Club
121 North Oxford Avenue
Ventnor, NY 08406

Viking Rowing Foundation
2006 Cornwall Avenue
Northfield, NJ 08225

Villanova University Crew
800 Lancaster Avenue
Villanova, PA 19085

The Virginia Boat Club
PO Box 26051
Richmond, VA 23260-6051

Walt Whitman Crew Boosters
5002 Rockmere Ct.
Bethesda, MD 20816

Warren Rowing Club
3015 Earlysville Road
Earlysville, VA 22396

Washington & Lee High School Crew
1300 North Quincy Street
Arlington, VA 22201

Washington College Crew
Washington College
Chestertown, MD 21620

West Catholic Rowing Association
2624 South Shields Street
Philadelphia, PA 19142

West River Rowing Club
2733 Fennel Road
Edgewater, MD 21037

West Potomac H.S. Crew
WP Crew Boosters
PO Box 6211
Alexandria, VA 22306

West Springfield H.S. Crew Boosters
   Club
West Springfield Crew
Box 2558
Woodbridge, VA 22193

Wharton Business School Rowing
   Association
111 Vance Hall
University of Pennsylvania
Philadelphia, PA 19104

Wildcat Rowing Association
Villanova University
800 Lancaster Avenue
Villanova, PA 19085

Wilkes University Crew Club
Purchasing Office
PO Box 111
Wilkes-Barre, PA 18766

William & Mary Rowing Club
Department of Recreation Sports
Box 2
Williamsburg, VA 23187

Wilmington Rowing Club
2213 Nassau Drive
Wilmington, DE 19810

Wilmington Youth Rowing Association
206 Holland Drive
Wilmington, DE 19803

Winchester Thurston School
555 Morewood Avenue
Pittsburgh, PA 15213

Woodbridge Crew, Inc.
PO Box 405
Occoquan, VA 22125

Yale Old Fellows Rowing
   Association
1938 Pine Street
Philadelphia, PA 19103

Yorktown High School Crew
5201 North 28th Street
Arlington, VA 22207

YMCA Three Rivers Rowing Association
3334 Benden Drive
Murrysville, PA 15668

MIDWEST

Ann Arbor Rowing Club
PO Box 3128
Ann Arbor, MI 48106

Austin Rowing Club
PO Box 1741
Austin, TX 78767

Bay Area Club of Houston
PO Box 580374
Houston, TX 77258

Bay City Rowing Club
400 W. Lafayette
Bay City, MI 48706

Camp Randall Rowing Club
851 East Gorham
Madison, WI 53703

Chicago Aquatic Center
400 East Randolph Street #2527
Chicago, IL 60601

Chicago River Rowing Association
400 E. Randolph Street, Suite 2415
Chicago, IL 60601

Chicago River Rowing Club
Membership Chairman
195 N. Harbor Drive, #2005
Chicago, IL 60601

Cincinnati Rowing Club
15 West Central Parkway
Cincinnati, OH 45202

Creighton University Crew
Student Board of Governors
Omaha, NE 68178

CSB/SJU Rowing Club
St. Johns University
PO Box 1869
Collegeville, MN 56321

Culver Miltary/Girls Academy Crew
Culver Military Academy
PO Box 2
Culver, IN 46511

Dallas Rowing Club
3217 Townsend Drive
Dallas, TX 75229

Des Moines Rowing Club
PO Box 872
Des Moines, IA 50304

Detroit Boat Club
185 Earl Ct.
Grosse Pointe Farms, MI 48236

Dublin High School Crew
PO Box 764
Dublin, OH 43017

Duluth Rowing Club
PO Box 655
Duluth, MN 55802

Ecorse Rowing Club
PO Box 29055
Ecorse, MI 48229-0055

Fort Forth Rowing Club, Inc.
3620 Manderly Place
Fort Worth, TX 76109

Friends of Detroit Rowing
6383 Vernmoor
Troy, MI 48098

Grand Rapids Rowing Club
PO box 3189
Grand Rapids, MI 49501

Grand Valley Rowing Club
9979 Bend Drive
Jenison, MI 49428

Grand Valley Crew
1 Kirkhof Center
Campus Drive
Allendale, MI 49401

Greater Columbus Rowing
  Association
PO Box 218131
Columbus, OH 43221

Greater Dayton Rowing Association
130 Wisteria Drive
Dayton, OH 45419

Gross Ile Rowing Club
PO Box 385
Grosse Ile, MI 48138

Ignatius Chicago Rowing
  Associates, Inc.
303 W. Madison Street, #800
Chicago, IL 60606

Illinois River Oarsmen
1227 E. Cox
Peoria Heights, IL 61614

Indiana Rowing Association
c/o City Fitness Club 516 South Main
Elkhart, IN 46516

Indianapolis Boat Club
PO Box 30339
Indianapolis, IN 46230

Indianapolis Rowing Center
PO Box 53223
Indianapolis, IN 46253

Iowa Rowing Association
PO Box 1463
Kansas State University
Manhattan, KS 66503-7579

Kansas City Rowing Club
PO Box 025635
Kansas City, MO 64102

Kansas State Rowing Association
PO Box 1463
Kansas State University
Manhattan, KS 66503-7579

Kansas State Women's Rowing
Department of Athletics – Women's
  Rowing
12 Ahearn Fieldhouse
Manhattan, KS 66502-3355

Kansas University Crew
213 Strong Hall
University of Kansas
Lawrence, KS 66045

Lansing Oar & Paddle Club
726 Touraine
E. Lansing, MI 48823

L'Aviron
PO Box 50320
Austin, TX 78763

Lincoln Park Boat Club
c/o Rowing Directory
4510 N. Grenview
Chicago, IL 60640

Loyola Academy Rowing Association
1661 Everett Road
Lake Forest, IL 60045

Macalester College Crew
1600 Grand Avenue
St. Paul, MN 55105

Macomb-YMCA Rowing Program
36691 Jefferson
Mt. Clemens, MI 48045

Manley Career Academy Crew
5208 S. Woodlawn Avenue, Apt. #3
Chicago, IL 60615

Marietta College Rowing Association
Box C-65
Marietta College
Marietta, OH 45750

Marquette University Crew
Org. Resource Center, AMU 140
PO Box 1881
Milwaukee, WI 53201

Mendota Rowing Club
PO Box 646
Madison, WI 53701

Michigan Rowing Association
1395 Coler Road
Ann Arbor, MI 48104

Michigan State University Crew
205 I.M. Sports West
Michigan State University
East Lansing, MI 48824

Michigan State University Men's Crew
312-A jenison Field House
E. Lansing, MI 48824

Milwaukee Rowing Club
3354 N. Gordon Pl.
Milwaukee, WI 53212-1810

Minneapolis Rowing Club
PO Box 583102
Minneapolis, MN 55458

Minnesota Boat Club
382 Winslow Avenue
St. Paul, MN 55107

Minnesota Sculls
7693 Babcock Tr.
Inver Grove Heights, MN 55077

Nebraska University Crew
1000 North 16th Street
Lincoln, NE 68588

North Suburban Crew, Inc.
2949 Harrison Street
Evanston, IL 60201

Northwestern University Crew
1732 N. Humbolt Blvd.
Chicago, IL 60647

Nortre Dame Rowing Club
PO Box 55
Notre Dame, IN 46556

Ohio Athletic Club
PO Box 2033
Columbus, OH 43216-2033

Ohio State Men's Crew Club
Ohio State University Men's Crew
Drake Union, 1849 Cannon Dr.
Columbus, OH 43210-1208

Ohio State University Crew
223 West 8th Avenue
Columbus, OH 43102

Ohio State University Women's Crew
Ohio Stadium SW-1950 Cannon Drive
Columbus, Ohio 43210

Oklahoma City Rowing Club
PO Box 20156
Oklahoma City, OK 73156

Pagosa Rowing Club
PO Box 3730
Pagosa Springs, CO 81147

Purdue Crew Club
1089 Recreational Gymnasium
Purdue University
West Lafayette, IN 47907

Quad City Rowing Association
PO Box 69
Moline, IL 61265

Rice Rowing Club
Office of Student Organization MS 526
PO box 1892
Houston, TX 77251-1892.

Rocky Mountain Rowing Center
c/o The Managers, Inc.
PO Box 647
Frisco, CO 80443

Rocky Mountain Rowing Club
Membership Coordinator
PO Box 6242
Denver, CO 80206

Rowing Club of the Woodlands
PO Box 8554
The Woodlands, TX 77387

Rowing Dock
PO Box 685162
Austin, TX 78768

Sooner Rowing Association
4400 One Williams Center
Tulsa, OK 74172

South Bend Scullers, Inc.
3431 South Twylckenham
South Bend, IN 46614

Sports Development Group
6147 Oak Street
Kansas City, MO 64113

St. Louis Rowing Club
PO Box 411094
St. Louis, MO 63141

St. Mary's Prep Rowing
3535 Indian Trail
Orchard Lake, MI 48324

Texas Crew, Recreational Sports
University of Texas
Gregory Gymnasium 33
Austin, TX 78712

Toledo Rowing Club
287 East Manhattan Blvd.
Oregon, OH 43608

Toledo Rowing Association
The Monro Steel Company
8201 West Central Avenue
Toledo, OH 43617

Topeka Rowing Association
4336 SE 25th Street
Terrace
Topeka, KS 66605

University of Chicago
c/o Sports Club Office
Bartlett Gym, 5640
S. University Avenue
Chicago, IL 60637

University of Chicago Women's Crew
400 East Randolph Street
#2527
Chicago, IL 60601

University of Cincinnati Rowing
   Club
221 Tangeman University Center,
   Loc 136
Cincinnati, OH 44107

University of Dayton Rowing Club
301 Oakwood Avenue
Dayton, OH 45409

University of Iowa Women's Crew
248 Carver Hawkeye Arena
Iowa City, IA 52242

University of Kansas Women's Rowing
Allen Fieldhouse, Room 227
Lawrence, KS 66045

University of Michigan Rowing Club
North Campus Recreation Building
University of Michigan
Ann Arbor, MI 48109

University of Michigan Women's Crew
Athletic Department
1000 South State Street
Ann Arbor, MI 48109

University of Minnesota
222 Second Street NE
Minneapolis, MN 55413

University of Minnesota Men's Crew
221 Cooke Hall
1900 University Avenue SE
Minneapolis, MN 55455

University of Minnesota Women's
   Crew
238 Bierman Building
516 15th Avenue SE
Minneapolis, MN 55455

University of Nebraska Crew Club
PO Box 880232
55 Campus Rec
Lincoln, NE 68588-0232

University of Notre Dame Women's
   Rowing
Rockne Memorial
Notre Dame, IN 46556

University of Texas Women's Crew
718 Bellmont Hall
Austin, TX 78746

University of Wisconsin Crew
1440 Monroe Street
Madison, WI 53706

Upper Arlington Crew Club
PO Box 211086
Columbus, OH 44199

Washington University Crew Club
One Brookings Drive Box 1067
St. Louis, MO 63130

Waterloo Rowing Club
225 Commercial Street
Waterloo, PA 50701

Wayne State University Crew
Div. of Health and Physical
   Education
Wayne State University
Detroit, MI 48202

Western Reserve Rowing Association
12700 Lake Ave #2112
Lakewood, OH 44107

Western Reserve Rowing
   Foundation
PO Box 991241
Cleveland, OH 44199

Wichita Rowing Association
335 West Lewis
Wichita, KS 67202

Wichita State University Crew
Heskett Center
1845 North Fairmount
Box 126
Wichita, KS 67260

Wyndotte Boat Club
PO Box 341
Wyndotte, MI 48192

Xavier University Crew
5695 Valley Forge Drive
Fairfield, OH 45014

SOUTHEAST

Academia Cubana de Remo Crew
PO Box 592812
Miami, FL 33159

AFG Rowing Club
1000 University Blvd. d-6
Kingsport, TN 37660

Alabama Crew Team
PO Box 866964
Tuscaloosa, AL 35486

American Barge Club
1321 NW 14th Street
Suite 214
Miami, FL 33136

Atlanta Junior Rowing Association
12235 Winding Oak Terrace
Alpharetta, GA 30005

Atlanta Rowing Club
Dan Look
8351 Roswell Road, Ste. 103
Atlanta, GA 30350

Augusta Port Authority
PO Box 2084
Augusta, GA 30903

Augusta Rowing Club
101 Riverfront Dr
Augusta, GA 30901

Augusta Sculling Center
One Seventh Street, Unit 1301
Augusta, GA 30901

Augusta State University Rowing
Student Activities
2500 Walton Way
Augusta, GA 30904

Barry University
Barry University Rowing 430
   Fernwood Rd
Key Biscayne, FL 33149-1834

Benedictine Military School
PO box 1960
Bluffton, SC 29910

Bulldog Rowing Club
701 Oxford
Houston, TX 77007

Cape Fear Academy Crew
813 Swift Wind Pl.
Wilmington, NC 28405

Cape Fear River Rowing
PO Box 1586
Wilmington, NC 28401

Catawaba Yacht Club
118 E. Kingston Avenue
Charlotte, NC 28203

Centenary College Crew Team
2662 Barbara Street
Bossier City, LA 71112

Charleston Regatta
PO Box 32338
Charleston, SC 29417-2338

Chattanooga Rowing
First Tennessee Building 701 Market
   Street. Ste 1500
Chatanooga, TN 37402

The Citadel Crew
Department of Physical Education
Charleston, SC 29409

Cincinnati Community Rowing Club
1226 Riverview Place
Covington, KY 41011

Clemson Crew
Women's Rowing
PO Box 31
Clemson, SC 29633

Crew Boosters of Winter Park, Inc.
PO Box 1003
Winter Park, FL 32789

Davidson College Crew Club
PO Box 1750
Davidson, NC 28036

Duke Men's Crew
105 Card Gym, Box 90548
Durham, NC 27708

Duke University Women's Rowing
Head Coach
118 Cameron Stadium
Durham, NC 27708

Edgewater High School Crew
1324 Indiana Avenue
Longwood, FL 32750

Florida Institute of Technology Crew
c/o Florida Tech.
150 W. University Blvd.
Melbourne, FL 32901

Florida I.R.A.
FL Tech- Dept of Athletics
150 W. University Blvd.
Melbourne, FL 32901

Florida Rowing Association
524 NW 32nd Ave.
Gainesville, FL 32609

Furman University Crew
PO Box 28537
3300 Poinsett Hwy.
Greenville, SC 29613

Georgia Tech Crew
350285 GA Tech Station
Atlanta, GA 30332

Governor's Council
Physical Fitness & Sports
Office of the Governor
The Capitol
Tallahassee, FL 32301

Greater Louisville Rowing
Foundation, Inc.
1307 Navajo Court
Louisville, KY 40207

Halifax Rowing Association, Inc.
313 S. Pametto Ave.
Daytona Beach, FL 32239

Harbor City Rowing Club
2900 Riverview Drive
Melbourne, FL 32901

Hollywood Rowing Club
PO Box 030071
Ft. Lauderdale, FL 33303

Island Rowing Club, Inc.
9570 South Tropical Trail
Merritt Island, FL 32952

Jacksonville Episcopal High School
Crew
4455 Atlantic Blvd.
Jacksonville, FL 32211

Jacksonville Rowing Club
PO Box 8741
Jacksonville, FL 32609

Knoxville Rowing Association
4313 Furen Road
Knoxville, TN 37901

Lake Brantley Rowing Association,
Inc.
PO Box 915653
Longwood, FL 32791

Lawrence Boat Club
3017 W. 8th Street
Lawrence, KS 66049

Leon High School Crew
PO Box 38154
Tallahassee, FL 32315

Lincoln Crew Boosters, Inc.
8067 Tennyson Drive
Tallahassee, FL 32308

Lookout Rowing Club
PO Box 11411
Chattanooga, TN 37401

Loyola University Crew
Box 1
6363 St. Charles Avenue
New Orleans, LA 70118

Margaret Currach Club, Ltd.
7712 Green Street
New Orleans, LA 70118

MAST Academy Rowing Club
3979 Rickenbacjer Causeway
Key Biscayne, FL 33149

The McCGPS
The McCallie School 500 Dodds Ave
Chattanooga, TN 37404

Melbourne High School Crew
PO Box 974
Melbourne, FL 32902

Memmian Rowing Club
31 McAlister Dr. #MR5090
New Orleans, LA 70118-5645

Miami Rowing Club
PO Box 593061
Miami, FL 33159

Miami Rowing and Watersports
Center
3832 Shipping Avenue
Miami, FL 33146

Montgomery Central Rowing and
Sculling
3318 Lexington Avenue
Montgomery, AL 36106

Naples Rowing Club
PO Box 2844
Naples, FL 34116

New Charleston Mosquito Fleet
184 E. Bay Street, Suite 201
Charleston, SC 29401

New Orleans Rowing Club
829 Baronne Street, Ste. 200
New Orleans, LA 70113

Northwestern St. University Rowing
Club
Rm 22 I.M. NSU Campus
Natchitoches, LA 71497

Oak Ridge Rowing Association
PO Box 4384
Oak Ridge, TN 37830

Orlando Area Rowing Society, Inc.
PO Box 71
Windermere, FL 34786

Orlando Rowing Club
PO Box 547802
Orlando, FL 32854

Palm Beach Rowing Association
1050 Powell Drive
Riviera Beach, FL 33404

Palm Beach Rowing Club
5403 Oliver Street North
Jacksonville, FL 32211

Palmetto Rowing Club
4 Brams Point Road
Hilton Head Island, SC 29926

Raleigh Oars Rowing Club – ROARS
PO Box 10864
Raleigh, NC 27605

Rocket City Rowing Club
2822 Lafayette Dr.
Huntsville, AL 35801

Rollins College Crew
1000 Holt Avenue – 2730
Winter Park, FL 32789

Sarasota Scullers Youth Rowing Program
2901 South Tamiami Trail
Sarasota, FL 34239

Sarasota Rowing Club
2631 Grand Cayman Street
Sarasota. FL 34231

Shane Watersports Center/Miami
Beach Rowing Club
6500 Indian Creek Drive
Miami Beach, FL 33141

South Orlando Rowing Association,
Inc.
PO Box 568782
Orlando, FL 32856-8782

Southern Intercollegiate Rowing
Association
2729 St. Augustine Trail
Marietta, GA 30067

Space Coast Crew Boosters
PO Box 372252
Satellite Beach, FL 32937

Sports Development Group
6147 Oak Street
Kansas City, MO 64113

St. Andrew Rowing Club, Inc.
PO Box 500065
Atlanta, GA 31150

St. John's Few Rowing Association
763 Egret Bluff Lane
Jacksonville, FL 32211

Staton College Prep Crew
1149 West 13th Street
Jacksonville, FL 32209

Tampa Rowing Club
PO Box 10102
Tampa, FL 33629

Treasure Coast Rowing Club
PO Box 1286
Palm City, FL 34991

Tulsa Rowing Club
715 W 21st
Tulsa, OK 74107

University of Alabama in Huntsville
Crew
University of Alabama
Huntsville, AL 35899

University of Central Florida
UCF- Dept of Athletics PO Box
163555
Orlando, FL 32816-3555

University of Georgia Rowing
201 Ramsey Student Ctr. for
Physical Activities
Athens, GA 30602

University of Miami Crew
Hecht Athletic Center
5821 San Amaro Drive
Coral Gables, FL 33146

University of North Carolina Crew
PO Box 2126
Chapel Hill, NC 27514

University of North Carolina Wilmington
c/o SGA 601 South College
Wilmington, NC 28403

University of Tennessee Rowing Club
2106 Andy Holt/Stuent Aquatic
Center
Knoxville, TN 37916

University of Tennessee Women's Rowing
117 Stokely Athletic Center
Knoxville, TN 37996-3110

UTC Rowing
UTC- EHLS Department
615 McCallie Avenue
Chattanooga, TN 37403

Vista Shores Rowing Crew
741 Robert E. Lee Blvd.
New Orleans, LA 70124

Washington University Crew Club
One Brookings Drive
Box 1067
St. Louis, MO 63130

Winter Park High School Crew
PO Box 1003
Winter Park, FL 32789

Wolf River Rowing Club
44 North Second Street, 9th Floor
Memphis, TN 38103

SOUTHWEST

ARCO Women's Olympic Training
Center
2800 Olympic Parkway
Chula Vista, CA 91915

Berkeley Crew, Inc.
235 San Carlos Avenue
El Cerrito, CA 94530

Berkeley Crew Club
1224 Oxford Street
Berkeley, CA 94709

Berkeley High School Women's
Crew
1152 Sutter Street
Berkeley, CA 94707

Berkeley Rowing Club
2817 Piedmont Avenue
Berkeley, CA 94705-2313

California Lightweight Crew
2630 Claremont Avenue
Berkeley, CA 94705

California Maritime Academy
Crew
200 Maritime Academy Drive
Vallejo, CA 94590

California Rowing Association
6682 Giannini Court
Castro Valley, CA 94552

California Rowing Club
2909 Glascock Street
Oakland, CA 94601

California Yacht Club
Steve Hathaway
431 W. 7th Street
Los Angeles, CA 90014

CSU Long Beach State Crew
312 St. Joseph Avenue
Long Beach, CA 90814

CSUS/LNRA/Capital Crew
CSUS Aquatic Center
1901 Hazel Avenue
Rancho Cordova, CA 95670

The Dirty Dozen
4 Commodore, #328
Emeryville, CA 94608

Golden Bear Rowing Association
2415 College Avenue, #14
Berkeley, CA 94704

Graham Recreational Rowers
PO Box 2278
Orange, CA 92669

Humboldt Bay Rowing Association
PO Box 750
Trinidad, CA 95570

Humboldt State University
Dept. of Athletics–Rowing
Arcata, CA 95521

Kent Mitchell Rowing Club
550 Hamilton Avenue, Suite 230
Palo Alto, CA 94031

Ketos Whale Boat Club
2906 San Bruno Ave, #2
San Francisco, CA 94134

Lake Merritt Rowing Club
PO Box 1046
Oakland, CA 94604

Long Beach Rowing Association
PO Box 3879
Long Beach, CA 90803

Los Angeles Rowing Club
PO Box 9398
Marina Del Rey, CA 90295

Los Gatos Rowing Club
12073 Marilla Drive
Saratoga, CA 95070

Loyola Marymount Rowing Association
7101 West 80th Street
Los Angeles, CA 90045

Marin Rowing Association
50 Drakes Landing Road
Greenbrae, CA 94904

Mills College Crew
500 MacArthur Blvd.
Oakland, CA 94613

Mission Bay Rowing Association
939 Scott Street
San Diego, CA 92106

Motley Rowing Club
256B Newport Avenue
Long Beach, CA 90803

Newport Beach Rowing Club
505 Begonia Avenue
Corona Del Mar, CA 92625

North Bay Rowing Club
PO Box 192
Petaluma, VA 94953

Oakland Strokes
10 Highland Way
Piedmont, CA 94611

Oakland Youth Rowing Club
1240 Stanyan Street
San Francisco, CA 94117-3817

Open Water Rowing Center
85 Liberty Ship Way #102
Sausalito, CA 94965

Orange Coast College Rowing
   Association
2701 Fairview Road
Costa Mesa, CA 92626

Pacific Rowing Club
PO Box 27458
San Francisco, CA 94127-0548

Positive Strokes Rowing
PO Box 2705
Alameda, CA 94501

Rio Salado Rowing Club
2100 North Central Avenue
Phoenix, AZ 85004

River City Rowing Club
PO Box 980401
W. Sacramento, CA 95798

Hawaiian Rowing College
300 Wai Nani Way, #1807
Honolulu, HI 96815

Salt Lake Sculling & Crew
3044 East 3135 South
Salt Lake City, UT 84109

San Diego Crew Classic
1218 El Carmel Place
San Diego, CA 92109

San Diego Rowing Club
1220 El Carmel Place
Sand Diego, CA 92109

San Francisco Bar Pilots Rowing Club
40 Capra Way
San Francisco, CA 94123

San Francisco Police Athletic Club
   Crew
366 Mississippi Street
San Francisco, CA 94107

San Francisco Rowing Club
1631 Larkin Street, #6
San Francisco, CA 94109

Santa Clara Crew
2740 Park Avenue, Apt. #7
Santa Clara, CA 95050

Santa Clara University Rowing
   Association
Santa Clara University
Santa Clara, CA 96053

Santa Cruz Rowing Club
PO Box 2544
Santa Cruz, CA 95063

Serra/Notre Dame High School
   Crew
451 West 20th Avenue
San Mateo, CA 94403

Sonoma Sculling Society
937 Ridge View Drive
Healdsburg, CA 95448

Southern California Boat Club
13555 Fiji Way
Marina Del Rey, CA 90292

St. Ignatius Crew
267 7th Avenue
San Francisco, CA 94118

St. Mary's College Crew
15945 Via Cordoba
San Lorenzo, CA 94580

Stanford Crew Association
Stanford University
Athletic Department
Stanford, CA 94305

Stanford Rowing Club
2130 Hanover Street
Palo Alto, CA 94306

Stanford University Men's Crew
Stanford University
Athletic Department
Stanford, CA 94305

Stanford University Women's Crew
Stanford University
Athletic Department
Stanford, CA 94305

Stockton Rowing Club
PO Box 2181
Stockton, CA 95201

"The" Rowing Club
3818 Piedmont Avenue
Oakland, CA 94611

UCLA Marina Aquatic Center
14001 Fiji Way
Marina del Rey, CA 90292

University of California at Berkeley
   Crew
University of California
61 Harmon Arena, #4422
Berkeley, CA 94720

University of California at Davis
   Crew
140 Recreation Hall
University of California, Davis
Davis, CA 95616

University of California at Irvine
729 Farad Street
Costa Mesa, CA 92627

University of California at Los
   Angeles Crew
405 Hilgard Avenue
Los Angeles, CA 90024

University of California at San Diego
   Crew
PE Dept. S-005
La Jolla, CA 92093

University of Southern California
   Crew
203 Heritage Hall – Women's Rowing
Los Angeles, CA 90089

University of California – Santa
  Barbara
UCSB Rowing
Rec. Center/Physical Activities
Santa Barbara, CA 93106

University of San Diego
5998 Alcala Park
San Diego, CA 95292

Western Intercollegiate Rowing
  Association
2611 Corona Drive
Davis, CA 95616

ZLAC Rowing Club
1111 Pacific Beach Drive
San Diego, CA 92109

NORTHWEST

Anchorage Navy
7729 Anne Circle
Anchorage, AK 99504

Anchorage Rowing Association
c/o TDA
703 West Tudor Road, Suite 102
Anchorage, AK 99503

Ancient Mariners Rowing Club
PO Box 95531
Sewattle, WA 98145

Bush School Crew
405 36th Avenue East
Seattle, WA 98112

Cascade Rowing
Pocock Memorial Rowing Center
3320 Fuhrman Avenue, E
Seattle, WA 98102

Charley McIntyre Rowing Club
710 Cherry Street
Seattle, WA 98104

Coeur d' Alene Rowing
Association
PO Box 1291
Coeur d'Alene, ID 83816

Commencement Bay Rowing Club
PO Box 1614
Tacoma, WA 98401

Conibear Rowing Club
3800 Lake Washington Blvd. S.
Seattle, WA 98118

Corvallis Rowing Club
6410 NW Sumac
Corvallis, OR 97330

Deschutes Rowing Club
200 Pacific Park Lane
Bend, OR 97701

Everett Rowing Association
PO Box 1774
Everett, WA 98201

Falcon Rowing Club
5103 8th Avenue NW
Seattle, WA 98107

George Pocock Rowing Foundation
3320 Fuhrman Avenue East
Seattle, WA 98102

Gonzanga University Crew
Athletic Department
Box 66
502 East Boone
Spokane, WA 99258

Gonzanga University Rowing Association
Jesuit House
Gonzanga University
Spokane, WA 99258

Green Lake Crew
5900 W. Green Lake Way N.
Seattle, WA 98103

Holy Names Academy
11 East Allision Street
Seattle, WA 98102

Humboldt State University Rowing
  Association
PO Box 393
Arcata, CA 95521

Kenai Crewsers Rowing Club
PO Box 7
Moose Pass, AK 99631

Lake Ewauna Rowing Club
1034 Riverside Drive
Klamath Falls, OR 97601

Lake Oswego Rowing Club
PO Box 369
Lake Oswego, OR 97304

Lake Union Crew
11 East Allison Street
Seattle, WA 98102

Lake Washington Rowing Club
910 N. Northlake Way
Seattle, WA 98103

Lakeside School Crew
14050 First Avenue NE
Seattle, WA 98125

Lewis & Clark College
LC Box 17
0615 SW Palatine Hill Road
Portland, OR 97219

Lute Varsity Rowing Club
Athletic Department PLU
Tacoma, WA 98447

Martha Mom's Rowing Club
500 NW 137th Street
Seattle, WA 98177

Moonstruck Rowing Club
11 East Allision Street
Seattle, WA 98102

Moss Bay Rowing Club
1001 Fairview Avenue North, #1900
Seattle, WA 98109

Mt. Baker Rowing/Sculling
Center
3800 Lake Washington Blvd. South
Seattle, WA 98118

Nonesuch Oar & Paddle Club – ID
PO Box 1713
Pocatello, ID 83204

Northwest Legends Rowing
PO Box 3301
Everett, WA 98203

Northwest Sculling Association
2840 Eastlake Avenue East
Seattle, WA 98102

OIT Rowing Club
College Union Building
Klamath Falls, OR 97601

Orcas Island Rowing Club
Star Route, Box 195
Olga, WA 98279

Oregon Association of Rowers
PO Box 11963
Eugene, OR 97440

Oregon Rowing Unlimited
415 North State Street
Lake Oswego, OR 97034

Oregon State Rowing
Association
103 Gill Coliseum
Oregon State University
Corvallis, OR 97331

Oregon State University Crew
103 Gill Coliseum
Corvallis, OR 97331

Overlake School Crew
20301 NE 108th
Redmond, WA 98052

Pacific Lutheran University
Crew
PLU Athletics
Tacoma, WA 98447

Portland Boat Club
PO Box 97
Lake Oswego, OR 97034

Portland Rowing Club
9905 SW Serena Way
Tigard, OR 97224

Portland/Vancouver Rowing
Association
10223 NW Dick Road
Hillsboro, OR 97124

Ranier Rowing Club
3708 North 38th
Tacoma, WA 98407

Rio Abajo Rowing Club, Inc.
1319 Aalapapa Drive
Kailua, HI 96764

Sammamish Rowing Association
PO Box 160
Bellevue, WA 98009

Seattle Pacific Crew
Seattle Pacific University
Seattle, WA 98119

Seattle Tennis Club
922 McGilvra Blvd. East
Seattle, WA 98112

Seattle Yacht Club Rowing Foundation
1807 East Hamlin Street
Seattle, WA 98112

Sound Rowers
2121 Montvale Ct. W.
Seattle, WA 98199

South Eugene High School Rowing
  Club
1545 East 30th Avenue
Eugene, OR 97405

Station L. Rowing Club
PO Box 10875
Portland, OR 97296

Union Bay Rowing Club
Charla Lambert
IMA–UW Box 354090
Seattle, WA 98195

University of Puget Sound Crew
1500 North Warner Street
Tacoma, WA 98416

University of Washington Crew
  House
University of Washington
Box 354070
Seattle, WA 98195

University of Oregon Crew
EMU Club Sports
Box 3600
Eugene, OR 97403

Vashon Island Rowing Club
PO Box 79
Vashon, WA 98070

Washington State University
Cougar Crew
3rd Floor CUB
Pullman, WA 99164

Western Washington University
  Crew
OM 365-WWU
Bellingham, WA 98225

Wilamette Rowing Club
55 SW Oriole Lane
Lake Oswego, OR 97034

RACES AND REGATTAS

JANUARY

The Beach Sprints, Long Beach, California

"Beat the Beast at Saints" Indoor Rowing Ergometer Championships, Vancouver, British Columbia

Colorado Athletic Club Monaco Indoor Rowing Benefit, Denver, Colorado

Ergotica (hosted by Portland Boat Club), Portland, Oregon

International Masters Rowing Regatta, Canning River, Perth, Western Australia

The Northern New England Indoor Rowing Championships, Waterbury, Vermont

The Old Colony Erg Sprints, Brockton, Massachussetts

The Pacific Rim Indoor Rowing Championships, Portland, Oregon

Royal Hawaiian Rowing Challenge, Honolulu, Hawaii

San Diego Indoor Classic Rowing Championships, San Diego, California

St. Louis Indoor Rowing Championship, St. Louis, Missouri

Tennessee Indoor Rowing Championships, Chattanooga, Tennessee

FEBRUARY

Adirondack Sprints, Saratoga Springs, New York

Arizona Rowing Challenge, Phoenix, Arizona

Atlanta Ergometer Sprints, Atlanta, Georgia

Bucknell Erg Sprints, Lewisburg, Pennsylvania

Bytown Boat Club Winter Crew Regatta, Ottawa, Ontario

C.R.A.S.H.-B. Sprints World Indoor Rowing Championships, Cambridge, Massachussetts

Canadian Indoor Rowing Championships, Toronto, Ontario

Ergomania '98, Seattle, Washington

Ergorama: High School Indoor Rowing Relay Championships, Columbus, Ohio

Erie Erg Challenge, Rome, New York

Golden State Indoor Rowing Championships, Sacramento, California

The Granite Sprints, Durham, New Hampshire

Great Baltimore Burn, Baltimore, Maryland

The Hammer Ergatta, Cleveland, Ohio

Indiana Indoor Rowing Championships, Elkhart, Indiana

Indoor Rowing Championships, Cincinnati, Ohio

Judge-Referee Clinic - Invitation, Alexandria, Virginia

Keuper Cup Regatta, Melbourne, Florida

La Conner, Swinomish Channel and Skagit Bay - SoundRowers, La Conner, Washington

Mayor's Cup, Orlando, Florida

The Michigan Indoor Spirits, Detroit, Michigan

Mid Atlantic Erg Sprints, Alexandria, Virginia

The Mid Winter Meltdown, Madison, Wisconsin

Mile High Indoor Rowing Sprints, Denver Colorado

The Monster Erg, Victoria, British Columbia

The Narden Ergatta, Buffalo, New York

Ohio Valley Indoor Rowing Championships, Marietta, Ohio

Pittsburgh Indoor Rowing Championships, Pittsburgh, Pennsylvania

The St. Valentine's Massacre, Traverse Island, New York

Sarasota Sprints, Sarasota, Florida

Shuffle Off to Buffalo Vlll, Buffalo, New York

Southern Sprints, Melbourne, Florida

Southwest Ergometer Amateur Tournament (S.W.E.A.T.), Dallas, Texas

Twin Oaks Rowing Invitational, South Burlington, Vermont

UMass Erg Sprints, Amherst, Massachussetts

Vesper Ergo Rodeo, Philadelphia, Pennsylvania

The Virginia Reel Richmond Regatta, Richmond, Virginia

MARCH

(Collegiate and scholastic match racing begins)

Augusta Invitational, Augusta, Georgia

Biscayne Bay Yacht Club Cup, Melbourne, Florida

Bradley Cup, Rollins —JU—Tampa

Callow Cup, Penn vs. Navy

Cherry Blossom Regatta, Occoquan Reservoir, Lorton, Virginia

Clemson Sprints, Clemson, South Carolina

Coyote Point, Burlingame, California

Crawford Bay Crew Classic, Portsmouth, Virginia

CSUS vs. Santa Clara, Sacramento, California

CSUS vs. Stanford, Sacramento, California

Dustbowl Regatta, Oklahoma City

Elk Lake Spring Regatta, Vancouver Island, British Columbia

Fawley Cup Regatta, Spokane, Washington

Florida Crew classic, Gainesville, Florida

Gainesville Crew Classic, Gainesville, Florida

Green Lake Spring Regatta, Seattle, Washington

Greenhead Sprints, Brigantine, New Jersey

Grimaldi Cup, New Rochelle, New York

Heart of Texas Regatta, Austin, Texas

Jacksonvile Invitational, Jacksonville, Florida

Julian Whitestone Regatta (high school), Washington, DC

Kelly Cup, Philadelphia, Pennsylvania

Keuper Cup, FIT vs. UCF, Melbourne, Florida

Lake Sammamish - SoundRowers, Issaquah, Washington

Lexus Invitational, Oak Ridge, Tennessee

Manhattan Invitational, New Rochelle, New York

Manny Flick Regatta, (junior men and women) Philadelphia, Pennsylvania

Mareitta vs. Mercyhurst (third crew welcome), Marietta, Ohio

Mayor's Cup Regatta, Clermont, Florida

Metro Cup, Orlando, Florida

Miami International Regatta, Miami, Florida

Miami Invitational Regatta, Miami, Florida

NYC Indoor Paddling Erg Sprints Regatta, New York, New York

Old Dominion University at William and Mary, Williamsburg, Virginia

The Ontario Indoor Rowing Championships, St. Catharines, Ontario

Palm Beach Rowing Regatta, West Palm Beach, Florida

Penn vs. Columbia and Yale (women), Philadelphia, Pennsylvania

Penn vs. Navy and Georgetown (women), Philadelphia, Pennsylvania

Peter Archer Annual Spring Regatta, Long Beach, California

President's Cup (college crews), Tampa, Florida

Purdue-Marietta Challenge Cup, Marietta, Ohio

River City Regatta, West Palm Beach, Florida

Run vs. Row Regatta, Alexandria, Virginia

Smith Cup, Princeton vs. Navy

Southeast Michigan Indoor Rowing Championships, Grosse Isle, Michigan

SSC Championships, Tampa, Florida

Stanton Invitational, Jacksonville, Florida

Stetson Sprints, DeLand, Florida

Swan Creek Sprints hosted by Swan Creek Rowing Club, Lambertville, New Jersey

Tennessee Cup, Oak Ridge, Tennessee

U Miami vs. U Tennessee, Miami Beach, Florida

UBC Invitational, Burnaby, British Columbia

Walter Mess Regatta (high school), Lorton, Virginia

APRIL

Adams Cup, Harvard-Navy-Penn

Alexandria Regatta, Alexandria, Virginia

American Lake Classic - SoundRowers, Tacoma, Washington

Arlett Cup, Northeastern vs. Boston University

Atlanta Cup, Brown vs. Dartmouth

Atlanta Rowing Festival, Atlanta, Georgia

Atlantic 10 Women's Championship, Colins, New Jersey

Atlantic Coast Collegiate Regatta, Clemson, South Carolina

Augusta Invitational Regatta, Augusta, Georgia

Baltimore Cup Regatta, Inner Harbor, Baltimore

Bay Lake Youth Regatta, Disney, Florida

Big Eight Championships, Manhattan, Kansas

Big Ten Women's Championships, Culver, Indiana

Biglin Cup, Dartmouth-Harvard-MIT

Blackwell Cup, Columbia-Princeton-Yale

Boone Invitational Regatta, Orlando, Florida

Brentwood Regatta, Vancouver Island, British Columbia

Bucknell Spring Invitational Rowing Regatta, Lewisburg, Pennsylvania

California Collegiate Rowing Championships, Sacramento, California

Carnegie Cup, Cornell vs. Princeton, Princeton, New Jersey

Cascade Sprints, Lakewood, Washington

Catholic Schools championships, Philadelphia, Pennsylvania

Charlie Butt Regatta, Washington, District of Columbia

Childs Cup, Princeton-Columbia-Penn

Cincinnati Invitational High School Regatta, Cincinnati, Ohio

Cincinnati Viking Cup, Cincinnati, Ohio

Commencement Bay Rowing Club Spring Regatta, Tacoma, Washington

Compton Cup, Harvard-MIT-Princeton, Cambridge, Massachusetts

Congressional Regatta, Washington, District of Columbia

Corvallis Invitational Regatta, Corvallis, Oregon

Creighton University Invitational, Omaha, Nebraska

Daffodil Invitational Regatta, Tacoma, Washington

Darrell Winston Regatta, Occoquan Reservoir, Lorton, Virginia

Dodge Cup, Penn-Yale-Columbia

Durand Cup, Dartmouth-Rutgers-Yale, New Brunswick, New Jersey

Fern Ridge Regatta, Eugene, Oregon

Florida Intercollegiates, Tampa, Florida

Founder's Regatta, Kansas State vs. Washburn, Topeka, Kansas

Geiger Cup, Columbia-Cornell-MIT

Goes Cup, Cornell-Navy-Syracuse, Annapolis, Maryland

Gonzaga Invitational, Spokane, Washington

Governor's Cup, Florida Institute of Technology Rowing Association, Melbourne, Florida

Grimaldi Cup, St. John's-Iona-Fordham-Manhattan-King's Point, Orchard Beach, New York

Hebda Cup, Wyandotte, Michigan

Husky Invitational, Seattle, Washington

Ingomar Sprints, Arcata, California

Jacksonville Rowing Championship, Jacksonville, Florida

John Bennett H.S. Invitational, Buffalo, New York

La Salle Invitational Regatta, Philadelphia, Pennsylvania

Lexington Invitational, Los Gatos, California

Long Beach Junior Invitational, Long Beach, California

MAAC Regatta, Philadelphia or Orchard Beach, New York

Manny Flick Scholastic Regatta, Philadelphia, Pennsylvania

Maple Bay Regatta, Vancouver Island, British Columbia

Marietta Invitational Regatta, Marietta, Ohio

Matthews Cup, Cornell vs. Penn

Mercyhurst Prep Invitational Regatta, Erie, Pennsylvania

Merrill Lynch Invitational Regatta, Indianapolis, Indiana

Metropolitan Championships, New Rochelle, New York

Midwest Rowing Championships, Madison, Wisconsin

Miller Cup, Los Angeles, California

New Jersey Scholastic Rowing Championships, West Windsor

Norwalk River Rowing Club Spring Challenge, Norwalk, Connecticut

Oakridge Scholastic Regatta, Oakridge, Tennessee

Occoquan Cup, Occoquan Reservoir, Lorton, Virginia

Occoquan Sprints, Occoquan Reservoir, Lorton, Virginia

Ohio Valley School Boys Regatta, Parkersburg, West Virginia

Open Ocean Regatta, Sausalito, California

Oxford-Cambridge Boat Race, Thames River, England

Patritot League Championships, Rome, New York

Penn vs. Dartmouth and Princeton (women), Philadelphia, Pennsylvania

Penn vs. Syracuse and Northeastern (women), Philadelphia, Pennsylvania

Platt Cup, Cornell-Princeton-Rutgers

Portland Invitational, Portland, Oregon

President's Cup Regatta, Poughkeepsie, New York

Princeton Invitational, Drexel-Vesper Boat Clubs-University of Rhode Island, Princeton, New Jersey

Regional Park Regatta, Occuquan Reservoir, Lorton, Virginia

S.I.R.A./Dogwood, Oak Ridge, Tennessee

San Diego City Championships, San Diego, California

San Diego Crew Classic (college crews), Mission Bay, San Diego, California

Sandy Run Regatta, Occoquan Reservoir, Lorton, Virginia

Seattle Sprints, Seattle, Washington

Southern Intercollegiate Rowing Association Championships, Oak Ridge, Tennessee

Space City Sprints hosted by Bay Area Rowing Club of Houston, Houston, Texas

Space Coast Invitational, Merritt Island, Florida

State Championships, F.I.R.A., Tampa, Florida

Stein Cup, Brown vs. Harvard

Sunflower State Championships, Wichita, Kansas

Tri-Cities Regatta, Oregon State University vs. University of Wisconsin

UCLA Classic, Los Angeles

Victoria Rowing's Community Corporate Challenge, Victoria, British Columbia

Victoria Sea Festival, Victoria, British Columbia

Washburn Open President's Regatta, Topeka, Kansas

Washington College Invitational Regatta, Chestertown, Maryland

Washington State University, University of Southern California

West Virginia Governor's Cup, Charleston, West Virginia

Wood Hammond Cup, Penn vs. Princeton, Philadelphia

MAY

Alcatraz Challenge, San Francisco, California

Allen Cup Regatta, Farmington, Connecticut

Baggaley Cup, Cornell vs. Dartmouth

Ballard to Bainbridge and Back - SoundRowers (open water), Seattle, Washington

BayFest, Brooklyn, New York

Bergen Cup, Philadelphia

Brooke Regatta, Wellsburg, West Virginia

Burk Cup, Penn vs. Northeastern

Cadle Cup, Georgetown-George Washington-Trinity-Johns Hopkins-Loyola-George Mason, Washington D.C.

Cascade Sprints, Tacoma Washington

Catholic League Championships, Philadelphia, Pennsylvania

Central Region Sprints Lexus Cup (NCAA women), Oakridge, Tennessee

Champion International Collegiate Regatta (Quinsigamond Rowing Association), Worcester, Massachussetts

Chattanooga Sprints, Chattanooga, Tennessee

Cincinnati High School Invitational, Cincinnati, Ohio

City League Championships, Philadelphia, Pennsylvania

Coast Guard Chalenge, Oakland, California

Cochrane Cup, Dartmouth-MIT-Wisconsin, Madison, Wisconsin

Commencement Bay - SoundRowers, Tacoma, Washington

Connecticut River Rowing and Paddling Race, Essex, Connecticut

Dad Vail Regatta (small school and non-Ivy League championships), Philadelphia, Pennsylvania

Dallas Spring Regatta, Dallas, Texas

Dr. White Invitational, Philadelphia, Pennsylvania

E.A.W.R.C. Eastern Sprints, Preston, Connecticut

East Arm Ice Breaker, Greenwood Lake, New York

Eastern Association of Rowing Colleges Sprint Championship (The Eastern Sprints), Lake Quinsigamond, Worcester, Massachusetts

Eastern Association of Women's Rowing Clubs Regatta, Lake Waramaug, Connecticut

Eastern New York Championships, West Point, New York

Founders Regatta, Gunnery School, New Preston, Connecticut

Gateway Regatta, St. Louis, Missouri

Goldthwaite Cup, Harvard-Princeton-Yale

Great Plains Rowing Championships, Topeka, Kansas

Great Whaleboat Race, San Francisco, California

Head of the Martindale, St. Catharines, Ontario

High School Midwest Championships, Cincinnati, Ohio

I.R.A. Regatta, Men's Collegiate Championships, Camden, New Jersey

Ice Breaker Sprints, Greenwood Lake, New York

Interscholastic Sculling Championships - NVSRA, Occoquan, Virginia

Lake Sammamich Junoir Regatta, Redmond, Washington

Madeira Cup, Cornell vs. Penn

Mathews High School crew Annual Regatta, Mathews County, Virginia

Mayor's Cup, Providence, Rhode Island

Memorial Day Regatta, St. Paul, Minnesota

Mercyhurst Prep Invitational Regatta, Erie, Pennsylvania

Metropolitan Intercollegiate Rowing Association Championships, Orchard Beach, New York

Mid-American Collegiate Rowing Association Regatta, Marietta, Ohio

Middle States Regatta hosted by the Schuylkill Navy, Philadelphia, Pennsylvania

Miller Cup Invitational, Marina Del Rey, California

N.E.I.R.A Regatta (Quinsigamond Rowing Association), Worcester, Massachussetts

National Capital Invitational, Washington, DC

National Collegiate Rowing Championships, Cincinnati, Ohio

NCAA Women's National Collegiate Rowing Championships and NCAA Women's Rowing Championships Schedule Summary, Gainsesville, Georgia

New England Rowing Championships, Worcester, Massachussetts

New York State Collegiate Rowing Championships, Rome, New York

Northern Virginia Classic Regatta, Lorton, Virginia

Northwest Regionals, Fern Ridge, Eugene, Oregon

NOVAs - NVSRA, Lorton, Virginia

NYS Scholastic Championships, Rome, New York

Oakland Cup, Oakland, California

Opening Day, Seattle, Washington

Oxnard All-American Regatta (Southern California Women's Collegiate Championship), Oxnard, California

Pacific Coast Championships (western collegiate crews), Sacramento, California

Pacific Rim Invitational, San Diego, California

Packard Cup, Syracuse vs. Dartmouth

Penn vs. Navy (lightweight men), Philadelphia, Pennsylvania

Quahog Bay Row-Around, Hamswell, Maine

Raccoon Straits Challenge (open water), Sausalito, California

Regata Internacional Club Espana hosted by Club Espana, Mexico City, Mexico

Riverside Sprints, Riverside Boat Club, Cambridge, Massachusetts

Sag Sprints, Collegeville, Minnesota

Schlitz/Old Milwaukee Waterloo Open Regatta, Waterloo, Iowa

Scholastic Rowing Association Annual Regatta, Middletown, Delaware

Scholastic Rowing Association of America Regatta (HS Nationals), Camden, New Jersey

Scholastic Sprints hosted by TRRA, Pittsburgh, Pennsylvania

Shawnigan Lake Regatta, Vancouver Island, British Columbia

Small Boat Race (sculling and pulling boats only), Newport, Rhode Island

South Niagara High School Regatta, Welland, Ontario

Special Olympics Regatta, Philadelphia, Pennsylvania

Spring Regatta, Narragansett Boat Club, Providence, Rhode Island

St. Louis Senior Olympics Sculling Competition, St. Louis, Missouri

Stanford Invitational, Palo Alto, California

State College Invitational, Sacramento, California

Stotesbury Cup, Philadelphia, Pennsylvania

Toledo International Rowing Regatta, Toledo, Ohio

US Rowing NW Regional Junior Championships, Vancouver, Washington

US Rowing NW Regional Open Championships, Vancouver, Washington

US Rowing Soutwest Regional Junior Championship, Sacramento, California

Woodlands Spring Regatta, Texas

JUNE

Alden Ocean Shell Association (AOSA), New Hamburg Regatta, Hudson River, New Hamburg, New York

AOSA Squamscott Scullers Regatta, Stratham, New Hampshire

Bay 2 Bay Peninsula YMCA, San Diego, California

Canadian Schoolboys, St. Catharines, Ontario

Charm City Sprints 1998 Entry Form, Baltimore, Maryland

Cincinnati Invitational Regatta, Cincinnati, Ohio

Derby Sweeps & Sculls Derby, Housatonic River, Derby, Connecticut

Empire State Regatta (Northeast regional championships), Buffalo, New York

Empire State Regatta, Albany, New York

Firecracker 12, Norwich, Connecticut

Harvard-Yale Regatta, Thames River, New London, Connecticut

Moosehead Rowing Regatta, Greenville Jct., Maine

National Intercollegiate Men's Championship, Cincinnati, Ohio

National Intercollegiate Rowing Association Nationals, Seattle, Washington

New Jersey Concept ll Dry Land Rowing Championship, Westfield, New Jersey

North Tahoe Rowing Classic, Kings Beach, California

Petaluma River Regatta, Petaluma, California

Philadelphia Style Regatta, Philadelphia, Pennsylvania

Poulsbo Lutefish Pull - SoundRowers, Poulsbo, Washington

Queen's Cup, Brooklyn, New York

Rat Island Regatta - Sound Rowers, Port Townsend, Washington

Regatta, Ecorse, Michigan

Rose Srts Show (three-mile stake race), Norwich, Connecticut

Row for the Cure, Hartford, Connecticut

Schuylkill Navy Regatta, Philadelphia, Pennsylvania

Somes Sound Rowing Classic, Southwest Harbor, Maine

Sons of Norway Regatta, Minneapolis, Minnesota

Stonewall Regatta V, Washington, District of Columbia

Syracuse Masters Sculling Regatta, Syracuse Regatta Association, Syracuse, New York

Tulsa Sprints, Tulsa, Oaklahoma

Twin Tiers Regatta (professional rowing for cash prizes), Tioga, Pennsylvania

U.S. Team Trials, Princeton, New Jersey

United States Rowing Association Men's and Junior Men's Nationals, Oak Ridge, Tennessee

United States Rowing Association Women's Collegiate National Championships

US Rowing National Championships, Indianapolis, Indiana

US Rowing NW Regional Masters Championships - Heats and Finals Schedule, Vancouver, Washington

US Rowing Youth Invitational, Cincinnati, Ohio

JULY

Alden Regatta on the Maumee, Maumee, Ohio

Atlantic Crew Classic, Fredericton, New Brunswick

California Henley, Redwood City, California

California Yacht Club Celebration of the Henley, Marina Del Rey, California

Cape May Superathlon, Cape May, New Jersey

Charger Classic, Liverpool, New York

Chicago Sprint Regatta, Chicago, Illinois

Detroit Boat Club Rowing Regatta, Belle Isle, Michigan

Diamond States Masters Regatta, Middletown, Delaware

Dominican Day Regatta, Toronto, Ontario

Duluth Invitational, Duluth, Minnesota

Elk River Challenge - Sound Rowers, Westport, Washington

Empire State Games Trials, Buffalo, New York

Festival Regatta, Lowell, Massachussetts

Festival Regatta, Merrimack River, Lowell, Massachusetts

Grand Regatta, Grand Rapids, Michigan

Henley Royal Regatta, Henley-on-the-Thames, England

Independence Day Regatta, Philadelphia, Pennsylvania

Isle of Shoals (8.5 miles, Alden Ocean Shells), Kittery Point, Maine

Kennebeck River Flat Water Drag Race, Norridgewock, Maine

Konxville Rowing Association Sprints, Knoxville, Tennessee

Lake Merritt Sprints Regatta, Oakland, California

Last Gasp Regatta, Pagosa Springs, Colorado

Lottie McAlice Regatta hosted by TRRA, Pittsburgh, Pennsylvania

Mid-Atlantic Regionals (open water, US lifesaving qualifier), TBA

Moby Dick Classic, New Bedford, Massachusetts

National Championships (and selection for the national teams), Carnegie Lake, Princeton, New Jersey, or Camden, New Jersey

National Women's Lifeguard Championships (open water), New York City, New York

Ontario Rowing Championships, Welland, Ontario

Ottawa Invitational Regatta, Ottawa, Ontario

Philadelphia Youth Regatta, Philadelphia, Pennsylvania

Pull and Be Damned Regatta (LeMans Start, shells and traditional pulling boats), Anacortes, Washington

Rainbow Regatta, Seattle, Washington

Rutherford Riverfront Sprints, New Jersey

South Niagra Master's Invitational Regatta, Welland, Ontario

St. Catharines Invitational, St. Catharines, Ontario

State Games Of Oregon, Vancouver, Washington

Sweeps and Sculls, Providence, Rhode Island

U.S.L.A. Trial Race, Long Branch, New Jersey

US Rowing Club National Championships, Syracuse, New York

Vashon Island Strawberry Festival - Sound Rowers, Vashon, Washington

West Side Rowing Club Masters Championships, Buffalo, New York

Woodstock Regatta, Toronto, Ontario

AUGUST

AOSA Head of the Miles, Easton, Maryland

AOSA Martin Oarmaster Fitness Regatta, Schroon Lake, New York

AOSA New Meadows River Cruise, Brunswick, Maine

Around the Island, Wildwood, New Jersey

Baltimore Ariel Regatta, Baltimore

Bayada Regatta (disabled rowers), Philadelphia, Pennsylvania

Canadian Championships, Montreal, Quebec

Canadian Masters Rowing Championships, Toronto, Ontario

Carnegie Lake Regatta, Princeton, New Jersey

Festival Regatta, Merrimack River Rowing Association, Lowell, Massachusetts

Firecracker Sprints (fours with coxswains), Nashua, New Hampshire

Fly Lake Regatta, Sisters, Oregon

Great Cross Sound - Sound Rowers, Seattle, Washington

Harlem River Regatta, New York City

Hogtown Heats, Toronto, Ontario

Libby Moore Foundation - Cross the Bay, Lewes, Delaware

Maine State Championship Regatta, Bridgton, Maine

Monterey Bay Crossing, Santa Cruz, California

Nike World Masters Games, Portland, Oregon

Ontario Recreational Regatta, Welland, Ontario

Ottawa Master and Recreational Regatta, Ottawa, Ontario

Pacific Northwest Tub Four Rowing Championships, Seattle, Washington

Peconic Bay Round Robin, New Suffolk, Long Island, New York

Regatta of the Americas, Welland, Ontario

Round Shaw Island - Sound Rowers, Shaw Island, Washington

Rowing Extravaganza, Seattle, Washington

Royal Canadian, Henley St. Catharines, Ontario

Summer Extravaganza - Green Lake Crew Rowing Center, Seattle, Washington

Sweeps and Sculls Regatta, Narragansett Bay, Providence, Rhode Island

United States Lifesaving Association National Competition, Chicago, Illinois

United States Rowing Association and National Women's Rowing Association Masters Nationals, Philadelphia, Pennsylvania

US Rowing Level 1 Clinic, Virginia

World Police and Fire Games, Redwood Shores, California

SEPTEMBER

Bainbridge Island Marathon - Sound Rowers, Bainbridge, Washington

Bayada Regatta, Philadelphia, Pennsylvania

Bridge to Bridge, San Francisco, California

Budd Bay - Sound Rowers, Olympia, Washington

Cayuga Challenge, Ithaca, New York

Clinics for coxswains and USRA judge-referees, Middletown, Connecticut

Coastweeks Row on the Mystic, Mystic, Connecticut

Dutch Shoes Regatta, Hudson River, Albany, New York

Green Mountain Head (three-mile stake race), Putney, Vermont

Hartford Riverfront Regatta, Hartford, Connecticut

Head of the Cuyahoga, Cleveland, Ohio

Head of the Des Moines, Des Moines, Iowa

Head of the Hudson, Albany, New York

Head of the Licking, Cincinnati, Ohio

Head of the Niagara, Buffalo, New York

Head of the Potomac, Washington, District of Columbia

Head of the Rideau - Ottawa R.C. Regattas, Ottawa, Ontario

Head of the Thames, Thames River, Norwich, Conecticut

Head of the Welland Canal Regatta, Welland, Ontario

King's Head X1 Regatta on the Schuylkill, King of Prussia, Pennsylvania

Master Nationals, Lake Placid, New York

Mighty Merrimack Rowing Race, Newburyport, Massachusetts

Numerica's Cup Regatta, Manchester, New Hampshire

Race to the Sea, Merrimack River, Newburyport, Massachusetts

Row for the Cure, Portland, Oregon

Seattle Sculling Challenge, Seattle, Washington

Seneca Invitational, Seneca Falls, New York

Southwest Masters Regionals, Sacramento, California

Three State Ocean Rowing Regatta, Mystic, Conneticut

Twelfth Annual Head of the Androscoggin, Greene, Maine

US Rowing Masters National Championships, Topeka, Kansas

USRA Level 1 Coaching Clinic, Hamilton, New York

Waterfront Sprints, Narragansett Bay, Providence, Rhode Island

Wye Island Regatta, Wye Mills, Maryland

OCTOBER

Annual Dock Race, Montauk (Long Island), New York

Bucknell Fall Invitational Rowing Regatta, Lewisburg, Pennsylvania

Catalina to Marina Del Rey Great California Yacht Club Rowing and Paddling Derbby (37 miles, open ocean)

Chattanooga Head, Chattanooga, Tennessee

Dallas B.L.A.S.T., Dallas, Texas

Five Rivers MetroParks Fall Reagatta, Dayton, Ohio
Head of Ross Island, Portland, Oregon

Head of Silcox, Tacoma, Washington

Head of the Brazos, Waco, Texas

Head of the Charles Regatta, Cambridge, Massachusetts

Head of the Clinton River Regatta, Mt. Clemens, Michigan

Head of the Connecticut, Middletown, Connecticut

Head of the Creek, Miami Beach, Florida

Head of the Des Moines, Des Moines, Iowa

Head of the Dog, Portland, Oregon

Head of the Eagle, Indianapolis, Indiana

Head of the Erie, Rome, New York

Head of the Estuary, Oakland, California

Head of the Housatonic, Shelton, Conneticut

Head of the Kaw Fall Rowing Classic, Kansas City, Missouri

Head of the Merrimack, Nashua, New Hampshire

Head of the Mississippi, Minneapolis Rowing Club, Minneapolis, Minnesota

Head of the Mohawk (three-mile stake race), Aqueduct Rowing Club, Schnectady, New York

Head of the Ohio hosted by TRRA, Pittsburgh, Pennsylvania

Head of the Patapsco, Baltimore, Maryland

Head of the Port of Sacramento, West Sacramento, California

Head of the Rock Regatta, Rockford, Illinois

Head of the Tennessee, Knoxville, Tennessee

Hogan-Fries Regatta (novices-only), Buffalo New York

Lake Samish Salmon Roe - Sound Rowers, Bellingham, Washington

Lobster Row, Santa Cruz, California

Mercer-Medina Sausage Pull - Sound Rowers, Bellevue, Washington

Mount Holyoke Women's Invitational Regatta, Hadley, Massachussetts

Navy Day Regatta, Philadelphia, Pennsylvania

New Hampshire Championships, Manchester, New Hampshire

Occoquan Chase, Lorton, Virginia

Oxford Rowing Triathalon and Relays, Oxford, Maryland

Philadelphia Sculling Regatta, Philadelphia, Pennsylvania

Quad Cities Rowing Classic, Moline, Illinois

Sculler's Head of the Potomac, Washington, D.C.

Ship Shield Regatta, Delaware River, Burlington, New Jersey

Sippican Ocean Regatta, Buzzards Bay, Marion, Massachusetts

Springfield Heritage Regatta, Springfield, Massachussetts

Stonehurst Capital Invitational Regatta, Rochester, New York

Tail of the Fox Regatta, De Pere, Wisconsin

Textile River Regatta, Merrimack River, Lowell, Massachusetts

Thomas Eakins Head of the Schuylkill, Philadelphia, Pennsylvania

Twin Islands Regatta, Richmond, California

University of Nebraska Fall Regatta, Lincoln, Nebraska

NOVEMBER

(Most Northeastern college crews end on the water practices)

Braxton Regatta, Philadelphia, Pennsylvania

Clinch River Recreational Regatta, Oak Ridge, Tennessee

Dexter Fall Regatta, Eugene, Oregon

Frostbite Regatta, Seattle, Washington

Head of the Lake, Seattle, Washington

Head of the Occoquan Regatta, Springfield, Virginia

Philadelphia Frostbite Regatta, Philadelphia

DECEMBER

United States Rowing Association Annual Convention

SOURCES FOR SHELLS AND EQUIPMENT

COXSWAIN'S EQUIPMENT

Feldmar Watch and Clock Center
9000 West Pico Blvd.
Los Angeles, CA 90035
(310) 274-8016

The Swiss Watchmaker
58 Church Street
Cambridge, MA 02138
(617) 864-1163

RECREATIONAL SHELLS

Adirondack Rowing
Peter Gallo
Queensbury, NY 12804
(518) 745-7699

Little River Marine
PO Box 986
Gainesville, FL 32602
(352) 378-5044

Pocock Rowing Center
3320 Furman Avenue
Seattle WA 98102
(206) 328-0778

Garofalo High Performance
  Shells
660 Franklin Street
Worcester, MA 01604
(508) 755-1457

Durham Boat Company
220 Newmarket Road (Route 108)
Durham, NH 03824
(603) 659-7575

Lowell's Boat Shop Inc.
459 Main Street
Amesbury, MA 01913
(978) 388-0162

ROWING CLOTHING

Alden Ocean Shells
PO Box 368
Elliot, ME 03903
1-800-477-1507

Boathouse Sports
4700 Wissahickon Avenue
Philadelphia, PA 19144
(215) 848-1855

RACING SHELLS

Alden Ocean Shells
PO Box 368
Elliot, ME 03903
1-800-477-1507

Empacher Eurow Sport L.L.C.
South Gerrish Street
Brighton, MA 02135-1704
(617) 787-1177

Vespoli USA
385 Clinton Avenue
New Haven, CT 06513
(203) 773-0311

Durham Boat Company
220 Newmarket Road (Route 108)
Durham, NH 03824
(603) 659-7575

Schoenbrod Racing Shells
596 Elm Street
Biddeford, ME 04005
(207) 283-3026

Pocock Rowing Center
3320 Furman Avenue
Seattle WA 98102
(206) 328-0778

Garofalo High Performance Shells
660 Frankllin Street
Worcester, MA 01604
(508) 755-1457

SHELL PARTS

Boathouse Sports
4700 Wissahickon Avenue
Philadelphia, PA 19144
(215) 848-1855

OARS

Alden Ocean Shells
PO Box 368
Elliot, ME 03903
1-800-477-1507

Durham Boat Company
220 Newmarket Road (Route 108)
Durham, NH 03824
(603) 659-7575

ROWING LESSONS

Adirondack Rowing
Peter Gallo
Queensbury, NY 12804
(518) 745-7699

Alden Ocean Shells
PO Box 368
Elliot, ME 03903
1-800-477-1507

ERGOMETERS AND ROWING MACHINES

Alden Ocean Shells
PO Box 368
Elliot, ME 03903
1-800-477-1507

Concept II, Inc.
105 Industrial Park Drive
(802) 888-7971

INDEX